A House of Her Own

A House of Her Own

*Women Writers of New England
and Their Homes*

BETH LUEY

McFarland & Company, Inc., Publishers
Jefferson, North Carolina

Edna St. Vincent Millay, excerpts from ["Women have loved before as I love now"], ["Well, I have lost you; and I lost you fairly";] and "Ragged Island" from *Collected Poems,* Copyright 1931, 1954, ©1955, 1982 by Edna St. Vincent Millay and Norma Millay Ellis. Reprinted with the permission of The Permissions Company, LLC on behalf of Holly Peppe, Literary Executor, The Millay Society, millay.org.

From the Mary Baker Eddy Collection: Daisette Stocking McKenzie, "Reminiscences of Daisette Stocking McKenzie, C.S.B., and William Patrick MacKenzie, C.S.B., as recorded by Daisette D.S. McKenzie, C.S.B.," typescript, n.d., Mary Baker Eddy Library, Boston, Mass., 27–28. Letters and Reminiscences; See M. Adelaide Still, "Reminiscences of the Time I Spent in Mrs. Eddy's Home May 1907 to December 1910," typescript, n.d., Mary Baker Eddy Library, Boston, Mass., 23; Calvin C. Hill, "Reminiscences of Calvin C. Hill," typescript, 1943, Mary Baker Eddy Library, Boston, Mass., 190; Gill, *Mary Baker Eddy,* 524–26; Eddy to James Ackland, January 21, 1990, L10638, marybakereddypapers.org
© The Mary Baker Eddy Collection. Used by permission.

ISBN (print) 978-1-4766-9224-1
ISBN (ebook) 978-1-4766-5147-7

LIBRARY OF CONGRESS AND BRITISH LIBRARY
CATALOGUING DATA ARE AVAILABLE

Library of Congress Control Number 2023042894

© 2023 Beth Luey. All rights reserved

No part of this book may be reproduced or transmitted in any form or by any means, electronic or mechanical, including photocopying or recording, or by any information storage and retrieval system, without permission in writing from the publisher.

Front cover image: "The birthplace of Mary Baker Eddy" in Bow, New Hampshire. She remembered the house fondly and visited it late in life. (Prints and Photographs Division, Library of Congress). *Background* Kolesov Sergey/Shutterstock

Printed in the United States of America

*McFarland & Company, Inc., Publishers
Box 611, Jefferson, North Carolina 28640
www.mcfarlandpub.com*

For Nora

Table of Contents

Preface — 1

Introduction — 3

CONNECTICUT — 7
1. Helen Keller — 8
2. Harriet Beecher Stowe — 21
3. Ida Tarbell — 31

MAINE — 43
4. Sarah Orne Jewett — 44
5. Mary McCarthy and Elizabeth Hardwick — 53
6. Edna St. Vincent Millay — 67
7. Celia Thaxter — 77

MASSACHUSETTS — 89
8. Louisa May Alcott — 90
9. Emily Dickinson — 99
10. Sojourner Truth — 108
11. Edith Wharton — 121

NEW HAMPSHIRE — 130
12. Mary Baker Eddy — 131
13. Sarah Josepha Hale — 141
14. Grace Metalious — 150

Table of Contents

RHODE ISLAND — 159

15. Elleanor Eldridge and Frances Green — 160
16. Charlotte Perkins Gilman — 167
17. Cynthia Taggart — 177

VERMONT — 183

18. Shirley Jackson — 184
19. Grace Paley — 197

Chapter Notes — 205
Bibliography — 219
Index — 227

Preface

In 2006, my husband and I moved into a house built in 1800 for the town's first Congregational minister. I soon learned that my house had a "Me Too" event involving the clergyman and the young woman who took care of his children. It was a complex story that told me a lot about the Reverend Weston, young Phebe Jenney, and the community they lived in. I was surprised to find that the church elders did not dismiss the young woman's story out of hand or accept Weston's denial without further investigation. That story became the first chapter in a book that collected a dozen stories that helped me understand my new hometown: *House Stories: The Meanings of Home in a New England Town*. I went on to write two other books about historic houses in Massachusetts. Both are titled *At Home*, and one covers the eastern part of the state and the other, the central and western parts. As I worked on these books, I uncovered a great variety of interactions between the houses and the people who lived in them. Some houses reflect their owners' personalities or ambitions; other houses shape them. Some provide a setting for family drama; others cause it.

Most houses deemed worthy of preservation belonged to famous people, so most of them belonged to men. That didn't exclude the stories of women, but they were often secondary to those of their fathers or husbands. With this book, I was able both to move beyond Massachusetts and to focus on the lives of the women themselves. Because the women were writers, they left written records—memoirs, poetry, fiction, investigative reporting, diaries, and letters. Many of them had inspired biographers to do extensive archival research, and I was able to draw on primary sources as well as published biographies. Others left little behind but their writing. Whenever possible, I included the financial as well as the literary aspects of their careers. Many of these women were savvy about the literary marketplace and how to bargain with publishers.

New England boasts many more women authors than I could include. I focused on those whose homes were important to them or to their writing. I tried to provide geographic balance, a variety of genres, and a time span beginning in the eighteenth century and ending in the twenty-first. In many cases, I was reading an author's work for the first time. At other times, I was returning to old favorites. Knowing where the writers lived made it possible to read their work with a sense of place and, often, a deepened feeling for the natural and built environments where they placed their stories. Whether I was in Sarah Orne Jewett's peaceful villages, Shirley Jackson's haunted houses, or Grace Metalious's Peyton Place, I felt at home. I hope I've succeeded in sharing that sense.

Introduction

"A house of her own": When I started writing about historic houses, I noticed something puzzling about the homes of writers. With few exceptions, the male writers inherited their houses or married into them: Henry Wadsworth Longfellow's elegant Cambridge home was a wedding gift from his father-in-law; Ralph Waldo Emerson bought his house with money from his first wife's estate; Robert Frost's first farm was a gift from his grandfather; Herman Melville financed Arrowhead with loans and gifts from his father-in-law. The women didn't inherit their houses; they earned them. Louisa May Alcott bought Orchard House with her fees for short stories; Edith Wharton built The Mount with her royalties (which exceeded her large inheritance); and Mary Baker Eddy's Christian Science books paid for her first and subsequent homes.

Literary historians frequently suggest that the difference in earning power between male and female writers is due to the difference in the kinds of books they wrote. Men, they argue, wrote serious fiction and poetry that did not sell, so they needed other sources of income, whether nonliterary employment or wealthy wives. Women, they claim, wrote flowery verse and light fiction, often sentimental, that other women would buy. As you will see, that is not the answer. We find women in this book earning money from serious nonfiction, and from poetry collections and novels that were critically praised. In the nineteenth century, they were earning money from magazines and newspapers that were purchased by fathers and husbands *for* women, but rarely *by* them.

The writers in this book might reverse Virginia Woolf's claim that "a woman must have money and a room of her own if she is to write fiction." They certainly wanted a quiet place to work, but they would add that *"a woman must write if she is to have money and a room of her own."* Susan B. Anthony expressed the need for all women, not just writers: "Woman must have a purse of her own." Many of the unmarried women in this book wrote in order to live independently. Widows wrote to support their families. Still others—daughters or wives of men who were incapable of supporting them—wrote to pay the mortgage. Writing was often also a source of pride and pleasure, but the women who wrote purely for the joy of it were few.

For most, writing was a business. Their letters and journals show them becoming skillful at negotiation and marketing. But writing also gave meaning to their lives. For some, it was a basic need that began at a very early age. As young girls, Edith Wharton, Grace Metalious, Edna St. Vincent Millay, Louisa May Alcott, and Charlotte Perkins Gilman all had lively imaginations and used writing as a way to express their vivid fantasies, sometimes alarming their parents. Emily Dickinson, living happily in the family home, wrote hundreds of poems from an undeniable urge to put ideas and feelings into words. Grace Paley, in a New York City jail for participating in a protest, felt "a pain in the area of my heart" when deprived of pen and paper.

New England was a good place to be a writer. Boston and nearby New York offered publishing opportunities in newspapers and magazines, and both cities were home to book publishing houses. In Boston, James Fields, of Ticknor and Fields and the *Atlantic,* nurtured young talent and encouraged many of the women in this book. His second wife, Annie, turned their home into a salon for the firm's established writers from the United States and England, and invited promising young authors to meet them. Lasting friendships formed among these women, and they encouraged and advised one another. In New York, Horace Greeley's progressive newspaper reviewed and publicized female authors' work. New York was also the home of the McClure Newspaper Syndicate, which arranged the publication of stories and poems throughout the country and paid generous fees for short stories, forcing the elite magazines to increase their payments to authors.

"A house of her own" came in many forms, from the cramped cottage where Cynthia Taggart lived as an invalid, to the middle-class homes of most of these writers, to the Berkshire mansion where Edith Wharton spent her summers. Two of our writers—Sarah Orne Jewett and Emily Dickinson—lived in their parents' homes. Most, though, bought houses with their earnings. The two women of color—Elleanor Eldridge and Sojourner Truth—paid for their houses by writing their memoirs, telling stories that were unimaginable to most of their readers, with the help of collaborators who had led more privileged lives.

As important as it was to have a *house,* few of these women had any time or affection for *housekeeping.* Often, the first publication fee or royalty check went to pay for household help or childcare. Charlotte Perkins Gilman married for the first time only after her fiancé signed a promise that she would not have to dust. Grace Metalious was such a terrible housekeeper that the publicity photo of her at her typewriter had to be taken in someone else's house.

Writers' houses, and the stories of how they were acquired, help us to know their owners. I found clues in many sources: the writers' own words, descriptions by others, the architecture and decor, even the name the writer gave her house. Louisa May Alcott's father named their home "Orchard House"; she called it "Apple Slump." The connection between writer and home is different for each woman in this book, but it was important in all of their lives. Whether the writing made the home possible, or the home made the writing possible, the two are inextricable.

A Note on Visiting

I have provided information on how to visit the houses that are open to the public. Their websites often provide numerous photographs, as well as biographical information. For the houses that are in private hands, an internet search for the street address (which I have provided whenever possible) will bring up a Google Maps image. If the house has been on the market in the past few years, realtors' sites will often provide photographs of the interior as well as the exterior.

Connecticut

1

Helen Keller

For many years, writing was the only way Helen Keller could communicate directly with more than one person at a time. She could not see, but she learned to read Braille and to identify people and objects by touch and smell. She could not hear, but she could feel the vibrations of music and movement. A companion could convey speech to her with a manual alphabet. Until middle age, she could not speak in a way that others could understand. But her mind was buzzing with thoughts and feelings that she wanted to share, and questions that she wanted to ask. She learned to write, first with pencil and paper and later with typewriters. Written language—her books and articles—became her way of reaching the world.

Childhood and the "Miracle"

Helen Keller was born on June 27, 1880, on her father's cotton farm in rural Tuscumbia, Alabama. The family home was a white clapboard house called Ivy Green. The first floor had a parlor, dining room, and two bedrooms, each with a fireplace; the second floor, two bedrooms and a box room. One of the downstairs bedrooms belonged to her father's sister, Evaline Keller. Helen was born in "The Little House," a small cottage on the grounds—one large room with a bay window, and a smaller playroom—that had been her parents' honeymoon cottage. After her birth, her parents moved into the main house, and Helen lived in the cottage with a nurse until she was 19 months old.[1]

Helen's father, Captain Arthur Henley Keller, a 42-year-old Civil War veteran, edited the local newspaper and farmed. He had been widowed in 1877 and married Helen's mother, Kate Adams, a year later. She was 22, and the Captain's two grown sons were not happy at his quick marriage to a woman only a few years older than they. Kate had grown up as the pampered daughter of a wealthy family with Northern roots. After her marriage, she became a farm wife, raising her own vegetables and making

1. Helen Keller

The cottage at Ivy Green, in Tuscumbia, Alabama, where Helen Keller was born. The main house, architecturally similar to the cottage, is nearby, off to the left. When Annie Sullivan arrived, she and Helen moved into the cottage to facilitate teaching. *Photograph courtesy of Mary Carton.*

butter, lard, bacon, and ham. She nevertheless found time to read and to become involved in the movement for women's suffrage.

In February 1882, Helen became suddenly and severely ill with a high fever, now thought to have been scarlet fever or meningitis. The fever subsided and she fell into a peaceful sleep, but when she woke up, she could not see or hear. As she recovered, frustration at her isolation and inability to communicate led her to lash out with violent tantrums. She shattered anything breakable and bit, kicked, scratched, and pinched her family. As Helen grew stronger, and her frustration more intense, her tantrums became more frequent and violent. The family was urged to put her into an institution, but Kate refused.

Kate remembered that in Charles Dickens' account of his 1842 tour of the United States, *American Notes,* he wrote about meeting Laura Bridgman, a deaf-blind woman who had been taught to read at the Perkins Institution for the Blind, in Boston. That now seemed an unlikely source of help, though: the person who had taught Bridgman was long dead. The Kellers did not give up. Captain Keller and his sister Evaline took Helen to meet Alexander Graham Bell, the inventor of the telephone, who had become interested in helping deaf people to hear. Bell told them that the Perkins Institution was still open, now directed by Michael Anagnos. In a letter to Bell written on April 20, 1887, Evaline Keller reported that Captain Keller had asked Anagnos "to procure if possible a governess who understood the methods of teaching both the blind and deaf." Anagnos trained Annie Sullivan, who had been educated at Perkins and had worked with Laura Bridgman, to teach children like Helen.

The Kellers knew little about the life of Annie Sullivan. She was deeply ashamed of her family tragedies and poverty and rarely talked about her childhood. She did not tell Helen about it until she was in her sixties. She had been born in 1866 to impoverished Irish immigrants at a time when the Irish were generally despised. Her father was an illiterate, alcoholic, abusive field hand on a farm near Springfield, Massachusetts. Her mother was crippled in a household accident. The couple had five children, two of whom died young. When Annie was five, she contracted trachoma—then a common cause of blindness. Her mother died when Annie was eight and was buried in a potter's field. Her father abandoned the children, and Annie and her brother Jimmie, crippled by a tubercular hip, were sent to the poorhouse at the State Infirmary. For many children, this was a death sentence. They lived side by side with adults carrying contagious diseases in a verminous, neglected building. No attempt was made to educate them. Only three months after they arrived, Jimmie died. Annie was shattered. He was, she later told Helen, "the only thing I have ever loved."[2] She spent four years in the poorhouse.

When the inspector of state charities, Franklin B. Sanborn, visited the institution in 1880, Annie called out to him, "Mr. Sanborn, I want to go to school." When asked what was wrong with her, she explained that she didn't see very well. In October, she was transferred to the Perkins Institution. She was fourteen years old and had never been to school. She learned to spell and read Braille, but she felt isolated. The other students were better dressed, had been in school longer, and did not hide their anti-Irish prejudice. She was often in trouble and was nearly expelled. But she made two influential friends: the director, Michael Anagnos, and the star inmate, the aged deaf-blind Laura Bridgman. Annie learned the manual alphabet that Bridgman used. She also had surgery at the Massachusetts

Eye and Ear Infirmary that allowed her to read, opening new worlds. In 1886, she graduated from Perkins as the class valedictorian.

The summer after graduation, while she was wondering how to earn her living, she received a note from Anagnos, enclosing Captain Keller's letter requesting a teacher. She returned to Perkins, where Anagnos and Bridgman completed her training. In January 1887, they decided she was ready, and in March she traveled to Tuscumbia. The miracle worker had arrived. Evaline told Bell, "She is succeeding admirably with our little girl. She has been with her two months, she can now spell nearly a hundred words on her fingers and knows the meaning of them, and knows the entire alphabet for the blind. It is astonishing how eager she is to learn."[3]

Evaline did not convey the drama of what Helen would call her "soul's awakening," the moment that would come to be known as the miracle of Helen's breakthrough. Here is Helen's version: "My teacher placed my hand under the spout. As the cool stream gushed over one hand she spelled into the other the word *water*, first slowly, then rapidly. I stood still, my whole attention fixed upon the motions of her fingers. Suddenly I felt a misty consciousness as of something forgotten—a thrill of returning thought; and somehow the mystery of language was revealed to me. I knew then that 'w-a-t-e-r' meant the wonderful cool something that was flowing over my hand. That living word awakened my soul, gave it light, hope, joy, set it free!"[4]

Education

For the next three years, Helen made remarkable progress. Annie recognized that Helen's intellect was very much intact. She told Anagnos: "I shall assume that she has the normal child's capacity of assimilation and imitation. I shall use complete sentences in talking to her and fill out the meaning with gestures and her descriptive signs when necessity requires it, but I shall not try to keep her mind fixed on any one thing. I shall do all I can to interest and stimulate it and wait for results."[5] Annie spelled Shakespeare, the Bible, and Greek classics for Helen, who was soon reading, in Braille, Longfellow and Whittier.

Especially impressive was Helen's writing. A year after Annie's arrival, Helen started a journal, writing with a pencil on paper placed over a special writing board. She kept up a correspondence with Alexander Graham Bell and wrote personal appeals to raise money for other children who needed special education. Annie supervised her letter writing, refusing to send any correspondence that was not letter perfect. Helen's later editors said that writing did not come naturally to her, and that it was not pleasurable—perhaps because of Annie's perfectionism. But pleasurable or not, she did it. In the summer of 1889, Annie and Helen went to Boston, where Annie spent several months receiving treatment for her eyes. Helen was taught at Perkins, where she had access to the library and to teachers in subjects that Annie could not cover. She learned French in three months. They then returned to Alabama.

Anagnos publicized an exaggerated version of Helen's accomplishments, emphasizing his institution's contribution over Annie Sullivan's. The two had a more fundamental disagreement than who should get credit, however. Annie tried to guard Helen's privacy, while Anagnos sought publicity. By the age of ten, Helen had become a public figure, even a celebrity. In May 1888, when Annie and Helen went to Boston for the Perkins Institution commencement, they stopped in Washington to respond to an invitation to visit President Grover Cleveland in the White House.

In 1891 Helen sent Anagnos "a little story that I wrote," "The Frost King," as a birthday gift. Anagnos printed it in *The Mentor,* the Perkins alumni magazine, and it was reprinted in the weekly *Goodson Gazette,* published by the Virginia Institution for the Education of the Deaf and Dumb and Blind. A reader informed the editor that the story was not original but a replication of a story by Margaret T. Canby—a story that Helen had probably read. Anagnos charged Helen with plagiarism and sent Annie a list of questions. Her response paints a very plausible picture of a twelve-year-old's thinking: "I cannot say positively whether Helen has, or has not a clear idea of the difference between original composition and reproduction. I do not know certainly that she has ever had an original idea. If she has not, of course, she cannot have a clear conception of what is meant by original composition. But supposing that she has been conscious of the birth of ideas in her own brain, it is not probable, I think, that she makes any wise discriminations between such ideas and others which she has unconsciously absorbed in her reading." Years later, Keller would write, "At that time I eagerly absorbed everything I read without a thought of authorship, and even now I cannot be quite sure of the boundary line between my ideas and those I find in books. I suppose that is because so many of my impressions come to me through the medium of others' eyes and ears."[6]

The trust between Anagnos and Annie and Helen could not be restored, and the damage to Helen's career as a writer was immeasurable. Margaret Canby had written to Helen, "Some day you will write a great story out of your own head, that will be a comfort and help to many." But as late as her early twenties, Helen believed that "this kind prophecy has never been fulfilled. I have never played with words again for the mere pleasure of the game. Indeed, I have ever since been tortured by the fear that what I write is not my own.... Had it not been for the persistent encouragement of Miss Sullivan, I think I should have given up trying to write altogether."[7] In 1894, that encouragement convinced her to write an account of her life for the magazine *Youth's Companion*. "I wrote timidly, fearfully, but resolutely, urged on by my teacher, who knew that if I persevered, I should find my mental foothold again and get a grip on my faculties." When it was published, it was preceded by a note: "Written wholly without help of any sort, by a deaf and blind girl, twelve years old, and printed without change."[8]

Helen wanted desperately to speak. She had made one attempt, at the Horace Mann School for the Deaf, but that had been unsuccessful. In 1894, she traveled to New York to study at the Wright-Humason School for the Deaf. She studied geography, French, German, and math in addition to speech. Their system, too, failed to help her, but the academic work was a step toward preparing for college. As a young child, Helen had announced that she wanted to go to Harvard and was disappointed to learn that women were not welcome. She could, however, hope to attend Radcliffe, where women were taught separately from men by Harvard faculty members and, since 1894, could earn degrees.

To prepare for the Radcliffe entrance examinations, she enrolled in the Cambridge School for Young Ladies in 1896. Annie used the manual alphabet to convey the lectures to her, as well as the contents of books that were not available in Braille. After three years at the school, she took the entrance exam. It was daunting. Annie was not allowed to accompany her, and the exam was given by the director of the school, Arthur Gilman, who had learned the manual alphabet to administer the test. Helen passed all her exams—German, French, Latin, English, and Greek and Roman history. Gilman was delighted: "I think I may say that no candidate in Harvard or Radcliffe was graded higher than Helen in English.... No man or woman has ever in my experience got ready for these examinations in so brief a time. How has it been accomplished? By a union of patience, determination, and affection, with the foundation of an uncommon brain."[9]

Helen needed all of those qualities at Radcliffe. She still relied on Annie to convey the content of lectures and some readings, and few faculty members or students knew the manual alphabet. In her second year, though, Professor Charles Townsend Copeland encouraged her. Copeland was a poet who, during his Harvard career, became known as a superb mentor and teacher of writing. "In some of her work," he wrote, "she has shown that she can write better than any pupil I had ever had, man or woman. She has an excellent 'ear' for the flow of sentences."[10]

While she was still a student, the *Ladies Home Journal* offered her $3,000 to write the story of her life, to appear in five monthly installments.

John Albert Macy, a Harvard instructor and magazine editor, learned the manual alphabet and helped Helen to transform the installments into the book *The Story of My Life,* published in 1903 by Doubleday, Page. An immediate best seller, it has never been out of print and was translated into dozens of languages. The royalties provided a small but reliable income.

By the time Keller graduated from Radcliffe with honors in June 1904, she was a recognized writer. She was also a home owner: she and Annie Sullivan had bought a farmhouse in Wrentham, Massachusetts, by selling stock given them by John S. Spaulding, a wealthy benefactor.

Wrentham

Keller and Sullivan had spent summers in a rented cottage on Wrentham's Lake Pearl from 1898 to 1903, and Keller had also spent time at Red Farm, the home of the literary critic Joseph E. Chamberlin and his family, near King Philip's Pond. Keller's love of nature, and the friends she and Sullivan had made in the town, made Wrentham an attractive place to settle. The spacious three-story house at 349 East Street had a large porch with a balcony above, opening from Keller's bedroom onto a yard with tall old trees.[11]

In 1905, Sullivan married John Macy, and he came to live with them. Keller remembered the years when the three lived together as happy and fruitful, "a sort of pre-existence—a dream of days when I wore another body and had a different consciousness." Although tensions soon arose in the marriage (the couple would separate in 1912), the author-editor relationship between Keller and John Macy was productive. A later editor described Macy as "the best critic she ever had.... He pruned her style of its wordiness, curbed her proneness to dogmatic preaching, and generally pulled her down out of the clouds." Macy said that Keller "writes well not by virtue of a facile gift, but by scrupulous revision, patient thinking, and diligent attention to the criticism of her instructors, and to the advice of Miss Sullivan. Labor is the secret of her advancement."[12]

Although Anagnos's publicity about Keller may have been self-serving and exploitative, it attracted the attention of people who were in a position to help her financially—to pay her tuition, living expenses, and support for Sullivan as well. Over the years, the two women received substantial funds from financial tycoons (John D. Rockefeller and Henry Huttleston Rogers of Standard Oil, Andrew Carnegie, John S. Spaulding) and financial support and professional assistance from writers and editors. Keller's letters include countless thank-you notes and expressions of gratitude. As she noted, though, "in spite of our income from Mr. Carnegie and the money we made ourselves our expenses were always a ravenous wolf devouring our finances."[13]

Living in Wrentham, with John Macy as resident editor, Keller continued to write. Macy helped her with a series of essays that appeared in the *Century Magazine* and was issued as *The World I Live In* in 1908. Keller wanted to clear away misconceptions about what it was like to be deaf-blind. She knew that most people thought she lived in darkness and silence, and she did not. "My hand is to me what your hearing and sight together are to you.... Out of doors I am aware by smell and touch of the ground we tread and the places we pass." She elegantly opens her world to the sighted and hearing. But in her preface, she raises a different issue—one that troubled her for many years: she did not want to be defined or limited by her disabilities.

Helen Keller on the porch of the home in Wrentham, Massachusetts, that she shared with Annie Sullivan and John Macy, ca. 1907. *Photograph by Lou A. Holman. Prints and Photographs Division, Library of Congress.*

> Every book is in a sense autobiographical. But while other self-recording creatures are permitted at least to seem to change the subject, apparently nobody cares what I think of the tariff, the conservation of our natural resources, or the conflicts which revolve about the name of Dreyfus. If I offer to reform the educational system of the world, my editorial friends say, "That is interesting. But will you please tell us what idea you had of goodness and beauty when you were six years old?" The editors are so kind that they are no doubt right in thinking that nothing I have to say about the affairs of the universe would be interesting. But until they give me opportunity to write about matters that are not-me, the world must go on uninstructed and unreformed, and I can only do my best with the one small subject upon which I am allowed to discourse.[14]

Her editors did not think she had nothing to say. To the contrary, they feared that her opinions would be unpopular and offend readers. She was willing to take that chance. For the rest of her life, she would speak out about her political and ethical convictions, and she would be listened to, admired, and sometimes criticized.

Finding Her Voice

Keller's desire to communicate more directly led her to try once more to learn to speak. Lecture tours were popular, and she wanted to share her ideas and increase her income by joining the circuit. In 1910 she began voice lessons with Charles White, a singing teacher who specialized in teaching people to make their voices more flexible and to strengthen the vocal cords. She also had surgery to replace her eyes with prosthetics. Her left eye protruded unattractively, and she felt that would detract from her stage presence. From then on, journalists would routinely refer to her beautiful blue eyes, unaware that they were not real.

Around 1908, Helen Keller had become a Socialist and a suffragist. Having learned to speak, she became outspoken. She published her political views in an essay collection, *Out of the Dark*, issued in 1913. Her image changed from that of a brave young woman overcoming disability to that of a brave young woman speaking her mind. As a Socialist, Keller opposed U.S. entry into World War I, a position that grew increasingly unpopular. She expressed support for the Bolshevik Revolution and for the efforts of Margaret Sanger and others to legalize birth control. She donated to the National Association for the Advancement of Colored People. Her "radicalism" deterred many people from attending her lectures.

When Annie Sullivan spent five months in Puerto Rico to improve her health, Kate Keller came to live with Helen in Wrentham. Helen had hired a new secretary, Peter Fagan, who shared her political views. They became romantically involved, despite her mother's opposition. As Helen remembered, "his love was a bright sun that shone upon my helplessness and isolation." Kate Keller had assumed since Helen first became deaf-blind that marriage and motherhood were simply not possible. Helen's attraction to Fagan and his obvious devotion did not change her opinion. The couple secretly applied for a marriage license, but Kate found out and banished Fagan from the house. He and Helen then planned an elopement that Kate thwarted. They tried once more to elope but were again found out. In 1929, writing in *Midstream*, she said "The brief love will remain in my life, a little island of joy surrounded by dark waters. I am glad that I have had the experience of being loved and desired. The fault was not in the loving, but in the circumstances."[15]

In 1917, they sold the house in Wrentham, and Helen Keller, Annie

Sullivan, and a new secretary, Polly Thomson, moved to 93 Seminole Avenue in Forest Hills, New York. It was a two-story house of brick and limestone with pointed gables and a large bay window. They called it "Castle on the Marsh." Although it was small—seven rooms—and ugly, it was home for more than twenty years.[16]

In 1918, Keller and Sullivan appeared in a silent film, *Deliverance*, that told the story of her life. It was not a realistic portrayal. In fact, it was ridiculous. As a visual record of Keller as a young woman, though, it is invaluable. A sparkling, attractive figure, she walks in a garden, rides in a biplane, dances, reads Braille, and writes letters. When the film opened in New York, Actors' Equity was on strike. True to her principles, Keller refused to attend. Instead, she marched in protest with the strikers.

More successful, and more profitable, was the vaudeville act that Keller, Sullivan, and Polly Thomson staged twice a day for four years, beginning in 1920. Set in a drawing room, the twenty-minute sketch told the story of how Sullivan taught young Helen language. It ended with a "message of hope and inspiration to all mankind." Keller wrote that she "found the world of vaudeville much more amusing than the world I had always lived in, and I liked it." Audiences were welcoming, and she wore stage makeup and evening gowns with sequins and chiffon. The women were well paid for their performances, earning two thousand dollars a week—as much as the highest-paid professional entertainers.[17]

On the World Stage

Keller continued to write books and magazine articles. She began a continuation of her autobiography, the book that became *Midstream*, but she rewrote it four times before it was ready for publication in 1929. At that point she declared, "There will be no more books"—a vow that she broke several times. Instead she would occupy herself with public speaking about human rights and ways of improving life for people with disabilities. She became a founder of the American Civil Liberties Union, and an advisor and fundraiser for the American Foundation for the Blind and for similar groups outside the United States. Recognizing that her more extreme political views would hinder her effectiveness in this visible role, she kept them mostly to herself until World War II.

In the 1930s she visited the British Isles, Brittany, Yugoslavia, and Japan, speaking about the need for better education and employment opportunities for blind people. World War II ended her travels temporarily, but she visited dozens of military hospitals, offering hope and encouragement to wounded soldiers and sailors.

The decade brought a personal tragedy as well. Kate Keller had died in 1921, and Helen was left without one of her most dependable supports. But the greater loss occurred when Annie Sullivan died on October 20, 1936, with Helen holding her hand. Sullivan's accomplishment had been publicly recognized fully only late in her life, with the 1933 publication of Nella Braddy Henney's biography, *Anne Sullivan Macy: The Story Behind Helen Keller*. It would be more than twenty years before Keller would complete her own biography of her teacher.

Shortly before she died, Annie Sullivan told Polly Thomson, "Thank God I gave up my life that Helen might live. God help her to live without me when I go."[18] Keller did live without Annie, but her death was a terrible loss. They had been together, with only a few months apart, for nearly half a century. Others filled in for Annie in practical ways—Polly Thomson as her secretary, Nella Henney as her editor, and many friends as companions. But there was never an emotional bond as strong as the one begun by the seven-year-old Helen and the 21-year-old Annie in the little cottage in Tuscumbia.

A New Home

In 1939 one of the trustees of the American Foundation for the Blind had a house built for Keller in Easton, Connecticut. She named it Arcan Ridge after a farmhouse she had visited in Scotland. Cameron Clark, a Connecticut architect, was hired to design a house that would meet the needs of a deaf-blind home owner. "Yours is a different understanding of architecture than that of my other clients," Clark wrote.[19] He understood that the house should be easily navigable and offer a variety of spaces, including an outdoor terrace. Clark honored Keller's traditional architectural taste by adapting Colonial Revival features to create a house that would work for her and be compatible with the neighborhood. The symmetry of a central hall with rooms opening off each side made it easy to orient oneself.

Arcan Ridge became Keller's home base as she traveled around the world on behalf of the blind. In 1946, she made a world tour for the American Foundation for the Overseas Blind, the first of many that would take her to every continent except Antarctica in the next decade. While she and Polly Thomson were in Paris, they received a phone call telling them that a fire had destroyed Arcan Ridge and all its contents, including Keller's manuscript of the book she was writing about Annie Sullivan. They decided to rebuild the house, based on the original plans. The many gifts and mementos that Keller had acquired over the years were destroyed, but new treasures soon replaced the old.

Helen Keller's house in Easton, Connecticut, ca. 1941. This is the back of the original house, which burned in 1946. The house that replaced it was identical except for an added enclosed dining porch. *Courtesy of the Historical Society, Easton, Connecticut.*

Keller traveled widely to increase understanding of the needs of blind people and to raise money to meet those needs. At home, *Teacher* was published in 1955, and four years later the movie *The Miracle Worker* was released. Keller had visited the set and met Patty Duke, who was playing the young Helen, and Anne Bancroft, who played Annie Sullivan. Both women won Academy Awards for their roles. Harvard University made Keller the first woman to be awarded an honorary degree, and Radcliffe College created the Helen Keller Garden, with a fountain named for Annie Sullivan.

There were changes in the household at Arcan Ridge. Polly Thomson had a stroke in 1957, requiring live-in nursing care until her death in March 1960. Two new companions, Winnie Corbally and Evelyn Seide, managed the house, accompanied Keller to public appearances, and read to her. In 1961, she suffered several minor strokes. She stayed at home most of the time and had to use a wheelchair. In 1964, Lyndon Johnson awarded her the Presidential Medal of Freedom, and he became the twelfth president she had met, following Grover Cleveland, William McKinley, Theodore Roosevelt, William Howard Taft, Woodrow Wilson, Warren G. Harding, Calvin Coolidge, Herbert Hoover, Franklin D. Roosevelt, Harry S Truman, and Dwight Eisenhower.

Helen Keller died on June 1, 1968, at Arcan Ridge. Her funeral was held at the National Cathedral, and her ashes were interred next to those of Annie Sullivan and Polly Thomson.

To Visit

Helen Keller's birthplace, 300 North Commons Street West, Tuscumbia, Alabama 35674, is open to the public. For details, go to www.helenkellerbirthplace.org. The house in Forest Hills burned down; Arcan Ridge and the house in Wrentham are not open to the public.

2

Harriet Beecher Stowe

In May 1850, Harriet Beecher Stowe traveled with three of her children from Cincinnati, Ohio, to Brunswick, Maine. Her husband, Calvin, would join them later to take up his duties on the faculty of Bowdoin College, his alma mater. Born in Litchfield, Connecticut, in 1811, Harriet grew up there and in Boston. In 1832, though, she had moved to Ohio when her father, the Rev. Lyman Beecher, became the head of the new Lane Theological Seminary. The Beechers lived in the president's house, a large Federal mansion painted a pale yellow with dark green shutters.[1]

Calvin Stowe had joined the Lane faculty in 1833, and Harriet became fast friends with his wife, Eliza. After Eliza died in a cholera epidemic, Harriet and Calvin were drawn together. They married in January 1836.

Although the couple had little money, and soon had many children, Harriet was determined to write. She had already collaborated with her sister Catherine on books about education, morality, and home management. Calvin encouraged her: his wife "must be a *literary woman*. It is so written in the book of fate."[2] She insisted on having some private space to write, and they created a small room next to the nursery where she worked three hours a day. Her sketches and magazine articles paid for household help. She gathered her New England sketches into a book she titled *Mayflower,* published in 1843.

The nearly two decades Harriet spent in Cincinnati were essential for her later writing. The theological and political debates about slavery that took place on the Lane campus could have been held anywhere, but living close to the South brought theory down to earth. She was exposed to people with a wide variety of attitudes toward slavery and saw slaveholders as human beings who were flawed but redeemable. She knew free and enslaved Black people, and she had visited a Kentucky plantation. A companion later wrote that in *Uncle Tom's Cabin,* scenes from that visit "were portrayed with the most minute fidelity."[3] Harriet had seen the fear of a free Black woman when her former owner was nearby, and she had helped her to flee. At an Underground Railroad station in Ripley, Ohio, she heard the story of a fugitive escaping across a frozen river with a baby in her arms. What she had seen and heard fed her imagination.

On her way to Brunswick, Harriet visited relatives. At her brother Edward's home in Boston, her sister-in-law Isabella described the "terrible things" happening in America. She then wrote to Harriet, "telling her of various heartrending events caused by the enforcement of the Fugitive Slave Law," which required residents of free states to return fugitives to their owners. "Now, Hattie," she wrote, "if I could use a pen as you can, I would write something that would make this whole nation feel what an accursed thing slavery is."[4]

Harriet did want to write about slavery, but the demands on her time were extraordinary. Calvin was still in Ohio, and the house they rented—the only one available—needed a great deal of work. It had been designed in 1806 by Samuel Melcher III, Brunswick's leading architect, for the Rev. Benjamin Titcomb. The two-story Colonial house had a center hall with front rooms on either side, a two-story ell, and a one-story kitchen ell. In the 1820s, the Reverend Titcomb had rented rooms to Bowdoin students, including Stephen and Henry Wadsworth Longfellow. Henry's letters to his mother had complained of the leaky windows and unbearable cold that the open fires could not alleviate. By 1850, coal stoves had been installed, but there was no indoor plumbing and the windows were still drafty. Harriet managed to paint, install a kitchen sink, and refurbish furniture before Calvin and the other children arrived in July. On July 8, Harriet gave birth to Charles Edward Stowe. Calvin added a Newfoundland dog named Bruno to the family. And in November, Calvin returned to Ohio for six months to teach at Lane. With the arrival of winter, it became clear that the coal stoves had not solved the heating problem. "If I sit in my bedroom and try to write my head aches and my feet are cold," Harriet told Calvin.[5]

Despite the poor condition of the house, the rent was higher than the Stowes had budgeted for. Harriet assured Calvin that she could earn enough from writing "an extra piece or two" to cover the expense.[6] With extraordinary energy, and the help of her sister Catharine, she sat down to write.

Uncle Tom's Cabin

In November 1850, Harriet broke the law. A fugitive slave named John Andrew Jackson arrived in Brunswick on his way to Canada and spent the night at the Stowes' house before moving on. The following March, Harriet had a vision in church of a slave being whipped to death. As soon as she got home she wrote down the vision and read the passage aloud to her children.[7] Throughout the spring and summer, she wrote installments for the *National Era*, with the first installment appearing on June 5, 1851.

Calvin returned to Brunswick in March, and Harriet's sister Catharine joined the family for four months to help manage the household. She described their daily routine during her stay: "At eight o'clock we are thro' with breakfast & prayers & then we send off Mr. Stowe & Harriet both to *his room at the college.* There was no other way to keep her out of family cares & quietly at work & since this plan is adopted, she goes ahead finely."[8] After Catharine left, Harriet wrote despite family cares. She had always spent two hours reading aloud to her family every evening. Now she read installments to the children as she completed them, and she read them to adult friends on Saturday evenings. She used her listeners' reactions to revise before sending the manuscript on to the publisher.[9]

Harriet Beecher Stowe's house at 63 Federal Street, near Bowdoin College, Brunswick, Maine, where she lived from 1850 to 1852, and where she wrote *Uncle Tom's Cabin*. In 1855 the house underwent a major renovation, changing the Federal-style house shown here to the Greek Revival structure now on the campus. *Beecher-Stowe Family Papers, Schlesinger Library, Harvard Radcliffe Institute.*

For forty weeks, readers of the *National Era* read her work, and before April 1, 1852, when the last installment appeared, Harriet signed a contract with John P. Jewett of Boston to issue the stories as a book. Jewett's extensive advertising, plus the wide circulation of the stories in the *National Era*, had created a large market. The first printing of the two-volume novel—5,000 copies—arrived on March 20, 1852, and sold out immediately. By the end of the first week, 5,000 more were sold; by the end of the year, 300,000. By February 1853 a million had been sold in the United States and England. That month the Stowes dined with Henry Wadsworth Longfellow (a college friend of Calvin's as well as a former tenant in the

Brunswick house), who noted in his diary, "At one step she has reached the top of the stair-case up which the rest of us climb on our knees year after year." Harriet earned $10,300 in three months, ten times as much as Calvin's annual Bowdoin salary.[10]

A New Home

Six months after the publication of *Uncle Tom's Cabin*, the Stowes moved to Andover, Massachusetts, where Calvin had accepted a post at the Andover Theological Seminary. The seminary's "old stone workshop," built in 1828, had been used as a carpentry classroom, but it was now unoccupied and in disrepair. Harriet saw the possibilities of the old Federal style building and paid for its remodeling at a cost of slightly under $3,000. She planned the renovation herself, separating the open space into rooms, installing fireplaces and window seats, and adding an Italianate piazza.[11] In the decade that the Stowes lived in the house, Harriet wrote *The Key to Uncle Tom's Cabin*—a collection of documents and other evidence to answer the novel's critics. Her sisters Mary Perkins and Isabella Hooker helped with the research. She wrote numerous stories and six books, including *Dred* (1856), *The Minister's Wooing* (1859), and *The Pearl of Orr's Island* (1862).

In 1861, when the Civil War began, Harriet closely followed news of the battlefront. Her son Fred had enlisted, and Calvin's Andover students had formed a military company. Harriet wrote about the war for the *Independent*, pressing Lincoln to free the slaves. In November 1862, she traveled to Washington. Her visit to the White House generated an anecdote that is the only thing that many people know about Harriet: that Lincoln greeted her with "So this is the little woman who wrote the book that made this great war!" Modern biographers agree that this never happened. Harriet *did* visit the White House, and she *did* meet Lincoln, but there is no first-person account of their meeting. Her son Charles first described the event in his 1911 biography of his mother, but there is no evidence that he had been there. No other family member recorded the conversation, and there is no record of the visit in Lincoln's papers. But we do know what happened when the news reached Boston that Lincoln had signed the Emancipation Proclamation on January 1, 1863. Harriet was at the Boston Music Hall, and the celebrating crowd began chanting her name.[12]

Retiring to Nook Farm

In 1862, the Stowes began looking for a place to spend their retirement. Harriet was 51, and Calvin was 60; their children were grown and

Harriet Beecher Stowe's house in Andover, Massachusetts, formerly a carpentry workshop, which Stowe remodeled in 1852. The Stowes lived here until they moved to Oakholm, in Nook Farm, in 1864. *Beecher-Stowe Family Papers, Schlesinger Library, Harvard Radcliffe Institute.*

the long struggle for emancipation was over. They no longer had strong ties to Cincinnati or Brunswick. With the professional connection to Andover ended, there was no reason to remain there. Harriet's many siblings were scattered across the country. Henry Ward Beecher had been in Brooklyn since 1847, where he had become nationally famous as the minister of a large, wealthy congregation. At the end of the Civil War, Lincoln would invite him to deliver the address at the ceremony at Fort Sumter. The other surviving brothers were preaching and teaching in Florida, Illinois, Massachusetts, and upstate New York. Sister Catharine had never stayed in one place for long. But two of the sisters had settled very near each other in Hartford, where they had joined a small community of reform-minded people known as Nook Farm. Mary Beecher Perkins was raising her family there while her husband practiced law. Isabella Beecher and John Hooker settled there as well. They had been deeply involved in abolition, and after the war Isabella began her lifelong work, advancing the cause of women's suffrage. The Stowes decided to join them.[13]

Nook Farm was a hundred-acre plot just outside Hartford's city limits. John Hooker and his brother-in-law Francis Gillette had bought the land in 1851 and sold building lots to like-minded people. No fences separated one household from another; rather, paths connected them. Residents wandered past one another's gardens and visited through open doors. Each house was unique, but they shared a common exterior aesthetic: dark brown, ornamented with balconies, gables, and towers. Many had conservatories.[14]

Harriet bought land at Nook Farm in 1862 and hired the architect Octavius Jordan to build a house that she named Oakholm. She supervised every detail of its design and construction, telling the publisher James Fields, "My house with *eight* gables is growing wonderfully.... I go every day to see it—I am busy with drains sewers sinks digging trenching—& above all with manure!"[15] The Stowes moved into the house in 1864. It was an expensive undertaking, and Harriet wrote *Oldtown Folks* and what the biographer Milton Rugoff describes as "a variety of potboilers" to pay the bills. Calvin contributed to the effort as well, when his *Origin and History of the Books of the Bible*, published by the Hartford Publishing Company in 1867, unexpectedly proved a popular success, earning $10,000 in royalties. Three years later, the Stowes bought a gothic house with an orange grove in Mandarin, Florida, where they spent the winters. Harriet published a collection of her Florida sketches as *Palmetto Leaves* in 1873.[16]

The Stowes' financial troubles grew worse when Harriet shocked public sensibilities with "The True Story of Lady Byron's Life" in the *Atlantic*. She had grown friendly with the poet's widow on her trips to England, and in 1856 Lady Byron had told her about Byron's incestuous affair with his half-sister, Augusta Leigh. Lady Byron died in 1860, and in 1869 Countess Guiccioli, Byron's last mistress, published her *Recollections of Lord Byron*. She cast Lady Byron as a villain whose coldness had driven the poet from England into exile and ultimately to his death. Harriet decided to defend Lady Byron by making the scandal public. She knew that she was taking a risk. As she told William Dean Howells, an editor at the *Atlantic*, "I tremble at what I am doing & saying but I feel that justice demands it of me & I *must* not fail."[17]

Neither Harriet nor Howells realized how great a risk it was. Outraged at the attack on Byron's character, many readers canceled their *Atlantic* subscriptions. Charles Dickens told the *Atlantic*'s publisher, James Fields, "Wish you had nothing to do with the Byron matter. Wish Mrs. Stowe was in the pillory." A New York newspaper predicted that even Harriet's lifelong friends would desert her. They did not. Certainly the residents of Nook Farm remained loyal. Mark Twain, a frequent visitor to Nook Farm who would soon build his own house next to Harriet's, wrote in the *Buffalo Express* that incest "has been committed, time and again. History furnishes examples enough, to say nothing of the current experience of society, and it is quite as possible that Byron may have added one to the horrid examples of unnatural vice in history as it is undoubted that other men of noted name and distinguished position did before him."

Harriet wrote *Lady Byron Vindicated* (1870) to defend both her friend and herself, but it changed nothing. As the biographer Joan Hedrick explains, the book "vindicated neither Lady Byron, the cause of woman's rights, nor Stowe's reputation."[18]

In 1871, the Stowes sold Oakholm and bought a smaller house under construction in Nook Farm, the one that we now visit. Far less ostentatious than Oakholm, it bears no name. Its gray-painted brick stands in contrast to its neighbors' dark brown exteriors. Its third story, below a steep roof, is gabled. The overall style is Victorian gothic, with a pointed arch over the front door and rounded arches over some of the windows. Despite its dark woodwork, the house is light and airy, with bay windows that provide views of the grounds. One entire wall has gothic-style bookcases built to hold the many editions of Harriet's works, as well as the other books that she and Calvin had collected. An eclectic variety of furniture gives the house a homey feel, as do the paintings, which include some of Harriet's watercolors of scenes from Florida, and the requisite proliferation of knickknacks. Two porches connect the house to the gardens and neighboring yards. With 12 rooms, it was large enough to accommodate visiting family members, but small enough to be managed by an aging couple with few servants. Calvin, Harriet, and their oldest children, twin daughters Eliza and Harriet, moved into the house in 1873.[19]

Scandal and Division

The Beecher family—with 11 siblings and half-siblings—had always stuck together. The brothers all became ministers, serving congregations around the country. The four sisters were close, and three of them were living within yards of one another. But in 1872 their brother Henry Ward Beecher became involved in a scandal that was aired in the newspapers and eventually the courts. Henry was the most famous minister in America and had served the congregation of Brooklyn's Plymouth Church for 25 years. In the midst of the anniversary celebrations, *Woodhull & Claflin's Weekly* featured the headline "The Beecher-Tilton Scandal Case." Beecher was accused of having an affair with Elizabeth Tilton, a parishioner and the wife of a friend, the editor Theodore Tilton. The evidence was complicated, contradictory, and ever-changing, and the witnesses well known. Elizabeth Tilton repeatedly admitted adultery and then withdrew her confessions. She had spoken about the events with Susan B. Anthony and Elizabeth Cady Stanton. Theodore Tilton was said to have been unfaithful to Elizabeth. Henry denied the affair, but rumors of the relationship and of other improprieties persisted. In 1873, the church's examining committee charged Theodore Tilton with slander and dropped him from the church.[20]

Newspapers were filled with reports, rumors, and opinions; pamphlets, broadsides, cartoons, and poems kept the affair in the news. Tilton—impoverished, disbelieved, and angry—resorted to the courts. On January 11, 1875, people crowded into the Brooklyn City Courthouse to hear *Theodore Tilton v. Henry Ward Beecher, Action for Criminal Conversation*. For the first time, the Beecher siblings did not present a united front. Isabella Hooker believed Henry to be guilty, and Henry's supporters openly questioned her sanity. She did not appear at the trial. Their brother Tom also believed Henry to be guilty but chose to remain silent. "In my judgment," he wrote to Isabella, "Henry is following his slippery doctrines of expediency."[21] He did not believe the truth would come out in court. Harriet believed Henry and was furious at Isabella. She sat in the front pew of his church and defended him to friends and family, but she remained in Florida during the trial. Catharine and William offered odd defenses, including the suggestion that if Henry had wanted a mistress he would have chosen someone younger.

Harriet Beecher Stowe with two of her grandchildren, Lyman Beecher Stowe and Leslie Stowe, at her second home in Nook Farm, ca. 1885. The children's father was Charles Edward Stowe, who lived nearby. *Beecher-Stowe Family Papers, Schlesinger Library, Harvard Radcliffe Institute.*

The trial lasted nearly six months, and after eight days of deliberation, the jury reported that it could not reach a verdict. Plymouth Church expelled the parishioners who had expressed belief in Beecher's guilt, and Beecher used his charm and eloquence to win over doubters. Three years later, on April 16, 1868, Elizabeth Tilton published a letter in the *New York Times* stating that she had in fact committed adultery with Henry Ward Beecher, and an accompanying editorial accepted the truth of the letter.

But few were listening, and even fewer believed her. Henry became the most popular and highest-paid lecturer in the country.

Old Age at Nook Farm

The scandals swirling around her defense of Lady Byron and Henry's adultery took their toll. Before Henry's trial, Harriet had been prolific. *Oldtown Folks,* which she had been working on since 1866, appeared in 1869; and three novels set in New York society—*Pink and White Tyranny, My Wife and I,* and *We and Our Neighbors*—were published in 1871 and 1873. She wrote only one book after the trial: *Poganuc People* was published in 1878. Perhaps, as the *New York Times* suggested, "she wisely stayed her pen while still it commanded readers." Perhaps she was simply tired.[22]

Although her popularity had been damaged by the Lady Byron episode, the literary community still revered her. In 1882 the *Atlantic* gave her a slightly belated seventieth-birthday party, the first woman to be so honored. John Greenleaf Whittier and Oliver Wendell Holmes read poems they had written for her, and she gave a speech about her hopes for America's freed slaves. Annie Fields, her publisher's widow, continued to visit, and in 1884 she brought along an admiring young writer—Sarah Orne Jewett—whose books were inspired in part by *The Pearl of Orr's Island.*

Then the personal losses began. Her brother Henry died in 1883; Calvin and her brother Jim, in 1886. Harriet stopped traveling to Florida and lived quietly at Nook Farm with her twin daughters. Her mind gradually failed, and she became simply a kindly presence. She walked a great deal, often to the home of her son Charley, two miles from Nook Farm. She visited her neighbors' homes, picking flowers. She played and sang beloved songs. When she died, on July 1, 1896, the *New York Times* paid tribute to her family, her work, and her life. Her death, the paper claimed, "is more than the ending of a woman's life of whatever degree of fame. It marks the extinction of genius in a family, and is one of the closing leaves in an era of our century…. Rarely, indeed, is there so much in a single life as memorable or so interesting as in that of the writer of probably the most widely read work of fiction ever penned."

To Visit

The Harriet Beecher Stowe House (*www.stowehousecincy.org*) at 2950 Gilbert Avenue, Cincinnati, Ohio, is open Thursday through Sunday, year round.

The house where Harriet wrote *Uncle Tom's Cabin,* 63 Federal Street, Brunswick, Maine, is owned by Bowdoin College. "Harriet's Writing Room," commemorating her contributions to American literature and history, is open to the public; visitors should check with the college about hours.

The Stowes' house in Andover, 80 Bartlet Street, is part of Phillips Academy and is not open to the public. Harriet, Calvin, and their son Henry are buried in the Phillips Academy cemetery.

The Harriet Beecher Stowe Center (*www.harrietbeecherstowecenter.org*) is open every day except Tuesdays and holidays. The Center offers a variety of tours, and all are interactive and conversational, with opportunities for visitors to ask questions, express opinions, and make suggestions. Located at 77 Forest Street, Hartford, Connecticut, it is only a few yards from Mark Twain's house.

3

Ida Tarbell

Ida Tarbell grew up in the newly opened oil fields of Pennsylvania in the 1860s. Her family's fortunes depended on the market for oil, increasingly controlled by John D. Rockefeller's Standard Oil Company. As "the Standard" tightened its hold, the Tarbells and their neighbors watched their livelihoods become more and more precarious. In 1902, Tarbell would publish the first of 12 articles disclosing Standard Oil's monopolistic tactics. Four years later, the U.S. Attorney General won a suit against the company for antitrust violations, and in 1911 the Supreme Court upheld the verdict. The trust was dissolved. But Tarbell was more than a "muckraker"—Theodore Roosevelt's derogatory name for investigative journalists. She was an accomplished biographer, researcher, and editor whose advice was sought by presidents.

Log Cabin to Mansion

Franklin Sumner Tarbell and his wife, Esther Ann McCullough, planned to raise their children on an Iowa farm. Franklin had gone west, leaving his wife and infant daughter Ida in Hatch Hollow, a small rural community in northwest Pennsylvania. They lived in the log house of Esther's family. In her eighties, Ida remembered that "no home in which I have ever lived has left me with pleasanter memories of itself. It was a Cape Cod house, a story and a half high, built of matched hewn logs, its floors of narrow fitted oak planks, its walls ceiled, its 'upstairs' finished, a big fireplace in its living room. There were spreading frame outbuildings to accommodate the multiple activities of a farm which was in my time a going concern."[1]

Ida was born on November 5, 1857, in the midst of a financial panic that the following year left Franklin stranded in Iowa. He walked all the way back to Hatch Hollow, arriving in 1859, just in time for Edwin Drake's first successful oil well to start producing. Franklin began building wooden oil tanks, and to be closer to his customers, he moved the family to Rouseville in 1860. It was a dreadful place—primitive, noisy, smelly, and dangerous—but profitable enough for Franklin to find a house for his family on a hill outside town. When iron oil tanks replaced wood, he began drilling for oil and selling timber.

In 1870, Franklin built a new home for his family in Titusville. Five years earlier, nearby Pithole had been a thriving city of 15,000, with enough people and money to support the Bonta House, a fancy hotel that had cost $60,000 to build. Now, five years later, the Pithole wells were dry, and Franklin was able to buy the hotel for $600. He used parts of it—including doors, windows, and elaborate woodwork—to build a large, Italianate two-story house with a tower on East Main Street. Its tall shuttered windows, second-floor balconies, cupola, and porch made an impressive sight. The center wing included a living room, dining room, spare room, and kitchen on the first floor, with three bedrooms on the second. Franklin drew on his skill as a barrel maker to create curved interior walls in some of the rooms.[2]

Learning and Teaching

Titusville, older than the oil boom, had established churches and good schools. In high school, Ida excelled in science and writing. She graduated at the top of her class and enrolled at Allegheny College in Meadville, Pennsylvania, affiliated with the Methodist Church. Women had only recently been admitted, and Tarbell was the only woman in the freshman class.

Allegheny College was a wonderful place for Tarbell. Jeremiah Tingley, a science professor, encouraged her ambitions in natural science. She was the editor of the college newspaper, a member of Ossoli (the ladies' literary society named after Margaret Fuller Ossoli), and made close friends. Her time there was so important to her that she bequeathed her papers to the college. But when she graduated, the only career that seemed available was teaching.

In August 1880, Ida Tarbell became the preceptress of the Poland Union Seminary in Ohio. It was an impressive title, but it simply meant that for $500 a year she would teach Greek, Latin, French, German, geology, botany, geometry, and trigonometry. It left her no time for writing. After two years she returned home to a town struggling to survive as Standard Oil drove profits down for independent producers. Her father again headed west, beyond Iowa to the Dakota Territories. Ida stayed home to care for her mother and grandmother. When her father returned, she started a new career.

Ida Tarbell's childhood home at 324 East Main Street in Titusville, Pennsylvania, built by her father in 1870. It was restored in 2007. *The Drake Well Museum, Pennsylvania Historical and Museum Commission.*

Editor

In 1874, a Methodist clergyman and a philanthropist founded the Chautauqua Institution on Lake Chautauqua in New York. They offered lectures and classes in music, art, physical education, and academic subjects in a village with attractive cottages and meeting places. Two years later, the Institution began publishing a newspaper, the *Chautauqua Assembly Daily Herald*. In the summer of 1883, the *Herald* announced: "This unique little paper will be enriched by the pen of Miss Ida M. Tarbell, a young lady of fine literary mind, endowed with the peculiar gift of a clear and forcible expression."[3] During the off-season, they published a monthly magazine, *The Chautauquan*.

Tarbell wrote articles, translated pieces from the *Revue des Deux Mondes*, took care of proofreading, and learned how to lay out the newspaper. She was, in effect, the managing editor, though her title was assistant editor. The magazine expanded to cover social and economic problems, with articles on topics such as temperance, women's rights, and the eight-hour day. During her eight years at the *Chautauquan*, the magazine circulation increased from 15,000 (1880) to 50,000.

Tarbell's time at *The Chautauquan* ended abruptly and unhappily. The editor, Rev. Theodore Flood, had always undervalued her work. In 1890 he named his inexperienced son associate editor. Tarbell resigned, along with two other young women on the staff. Her next move—startling to her family—was to go to Paris and support herself as a writer. She had become interested in Manon Phlipon de Roland (1754–1793), a French writer and hostess of an influential salon, who was sent to the guillotine during the Terror. Tarbell had written an article about her for *The Chautauquan*, but she wanted to write a full biography.

The two young women who had left *The Chautauquan* with her, along with another friend, joined her. With four of them sharing rent, they thought, the adventure would be affordable. They arrived in Paris in August 1891 and found an apartment in a boardinghouse at 5, rue de Sommerard in the Latin Quarter.[4]

Writer

Although Tarbell and her friends succumbed to many of Paris's temptations—sightseeing, cheap restaurants, parks—she immediately began writing. She rose at 6:00, wrote from 8:00 to 12:00, and scoured French newspapers for leads. Before leaving the United States, she had arranged with several newspapers to buy news and feature articles. Her first sale, though, was a short story, "France Adorée," which she sold to *Scribner's* for $100. Soon her articles were appearing in the *Chicago Union Signal*, the *Pittsburgh Dispatch*, the *Boston Transcript*, and the *Cincinnati Times Star*. She sold articles to *Harper's Bazaar* and the McClure newspaper syndicate. She probably took special pleasure in the $100 that Theodore Flood paid for two articles in *The Chautauquan*. She also found time to work on her biography of Madame de Roland.

In the spring of 1892, her roommates went home, and Tarbell moved with her landlady to a house at 17, Rue Malebranche.[5] Her work was becoming well known at home, and American editors began to pay court. Samuel McClure, head of the newspaper syndicate, invited her to join him in New York, where he was starting a new magazine. She agreed instead to freelance for him while working on her book. Edward Burlingame, the editor of *Scribner's*, promised that his magazine would publish an article on Roland and that their book publishing arm would issue the title when it was ready. *Madame Roland* was published in 1895.

As productive as she was, she wasn't always getting paid. The Panic of 1893 had left newspapers and magazines strapped for cash. In 1894 she struck a deal with McClure. He would pay her passage home, and in

October she would join his staff at a salary of $2,100. She returned to the United States that summer, and McClure summoned her to New York in July for a special assignment.

In the 1790s, Napoleon Bonaparte had begun his rise to power. As the centennials of his victories approached, public interest in his life grew. Gardiner Hubbard, a wealthy Washingtonian and founder of the National Geographic Society, had agreed to let McClure publish the engravings of Napoleon that he had collected to illustrate a biography of the emperor. Tarbell was to write the biography. She moved to Washington, living on Hubbard's estate, Twin Oaks, and using his library as well as the Library of Congress and the papers of the State Department.[6]

Tarbell finished the first article in only six weeks. When it appeared in November 1894, the circulation of *McClure's Magazine* jumped from 24,500 to 65,000. By the time the series ended in April 1895, circulation had risen to 100,000, and by the turn of the century, to 250,000. The *Boston Globe* reviewed her work: "It is familiar with the latest as well as with older data, and is so painstaking in research that it brings out much that is new to most readers. It recognizes the scientific spirit of modern historical criticism, and is firsthand and attractive in style."[7] McClure's book publishing arm issued the series as *A Life of Napoleon Bonaparte* in 1901, and Tarbell supplemented it with *A Sketch of the Life of Josephine*. She was still receiving royalties from the Napoleon book in 1938.

Tarbell's next assignment was a series of articles about Abraham Lincoln based on the recollections of people who knew him. When she consulted John Nicolay and John Hay, Lincoln's private secretaries, who had co-authored a ten-volume biography, Nicolay insisted that they had found and published everything that was to be found. Unconvinced, she turned to public records from courts and local and county governments, local histories, newspapers, and interviews. She was living in an apartment at 191 I Street NW, in Washington but traveled to Kentucky, Indiana, and Springfield, Illinois.[8] She discovered new sources and amassed a collection of anecdotes, most of which proved untrue when investigated. Lincoln's son Robert gave her a daguerreotype of Lincoln as a young man, without a beard, that had never been published. That portrait appeared with her first article in November 1895. The series continued with edited manuscripts by people who had known the president and then 20 articles with Tarbell's byline. Though never trained as a historian, Tarbell had become a thorough, careful researcher who was able to present a much-studied subject in a new light. Her book *The Life of Abraham Lincoln* was published by Doubleday, McClure in 1900 and reprinted many times.

Muckraker

In May 1899, Tarbell became the managing editor of *McClure's*. She shared a two-bedroom apartment at 40 West 9th Street in Greenwich Village with two cats.[9] Tarbell decided to tackle the topic of monopolies. Of course, Standard Oil was very much on her mind because of its impact on her family and all of the people who, like them, had struggled against the trust. And Standard Oil wasn't a faceless entity. Because it was equated in most people's minds with John D. Rockefeller, the narrative could be more interesting. In September 1901, McClure approved a three-part feature on Standard Oil. Tarbell told her research assistant that her goal was to produce "a narrative history of the Standard Oil Company. I am to do it, and shall go about it as I would any other piece of historical work in which I had to draw almost entirely from original sources. It is in no sense a piece of economic work, nor is it intended to be controversial, but a straightforward narrative, as picturesque and dramatic as I can make it, of the great monopoly."[10]

It turned out to be far more difficult than she expected: Many people "believed that anybody going ahead openly with a project in any way objectionable to the Standard Oil Company would meet with direct or indirect attack. Examination of their methods had always been objectionable to them. 'Go ahead, and they will get you in the end,' I was told."[11] With a combination of courage, determination, and research skills, Tarbell plowed ahead. One document vital to her argument was *The Rise and Fall of the South Improvement Company,* a pamphlet that detailed how Standard Oil had manipulated railroads to freeze out competitors. To suppress it, Standard Oil had bought all the copies—except one, which Tarbell found in the New York Public Library.

With enough documents in hand, she wanted to interview the principals. Rockefeller's associate Henry Huttleston Rogers asked his friend Mark Twain to introduce him to Tarbell. Rogers was concerned about the company's image and thought that he could exert some control over what Tarbell would write. Their first meeting took place at Rogers' home on East 57th Street. It began with reminiscences about Rouseville:

> We forgot our serious business and talked of our early days on the Creek. Mr. Rogers told me how the news of the oil excitement had drawn him from his boyhood home in New England, how he had found his way into Rouseville, gone into refining. He had married and put his first thousand dollars into a home on the hillside adjoining ours.
> "It was a little white house," he said, "with a high peaked roof."
> "Oh, I remember it!" I cried. "The prettiest house in the world, I thought it." It was my first approach to the Gothic arch, my first recognition of beauty in a building.[12]

When they got down to business, they agreed that she would tell him what she was working on, and he would provide documents and explanations. He would have no say in what she wrote. They continued to meet for two years, almost always at his office. His information always had to be checked against other sources, and he often evaded her questions. He was never able to arrange a promised meeting with Rockefeller.

Tarbell got more cooperation from other sources, including the congressional Industrial Commission and the Interstate Commerce Commission. No matter what the source of her information, she checked and rechecked it. She worked at home, looking in at the office once a day. By mid-1902, she had drafts of three articles, which—like all articles in *McClure's*—had to undergo review by the editors. Finally, the first article was published in November 1902. Its appearance and reception allayed the fears of her Titusville neighbors, and they began to share their experiences. People brought her documents and information about a Standard Oil practice that she had only suspected: they spied on their competitors and detractors. Her article on that subject so infuriated Rogers that he would no longer meet with her. (They did meet by accident in 1907 and spent time together at his home.)[13] The series ended in November 1904, followed by the publication of the two-volume *History of the Standard Oil Company*, with more than 200 pages of documentation.

The book was a commercial and critical success. Newspapers wrote about it and published Tarbell's picture. One magazine, *The Critic*, wrote: "Her *History of Standard Oil* is to the present time the most remarkable book of its kind ever written in this country." Decades later, a friend asked Tarbell, "If you could rewrite your book today, what would you change?" "Not one word, young man, not one word." In 1999, New York University's journalism school ranked it fifth among the 100 best works of journalism in the 20th century.[14]

Tarbell's book provided ammunition for the federal antitrust lawsuit that began in 1906 and ended with the breakup of the trust in 1911. It also spurred the publication of more investigative reporting, not only by the *McClure's* journalists whom Theodore Roosevelt labeled "muckrakers," but also by other magazines. Even the *Ladies' Home Journal* joined in with an exposé of patent medicines.

Tarbell used her royalties to buy a Connecticut farm. She named it Twin Oaks, after the Hubbard estate in Washington. The resemblance ended with the name. Her Twin Oaks was a two-story frame house with a central chimney, built in the late eighteenth century. Fireplaces and stoves provided the only heat. The graceful Greek Revival entrance, probably added in the mid–19th century, features side and transom windows and a portico with Doric columns. The main part of the original house had been expanded before she bought it. The property also had barns and a small cottage. She furnished it with antiques bought locally and covered the floors with rush mats.

Tarbell had not planned to farm: "I wanted something of my very own with no cares," she wrote, "but … things happened: the roof leaked; the grass must be cut if I was to have a comfortable sward to sit on; water in the house was imperative." Soon she was planting crops and flowers; having fields plowed; and raising horses, a cow, a pig, and chickens. To ensure that she didn't go broke, she decided to spend "only what I could lay aside from income, that I would divide this appropriation into three parts—one for the land, one for the house, one for furnishing. As the budget was very small it meant that a thousand things that I wanted to do went undone, and still are undone. But it meant also that I had little or no financial anxiety."[15]

Tarbell, always attentive to her financial situation, had become increasingly cautious since 1905, when her father died and she took his place at the head of the family. Twenty years later, she wrote that the farm "had become the family home. Here my mother had come to pass the last summers before her death in 1917; here my niece Esther had been married under the Oaks; here my niece Clara and her husband Tristram Tupper,

Ida Tarbell's house, Twin Oaks, ca. 1910. Tarbell bought the house at 320 Valley Road, Easton, Connecticut, in 1905 with the royalties from her exposé of Standard Oil. She dug a new well and brought running water into the house; the area had no electricity until the 1930s. *Historical Society of Easton, Connecticut.*

battered by war service, had come in 1919 to live in our little guest house....
A hundred associations gave the place a meaning and dignity which I
had never expected to feel in any home of my own, something that only
comes when a place has been hallowed by the joys and sorrows of family
life."[16]

New Ventures

Sam McClure had built up his magazine with the help of his partner John Phillips and writers like Tarbell, Lincoln Steffens, Ray Stannard Baker, Finley Peter Dunne, and Albert Boyden. The reporters were becoming disillusioned with McClure, whose extramarital affairs and overambitious business plans were making their jobs difficult. In 1906, they decided to leave. They agreed to finish the projects they were working on and accepted severance packages.

The writers pooled their resources, enlisted friends to invest, and bought *The American Magazine*, an arrangement that lasted until 1915, when they sold it to the Crowell Publishing Company. Tarbell wrote about the history of tariffs and, to bring the topic down to earth, she published "Every Penny Counts," demonstrating the negative impact of tariffs on consumers. President Woodrow Wilson, impressed by the articles, invited her to join the Tariff Commission in 1916, but she declined.

When Tarbell was growing up, two subjects were discussed in the family home. Her father talked about Standard Oil, and her mother talked about women's rights. Ida had had the last word on the oil monopoly, and now she took up the role of women. She was at odds with her mother and sister, who were staunch proponents of women's right to vote. Tarbell supported the rights of working women to a fair wage and reasonable hours, but she insisted that middle-class women should stick to their traditional roles. Their job was to take care of their homes and families and to train their domestic help properly. Women's suffrage was unimportant because it would make no difference in the way the country was governed. This, coming from a woman who had won such a prominent place in a very male profession, and exerted such public influence, came as an unpleasant surprise. Her articles on the subject were collected in *The Business of Being a Woman*, published by Macmillan in 1914. She infuriated many prominent women, including Charlotte Perkins Gilman and Helen Keller, and puzzled many others. Jane Addams, the founder of Hull House, concluded, "There is some limitation to Ida Tarbell's mind."[17]

After she resigned from *The American Magazine*, Tarbell wrote as a freelancer, but she also went on the lecture circuit. It was grueling work for a woman approaching 60. Her first tour took her to 49 towns in 49 days and paid her $2,500. In 1916 and 1917, she went on tour twice a year for five to six weeks, traveling by train. She was still managing the farm. And then war broke out.

World War I

When the United States entered the war, President Wilson appointed Tarbell to the Women's Committee of the Council of National Defense. In 1917, Tarbell's mother died, and Ida collapsed from stress and overwork. She spent three months at the Johns Hopkins Hospital and was diagnosed with Parkinson's Disease. Yet January 1919 found her in Paris reporting on the armistice and the Treaty of Versailles for the *Red Cross Magazine*. Her articles were collected in *Peacemakers—Blessed and Otherwise*. On her lecture tours, she spoke about the importance of the League of Nations. Her writing and lectures were now being managed by a literary agent, Paul Reynolds, whom she described as "the salvation of my old age!"[18]

Tarbell spent more and more time at the Connecticut farm, writing in her library every morning. In addition to articles in *The New Republic, McCall's, Collier's,* and *Century*, she published *In the Footsteps of the Lincolns* and biographies of Elbert H. Gary, the founder of U.S. Steel, and the businessman and diplomat Owen D. Young. *McCall's* sent her to Italy to write a four-part series on Mussolini, for which she was paid $25,000. President Warren G. Harding appointed her to his 1921 Unemployment Conference, where she served alongside Herbert Hoover, then secretary of commerce. Her frugality and conservative investments allowed her to survive the 1929 stock market crash with very few losses. She continued to write, but she retired from the lecture circuit in 1932.

Paul Reynolds had been urging Tarbell to write her autobiography, and she set to work sometime around her 80th birthday. She found it "a surprising adventure," revealing feelings, ideas, and memories that she had forgotten. And she never stopped working because, she wrote, "I know I should find this end of life less satisfactory if it were not a working end, conditioned as it must be by certain concessions to years, easements necessary if I am to keep vigor for my two or three hours a day at my desk and, once accepted, becoming more and more enjoyable."[19] Macmillan published *All in the Day's Work* in 1939, and Tarbell posed for a picture in front of the house on Main Street. When she died, on January 6, 1944, she was buried in Titusville's Woodlawn Cemetery, next to her parents.

To Visit

The Titusville house, at 324 East Main Street, has been restored to its late-19th-century appearance, and the first floor is a museum open to the public. For more information or to schedule a visit, call Oil Region Alliance at (814) 677–3152 or email info@oilregion.org

Maine

4

Sarah Orne Jewett

Sarah Orne Jewett was born in her grandfather's home in South Berwick, Maine, in 1849, and died there 59 years later. In her writing, she immortalized the houses, landscapes, history, and people of Maine. She traveled beyond the state's borders, but her writing did not.

Family

Four generations shared the house in South Berwick: Sarah's great-grandfather, Dearborn Jewett; grandfather Captain Theodore F. Jewett; his second wife, Mary; his older son, William; his younger son, Theodore; Theodore's wife, Caroline (Frances) Perry; and Theodore and Frances's daughters, Mary and Sarah. Frances was the daughter of Dr. William Perry, Theodore's former partner in a medical practice in Exeter, New Hampshire.

Fortunately, the house was large. It was built in 1744 for John Haggens, a successful merchant, whose family lived there until 1819. With two stories, large rooms, and high ceilings, it was big enough for the Jewetts. Elaborately carved woodwork—cornices, mantels, and staircases—marks it as the home of a prosperous family. Decorative plasterwork and a wide staircase give the first- and second-floor halls a spaciousness that carries over into the landing between the two floors, with a window seat and light streaming through an arched window. The main part of the first floor contains a parlor, library, dining room, and breakfast room, with the kitchen housed in an ell adjoining a pantry and shed. The second floor has four bedrooms in the main part of the house, with maid's quarters in the ell.[1]

Captain Jewett moved from Portsmouth, New Hampshire, to South Berwick in 1820. He rented the house while Haggens' estate was being settled and purchased it in 1839. He had become a timber merchant—a prosperous occupation in a shipbuilding town—but his years at sea provided him with endless stories to entertain his granddaughters. As Sarah wrote

4. Sarah Orne Jewett

Sarah Orne Jewett's House in South Berwick, Maine, ca. 1910. Jewett was born here in 1849 and died here at the age of 59. She redecorated many of the rooms, but the basic structure of the house remained as it had been in her childhood. She did most of her writing here. *Schlesinger Library, Harvard Radcliffe Institute.*

in her memoir, "Looking Back on Girlhood," "He was a sea-captain, and had run away to sea in his boyhood and led a most adventurous life, but was quite ready to forsake seafaring in his early manhood." She always remembered the stories he had told of their ancestors' roles in the Revolution, life at sea, and the War of 1812. Many of the old sailors in Sarah's stories trace their roots to Captain Jewett, his friends, and the seafaring friends of her Exeter relatives. By the time Sarah was writing, both shipping and shipbuilding had nearly vanished from Berwick, replaced by textile mills, but the stories of those older times survived.[2]

Sarah's other grandfather, Dr. William Perry, was an avid reader with an extensive library that he happily shared with his granddaughters. Sarah and Mary often visited their Exeter relatives, occasionally spending a whole summer. In her late forties, Sarah wrote to a friend, "I have had to go to Exeter several times lately, where I always find my childhood going on as if I had never grown up at all, with my grand-aunts and their old houses and their elm-trees and their unbroken china plates and big jars by the fireplaces."[3]

In 1854, when Sarah was five, Dr. Jewett and his family moved into a Greek Revival house that Captain Jewett had built for them in his garden. A third daughter, Caroline Augusta, was born soon after they moved. The house was smaller and less elegant than the captain's house, but it was comfortable, with a separate entrance opening into a wing for Dr. Jewett's office. Sarah and her sisters moved freely between the two houses. As her biographer Paula Blanchard notes, Sarah's "character was influenced by two quite different surroundings, merged so closely that the line between them was blurred under common grass and trees. One boldly commanded attention at the main intersection, as nearly aristocratic as New England democracy allowed; the other was comfortable and nondescript, a purely functional house of no pretensions whatever."[4]

The new house was not as grand as the old, but it was a reader's dream. Sarah suffered from what we now know to be rheumatoid arthritis, and when she was ill and confined to the house, reading became a lifeline. She remembered that "the old house was well provided with leather-bound books of a deeply serious nature, but in my youthful appetite for knowledge, I could even in the driest find something vital."[5] Those serious books included her father's botanical journals and medical books, and in both her life and her fiction, medicine and herbal remedies played a part. Her mother and grandmother introduced her to lighter reading, like Jane Austen's *Price and Prejudice,* George Eliot's *Scenes of Clerical Life,* and the works of Margaret Oliphant. Dr. Jewett subscribed to the *Atlantic Monthly* and *Punch,* and Sarah herself shared 17 magazine subscriptions with friends at school. The family read aloud in the evenings, and Sarah read to her grandmother every day. One of the books she read in her early teens, Harriet Beecher Stowe's *The Pearl of Orr's Island,* is set on Maine's seacoast, showing her that the lives of people around her were worthy literary subjects. When she reread the book as an adult, she found it "just as clear and perfectly original and strong as it seemed to me in my thirteenth or fourteenth year, when I read it first. I never shall forget the exquisite flavor and reality of delight that it gave me."[6]

Jewett lived with her mother and sister Mary in one or the other of those two houses her entire life, although beginning in 1881 she spent part of the year with Annie Fields in Boston. South Berwick was where she wrote. The landscape, its houses, and the people who lived there in the past and present became her subjects.

A Writing Life

Jewett began writing for publication soon after she graduated from the Berwick Academy in 1865, with stories for children written under pseudonyms. In 1869 her story "Mr. Bruce," written under the name A.C. Eliot, appeared in the *Atlantic Monthly.* She began to believe that writing was the path shown her by God, that it was the way she could live a useful life. Writing became both a vocation and a profession. On July 1, 1873, she wrote to the editor Horace Scudder, "I am getting quite ambitious and really feel that writing is my work—my business perhaps; and it is so much better than making a mere amusement of it as I used."[7]

She was businesslike about her writing. She kept to a schedule, writing letters in the morning and fiction in the afternoon. She committed to spending five hours a day writing, and she set goals for the number of stories she would complete each year. She sought advice from her editors and asked Scudder to explain the intricacies of copyright: "I know there is something about a thing's being 'copyrighted' or not, which may hinder their being used over again. At any rate, I should like to know if there is anything for me to do about it." She was not discouraged by rejection. She simply set rejected stories aside to be included in later collections. In 1873, still a novice, she understood where her talents lay, telling Scudder, "I don't believe I could write a long story.... In the first place I have no dramatic talent. The story would have no plot.... It seems to me I can furnish the theatre, and show you the actors, and the scenery, and the audience, but there never is any play." This did not concern her, though. "If the editors will take the sketchy kind and people like to read them, is not it as well to do that and do it successfully as to make hopeless efforts to achieve something in another line which runs much higher?"[8]

Jewett's early success was based on her ability to portray the scenery and characters around her. She is known as a "local color" writer—now sometimes a dismissive description, but at the time a sought-after quality. The way she captured the beauty, atmosphere, and people of the Maine coast captivated readers. Over time, she learned to add plot, and the sketches grew into stories and novels. Her most famous work was set in two fictitious towns, Deephaven and Dunnet Landing. The Deephaven saga began in 1873 with the publication of "The Shore House" in *The Atlantic*, followed by "Deephaven Cronies" in 1875 and "Deephaven Excursions" in 1876. In April 1877, the Boston firm of James R. Osgood and Company published *Deephaven*, a collection of 13 sketches in which two young women from Boston spend a summer in a seaside village. The men and women of the town entertain them with stories of times past, and the young women come to appreciate the town's past and present, its fisherman and farmers, and most of all the women who made rewarding lives for themselves in difficult circumstances. Offering the sort of moral that Jewett found hard to resist, one of them says, "I have understood something lately better than I ever did before,—it is that success and happiness are not things of chance with us, but of choice ... it is our own fault if the events of our lives are hindrances; it is we who make them bad or good."[9]

A year later, building on the success of *Deephaven*, Osgood published *Play Days: A Book of Stories for Children,* all of which had been published in magazines, and in 1879 *Old Friends and New,* a collection of mostly previously published stories. *Country By-Ways,* another collection, was published by Houghton Mifflin, the successor to Osgood's publishing house. It was dedicated to Jewett's father, who had died in 1878. Seven stories that had appeared in journals, plus one new story, were published as *The Mate of the Daylight, and Friends Ashore* in 1884, the same year that *A Country Doctor*—her first novel—appeared.

A Country Doctor is semi-autobiographical. Its heroine is the ward of a country doctor who decides not to marry but to devote herself to a God-given calling. In her case it is medicine, but it is easy to see in her the young Sarah making the decision to dedicate herself to writing. A year later a second novel, *A Marsh Island,* was published after being serialized in the *Atlantic.* Houghton, Mifflin published another story collection, *A White Heron and Other Stories,* in 1886. This record of publication demonstrates not only how prolific a writer she was, but how canny she was about maximizing her income from her writing. Each story was used at least twice, and as new stories appeared in magazines, they called attention to the books. She had once told an editor that she didn't consider writing a "bread and butter affair" but admitted that "such a spendthrift as I could not fail to be glad of money."[10]

All of those stories had been written in her childhood home— the more modest of the two houses—but in 1887 Sarah, Mary, and their mother moved into the "big house," while her sister Caroline Eastman and her family moved into the smaller house. The new arrangement echoed the geography of Sarah's childhood, with the older generation in the older house and the younger next door. Mary and Sarah redecorated, keeping the earlier style in many rooms (muskets over the kitchen hearth, and landscapes and family portraits in the parlor), but they incorporated contemporary styles with Arts and Crafts wallpapers and carpets in the entry hall and bedrooms. Jewett could write at desks in the library, her bedroom, and the upstairs hall. The library has ample shelving for many books, and the bedrooms are spacious and decorated with colorfully painted woodwork and tiles surrounding the fireplaces.

Jewett returned to writing for children with the publication of a popular history, *The Story of the Normans* (1887) and *Betty Leicester, A Story for Girls* (1889). Houghton, Mifflin also issued two more collections of previously published stories—*Tales of New England* and *Strangers and Wayfarers.* Much of her time from 1889 to 1891 was devoted to caring for her mother, who died in October 1891. Nevertheless, *A Native of Winby and Other Tales,* published in 1893, contained one new story.

In 1889, in a break from caring for her mother, Jewett visited Alice Longfellow in Martinsville, Maine, and returned to the area in 1895 and

1896. She immortalized the landscape in a series of sketches for the *Atlantic Monthly*, beginning in January 1896. That November they were collected and expanded in *The Country of the Pointed Firs*. The stories center around a mature woman who has chosen writing as her vocation. She comes to live for a time in the fictional Dunnet Landing and becomes a full participant in village life. One critic has argued that *Deephaven* was a rehearsal for *The Country of the Pointed Firs*, "the great final performance, in the course of which a world would be created."[11] That world brought together the people of the Maine coast whom she had known since childhood, the stories (true and apocryphal) she had heard, and the morals she wanted to convey.

Jewett's critical and popular reception is built on her writing for high-end publications—the *Atlantic Monthly*, *Harper's*, *Scribner's*, and *Century*—and on the novels and collections of stories published by prestigious Boston firms. But she also wrote for non-elite magazines and for newspaper syndicates, expanding her audience to readers beyond eastern cities who could not afford to subscribe to the *Atlantic*. Jewett wrote for the *Woman's Home Companion*, *Everybody's*, *Romance*, and *Pictorial Review*. Syndicates like those run by Samuel S. McClure and Irving Bacheller made money by paying authors for the rights to a story (usually $150) and then selling it to as many newspapers as possible. They needed well-known authors in their stables to convince newspaper editors to subscribe to their service. In September 1884, Samuel S. McClure called on Jewett to recruit her for the newspaper syndication service he was starting. He told Jewett he would take as many stories as she could write.

McClure had much to offer. The syndicates usually paid about three times what the high-end magazines offered, and authors could use their rates to bargain with other editors. Elite publishers considered it "ungentlemanly" to compete with one another, but that put authors at a disadvantage. Book historian Charles Johanningsmeier explains that the syndicates "helped usher in an era of competitive bidding among publishers" and quotes William Dean Howells as claiming that they "no doubt advanced the prosperity of the short story by increasing the demand for it."[12]

The syndicates also welcomed a greater variety of subject matter, treatment, and length than the literary magazines, and they gave their more famous authors a great deal of leeway. Jewett could write a short story for one-time publication or a long story that would appear in three or four installments, and she often set her own deadlines. She could also experiment with genres and styles that elite magazine editors would not countenance. Perhaps most important, the syndicates expanded readership exponentially. One of Jewett's syndicated stories, "Stolen Pleasures," appeared in five newspapers, including the *Detroit Free Press*, which sold

18,000 copies a day in 1885—almost twice as many copies as the *Atlantic* sold in a month.[13] In addition, some of those thousands of readers might enjoy Jewett's story enough to buy one or more of her books.

Selling stories to print media that catered to a wide range of readers, bargaining with publishers for higher fees and royalties, and seeing her works broadcast across the continent, Jewett had become a financial actor in the literary marketplace. She came to relish the business side of writing, "frankly enjoying the novelty of making money," as Blanchard notes. Although she had received a share in her parents' estate, she was prouder of her writing income, which amounted to $75,000 by the end of her life. She invested in U.S. Steel, the Pennsylvania Railroad, and other large corporations, but there was enough left for travel, redecorating the house, new horses, charitable causes, and the occasional frivolous purchase.[14]

A Writing Community

Writing was the foundation of Jewett's friendships and social life. In the 1870s, she began spending time away from Berwick, making friends in Boston, Newport, and summer resorts in eastern New England. In Boston, she met Mary Bucklin Davenport Claflin, an editor and writer on New England subjects from a generation earlier, whose writing influenced her work. Through Claflin, she met Harriet Beecher Stowe and John Greenleaf Whittier, who became one of her strongest supporters. Harriet Waters Preston, a translator and author of novels about New England life, became a friend and advisor. Sarah Chauncey Woolsey, who wrote for children under the name Susan Coolidge, may have inspired "A. C. Eliot."

The editors who published Jewett's work also became her friends. She dedicated *Deephaven* to Mary Greenwood Lodge, a writer and editor of *St. Nicholas Magazine*. William Dean Howells was both mentor and friend, providing valuable advice. Horace Scudder, editor of the *Riverside Magazine for Young People* and later of the *Atlantic Monthly*, played a similar role. But Jewett's closest professional and personal friends were James T. and Annie Fields.

James Fields became a partner in the publishing firm Ticknor & Fields in 1845, and he had become the editor of the *Atlantic Monthly* in 1861. When Jewett met him, he had retired from the firm. James and Annie had married in 1854. The historian Richard Brodhead's description of the couple's role in American letters shows how important this friendship was to writers: "Fields had gained monopolistic hold on the writings of Hawthorne, Emerson, Longfellow, and their likes and contrived the means to identify them as classics. He then transferred this cachet to the new authors his publishing instruments brought to public life, for instance William Dean Howells and Henry James. The high-spirited and immensely attractive Annie Fields, his much younger wife, supplemented his business dealings by travelling with him and making literary contacts abroad, then by creating the Bostonian salon where foreign literary dignitaries, still-living but already canonized American authors, and young aspirants to high letters could meet and realize a literary world."[15]

Through James and Annie Fields, Jewett met her fellow authors, many of whom became mentors and friends. Ticknor & Fields's British authors included Anthony Trollope, William Makepeace Thackeray, Henry James, and Charles Dickens, all of whom enjoyed Annie's hospitality. American authors, also frequent visitors, included Oliver Wendell Holmes, Henry Wadsworth Longfellow, James Russell Lowell, William Dean Howells, Ralph Waldo Emerson, Nathaniel and Sophia Hawthorne, Harriet Beecher Stowe, Celia Thaxter, and John Greenleaf Whittier. Whittier became an especially close friend, praising Jewett's writing and sharing complaints about arthritic pains. In 1879 he told her, "When tired and worried I resort to thy books and find rest and refreshing. I recommend them to everybody, and everybody likes them. There is no dissenting opinion; and already thousands whom thee have never seen love the author as well as her books."[16]

In 1881 James Fields died. Jewett had become so close to the couple that, according to Blanchard, James "had mentioned Sarah Orne Jewett to his wife as the friend he would choose for her above all others."[17] Jewett, though ill with the rheumatoid arthritis that grew more painful as she aged, visited in November. The two women lived together for three months. In February Sarah returned to Berwick, but not before the friends had agreed to travel to Europe together in May. For the next twenty years, Jewett spent winters and summers with Fields in her Boston home and at Gambrel Cottage, her country house in Manchester. They traveled to Europe four times and frequently toured the United States. Their relationship, often described as a "Boston marriage," was one of deep emotional commitment. They cared for each other in illness, read together, and—when apart—wrote affectionate letters. Jewett spent spring and fall in South Berwick with her mother and sisters, and that was where she wrote, but Boston became her emotional home.

Mortality

Most of the characters in Jewett's stories are middle-aged or elderly. Children are absent, and young adults are rare. That was an accurate reflection of villages like Deephaven and Dunnet Landing. Maritime economies were in decline, and young people left to find work. The people she wrote about were aging and dying along with their villages and way of life. Jewett was younger than her characters, but she was keenly aware of her own mortality. The rheumatoid arthritis that had caused manageable disability when she was young took a greater toll as she aged. Beginning in the late 1880s, her vacations with Annie often took them to spas and hot springs in hope of relief. She also began to suffer from eye problems that prevented her from reading. Writing became a physical struggle, but she managed to complete a historical novel set in South Berwick, *The Tory Lover*, serialized in the *Atlantic* in 1900–1901.

On September 3, 1902, Jewett celebrated her 53rd birthday with a carriage ride. The horse stumbled, and she was thrown from the carriage, suffering a concussion and a neck injury. Annie Fields came to stay while she recovered but returned to Boston after a few weeks. On October 24, Fields suffered a mild stroke that kept her confined to her room for three months. The two women—ill and apart—worried constantly about each other. They were not able to be together again until April 1903.

Jewett never recovered fully from the aftereffects of the carriage accident. Until 1906 she could not write or travel; sometimes she could not even read. But in 1908 she was able to form a new and important friendship with a young writer, Willa Cather. Jewett became her mentor, advising her on her work and her life. And, as Blanchard notes, "in her partnership with Annie, Jewett offered authentication of another sort," giving Cather courage to live with her friend Edith Lewis. Cather repaid her friendship by dedicating *O Pioneers!* to Jewett and by editing a selection of Jewett's work, with a critical preface that framed Jewett's reputation for many years.[18]

On March 9, 1909, at Annie's home in Boston, Jewett was paralyzed on one side by a stroke. In April, she was moved to the front guest room in the old house in South Berwick where she had been born. She died there on June 23, at the age of 59. Annie Fields died six years later.

To Visit

The Sarah Orne Jewett House, the older of the two, is at 5 Portland Street, South Berwick, Maine. The newer house is a visitor center and gift shop. See the website for hours and other information: historicnewengland.org.

5

Mary McCarthy and Elizabeth Hardwick

Mary McCarthy and Elizabeth Hardwick became neighbors in 1967, when McCarthy and her fourth husband, James West, bought the Daniel Johnson House in Castine, Maine. Hardwick had spent summers in the town since her marriage to Robert Lowell in 1949. The women had met in the 1940s and shared similar careers, political views, friends, and enemies. Both were successful essayists and novelists, and both helped to found influential magazines. They remained friends for half a century.

A Catholic Girlhood and the Vassar Girl

Mary McCarthy was born to Roy and Tess Preston McCarthy on June 21, 1912, and by 1917 she had three brothers. In 1918, en route to Roy's parents' home in Minneapolis, Roy, Tess, and the children came down with Spanish influenza. Roy died on November 6, and Tess the next day. Their grandmother sent the four orphans to be cared for by her middle-aged sister and her husband, Margaret and Myers Shriver, providing money and a small, shabby house down the street from their palatial home.[1] The children were neglected and poorly fed. The Shrivers beat them "all the time, as a matter of course," Mary remembered, "with the hairbrush across the bare legs for ordinary occasions, and with the razor strop across the bare bottom for special occasions."[2] In 1923 the children's maternal grandfather visited and was shocked at their condition. Two of the boys went to live with the McCarthy grandparents, while one stayed with the Shrivers. Mary returned to Seattle with Grandfather Preston.

The Prestons lived at 712 35th Avenue, an 1891 Victorian house with ten-foot ceilings, inlaid wood floors, and five fireplaces. The elegant first-floor rooms included a parlor, sitting room, dining room, and library. The second floor was divided into two suites—one for her grandparents, one for her Uncle Harold, and the bedroom that had been Mary's mother's, newly redecorated for her.[3] The servants—a chauffeur, cook, and maid—had rooms on the third floor. Tess had wanted the children to be raised as Catholics, so Mary was sent to Forest Ridge Convent of the Sacred Heart. She transferred briefly to the nearest public high school, where she did poorly and—her grandfather rightly feared—became too interested in boys. She moved to the Annie Wright Seminary, an Episcopal boarding school for girls in Tacoma, graduating as the valedictorian. With encouragement and recommendations from her teachers, she was accepted at Vassar.

At Vassar, Mary had excellent literature professors and a few close friends with whom she stayed in touch for years. She helped found an upstart avant-garde magazine, *Con Spirito*, with literary colleagues, including the future poets Elizabeth Bishop and Muriel Rukeyser. Her seven senior-year roommates made a lasting impression. New York socialites with whom she had little in common, they were appalled to see themselves decades later in McCarthy's most famous novel, *The Group*.

On a trip to New York, McCarthy met an actor, Harold Johnsrud, who was eight years older than she. For the next four years, they spent weekends, holidays, and some summers together. Shortly after graduation, on her 21st birthday, they were married. He acted occasionally and worked on writing a play; she wrote reviews for the *New Republic* and *The Nation* and worked part-time for an art gallery. They lived in either luxurious borrowed apartments or barely tolerable rented ones. Despite relative poverty, they entertained, partied, and spent time with literary and theater folks. Neither was faithful to the other. The marriage lasted until 1936, when McCarthy headed for Reno to get a divorce. On the train, she slept with a man she had met in the dining car, whom she later immortalized as "The Man in the Brooks Brothers Shirt."[4]

Partisan Review

In college, McCarthy had not been interested in politics, but in New York she found herself among people who were passionate about Soviet communism. In 1936, a fellow party guest asked her whether she thought Leon Trotsky was entitled to a trial. She asked naively what Trotsky had done, and after he explained, she agreed that he should have a hearing and the right of asylum. In the following weeks, she became aware of the rift between the Stalinist and Trotskyite wings and sided with the Trotskyites.

At political meetings, she met Philip Rahv, who together with a few friends was plotting to take over the Stalinist *Partisan Review* and change both its politics and its intellectual slant: It would be a literary as well as a political journal, and they would solicit material from outstanding writers. In 1935, McCarthy had become a household word—at least in New York's literary households—with a five-part series for *The Nation*, "Our Critics, Right or Wrong," coauthored with Margaret Marshall.[5] They had eviscerated nearly everyone writing literary criticism for debasing readers' tastes, ignoring modernist writers, patronizing their readers, and other failings. She was invited to become the theater reviewer for the new magazine, bringing her sharp eye and tongue to the assignment. The magazine's first issue, in December 1937, included contributions from the poets Delmore Schwartz and Wallace Stevens, the artist Pablo Picasso (writing about Francisco Franco), the writer James Agee, the philosopher Sidney Hook, and the critics Lionel Trilling and Edmund Wilson.

McCarthy's political life became her personal life. She and Philip Rahv began living together in 1936, but during their affair she began another affair—with Edmund Wilson, the author of several books, twice widowed, and 17 years her senior. They were married on February 10, 1938, and she soon became pregnant. She quickly realized that the marriage had been a mistake. Wilson drank heavily, and when drunk he was violent. She once ended up in the hospital with a black eye that Wilson had given her; he claimed it was self-inflicted. Their son, Reuel Kimball Wilson, was born on Christmas, 1938. The following fall, Wilson bought a house in Wellfleet, on Cape Cod. Isolated from her New York friends, McCarthy became a wonderful cook, raised her son, and, with Wilson's encouragement, began to write fiction.

Back in Manhattan, Elizabeth Hardwick was following in McCarthy's footsteps. Hardwick was born in Lexington, Kentucky, on July 27, 1916, the eighth of the 11 children of Eugene and Mary Ramsey Hardwick. She completed her undergraduate program at the University of Kentucky in 1938 and stayed another year to earn a master's degree. Yearning for the bohemian intellectual life of New York City, she enrolled in a Ph.D. program in English literature at Columbia. She quickly realized that an academic career was not a sensible goal for a woman at the time, and she began writing fiction. Her short stories were published in *The Yale Review* and *The Sewanee Review*, and she sent a hundred pages of a novel to an editor at Harcourt, Brace. He offered her a contract for what became *The Ghostly Lover*, published in 1945. After reading it, Philip Rahv invited her to write for the *Partisan Review*. The anti-Stalinist views she had developed in college made her at home with the magazine's editors and writers, including Mary McCarthy.

Hardwick's first contribution to the *Partisan Review* was the short story "The Mysteries of Eleusis," in spring 1945. The fall issue included her review of Richard Wright's *Black Boy* and an essay, "Poor Little Rich Girl," and in September her short story "The Temptations of Dr. Hoffmann" appeared. Hardwick and Mary McCarthy both published reviews in the November-December issue for 1946.

Marriages

In 1947, at a party hosted by Philip Rahv and his wife, Hardwick met Robert Lowell, then married to another *Partisan Review* writer, Jean Stafford. They began an affair the next year, when both were in residence at the Yaddo artists' retreat. Their mutual friends at the magazine warned Hardwick against becoming involved with Lowell, whose formidable reputation as a poet (he had just won a Pulitzer Prize) was matched by a reputation for violence during the manic stages of his bipolar disorder. His friends called him Cal, short for either Caligula or Caliban. In April 1949, when he was hospitalized at Baldpate Hospital in Georgetown, Massachusetts, after a manic episode, Hardwick wrote frequently and visited. She told McCarthy, "I was a gratifying hit with doctors and patients at Baldpate and for most purposes have gotten Cal committed to my care."[6] They were married on July 28, 1949, at his parents' country house in Beverly Farms, Massachusetts. McCarthy was Hardwick's matron of honor.

By the time of Hardwick's wedding, McCarthy had left Edmund Wilson. He had continued to drink heavily and controlled both her life and her money. The depositions taken during the 1945 divorce proceedings are chilling, no matter which of them one believes. She testified:

> Directly after our marriage I discovered that he was addicted to drink and our life together became a series of violent episodes. After I became pregnant he began beating me with his fists, he would kick me out of bed and again when I was on the floor. A short time before our son was born he knocked me down in the kitchen and kicked me in the stomach. At times he would hold me down on the bed and when I opened my mouth to scream he would hit me on the face and about the body. I was distraught and did not know what to do in my condition. Since the birth of our son I have tried to see this marriage through but from its inception to the present time I have been compelled to suffer physical and mental humiliation at the hands of the defendant.

He responded:

> At no time did I ever attack her. I have found it necessary to protect myself against violent assaults by her in the course of which she would kick me, bite me, scratch me and maul me in any way she could. She has even gone so far as to break down a door to my study to get at me and she has on other occasions pushed paper under the door to my study and set fire to it.

Plaintiff is the victim of hysterical delusions and has seemed for years to have a persecution complex as far as I am concerned. She seems to believe that I have attacked her and struck her on occasions when nothing of the sort has happened.[7]

Despite the turmoil, both were extremely productive during the seven years of their marriage. Wilson published several collections of critical essays and a volume of short stories. McCarthy wrote reviews and essays, sold short stories to *The New Yorker* and *Mademoiselle*, published *Memories of a Catholic Girlhood*, and completed two novels, *The Company She Keeps* and *The Oasis*.

After the divorce, McCarthy spent a year teaching at Bard College, an experience that she later used in her novel *The Groves of Academe*. She began seeing Bowden Broadwater, a researcher at *The New Yorker*, who was eight years her junior. They spent the summer of 1946 in Europe and married in December, living with Reuel in Broadwater's sister's tiny, primitive apartment at 57th Street and Third Avenue. Broadwater worked on and off in editorial positions but mostly devoted himself to McCarthy's career by taking over the housework and protecting her from interruptions. She knew what a gift that was: When she delivered the commencement address at Vassar thirty years later, she told the audience, "Being an artist or a serious craftsman of any kind takes a lot of time and practice and can rarely be tucked into the housewife's spare moments, between vacuuming the carpets and warming the baby's bottle."[8]

In 1949, McCarthy won a Guggenheim fellowship and sold stock in her family's grain elevator company. Newly prosperous, she and Broadwater bought an 1850 farmhouse on Union Street in Portsmouth, Rhode Island. They did much of the renovation themselves. In a letter to Hardwick, McCarthy described the decor: the kitchen was "royal blue with white wainscoting and woodwork, dark blue linoleum floor, and a wonderful new gas stove"; the sitting room was "a dream-yellow with green furniture and little red table and white woodwork." There was also a dining room, library, parlor, a "white and gold" bedroom for her and Broadwater, and a bedroom for Reuel.[9]

With Broadwater's encouragement and housekeeping, McCarthy wrote prolifically and began to command larger fees. In February and March 1950, a ten-part series, "Greenwich Village at Night," for the *New York Post* brought her $800. The *New Yorker* paid her $3,000 for several stories. An article about Vassar for *Holiday* brought in $1,000. She wrote reviews, essays, and short stories for other magazines as well. In 1952 she published *The Groves of Academe*—a satire of academic life during the era of Joseph McCarthy and the House Un-American Activities Committee.

Elizabeth Hardwick's marriage did not provide either encouragement or help with housekeeping. Lowell's manic episodes, usually preceded by affairs with younger women, recurred nearly every year, and he would spend the following weeks or months in a psychiatric hospital. During those times, he belittled Hardwick and her work. When he was healthy, he wrote and took temporary teaching positions. They lived in unsatisfactory apartments where she kept house and continued to write stories and reviews. Neither of them was earning much, and the hospital stays were expensive.

With the money Lowell had earned from teaching, and a few dollars left from an earlier Guggenheim fellowship, he and Hardwick went to Europe, where Americans could live fairly cheaply. They sailed at the end of September 1950 and spent several months in Florence. They next moved to Amsterdam and in May went on to Salzburg, where Lowell taught in July and August. In October they rented an apartment in Rome, where Hardwick discovered the key to combining work and marriage. She and Lowell had separate rooms, and she was working on a novel. She told a friend, "The sudden privacy is overwhelmingly exciting."[10]

They returned to the United States in January 1953 so that Lowell could take up temporary teaching posts. Hardwick was still working on her novel, but she was also writing important reviews, including a critical evaluation of Simone de Beauvoir's *Second Sex*. (She and McCarthy were among de Beauvoir's few female detractors.) Hardwick also published thoughtful review essays: "Memoirs, Conversations and Diaries" and "Anderson, Millay and Crane in Their Letters."[11]

In February 1954 Lowell's mother died in Italy, and he went there to deal with funeral arrangements. When he returned, he was hospitalized again—for the fourth time in as many years. Hardwick decided she would divorce him in May, telling a friend, "My heart tells me I should get out of this difficult marriage, that I will only have all these months and months of agony to go over again after a few years, that a mentally disturbed person simply cannot give enough."[12] But they would remain married for 16 more years, and then the divorce would come at his instigation.

In 1955 Lowell and Hardwick moved to Boston to be near his psychotherapist, the libraries they both needed, and Lowell's teaching job at Boston University. Hardwick began editing the letters of William James, archived in Harvard's Houghton Library.[13] The trustees under Lowell's mother's will bought them a four-story Federal-style row house at 239 Marlborough Street that they filled with family furniture. Each had a bedroom and study.[14]

Hardwick was writing for the *Partisan Review*, the *New Yorker*, and *Encounter*, a British magazine. Her novel, *The Simple Truth*, was published in February 1955. The reviews were mixed, and some suggested that the book did not exhibit the excellence of her essays and shorter fiction. She didn't attempt another novel for twenty years.

In 1956, Hardwick was surprised to find herself pregnant at the age of 40. She was told to avoid travel and exertion, but that did not preclude writing. On May 12, the *New Yorker* published "The Oak and the Axe," her story about a disastrous marriage. Their daughter, Harriet, was born on January 4, 1957. Hardwick hired a full-time baby nurse, giving herself time to write. From the winter of 1957 through the spring of 1959, Lowell was in and out of psychiatric hospitals and in and out of affairs with young women. Hardwick was again trying to sort out her feelings, writing to the poet Allen Tate, "this deranged person does a lot of harm.... He is terribly demanding and devouring. I feel a deep loyalty and commitment to him, and yet at the same time I don't know exactly what sort of bearable status quo I can establish with him."[15]

During Lowell's frequent absences and with tactics to manage his demands when he was at home, Hardwick continued to write for the *New Yorker* and *Harper's*. She became the theater critic for *Partisan Review*, a role pioneered by Mary McCarthy, and echoed McCarthy's 1935 dissection of reviewers in "The Decline of Book Reviewing," published in *Harper's* in October 1959. Fourteen years after McCarthy had written, Hardwick found book reviewers still uncritical and more interested in publicizing the books of friends than in expressing intelligent opinions.

Maine and Manhattan

In the 1930s, Lowell's Aunt Harriet Winslow had bought a house in Castine, Maine, where she escaped the summer heat of Washington, D.C. Lowell and Hardwick visited soon after their wedding, and in 1953 Aunt Harriet bought the "brickyard house" on Water Street, a former dormitory for brickyard workers, for the couple to use. The barn became Lowell's study. As Harriet found travel more difficult, her original house, at 29 School Street, on the town common between the Adams School and the Witherle Library, soon became the couple's summer headquarters. The Federal–style house had eight rooms and two baths, with an attached barn and a garden. The rooms were small, with low ceilings and exposed beams. When Harriet Winslow died in 1964, she left both properties and money for upkeep to Hardwick rather than to her nephew, because she was concerned about his instability.

Castine gave Hardwick a place to escape the social demands of Boston and New York. She shopped, spent time in local cafes, and got to know her neighbors. With Lowell writing in the barn, she could write undisturbed in the house. But Maine was cold in winter, and Hardwick needed to be in New York to see editors and spend time with colleagues. In 1961, Lowell sold the Boston house, and they bought the top-floor duplex apartment at 1 West 67th Street, in an 18-story building known as the Hotel des Artistes. Built in 1917, its gothic facade is decorated with gargoyles of painters, sculptors, and writers. It was built for successful creative people and offered a swimming pool, squash courts, and a restaurant that—at least in the early years—sent meals to the apartments via dumbwaiter. Their living room had a twenty-foot ceiling and skylights, with a balcony on the second floor. Lowell used the servant's room as his study.[16]

Lowell immediately left for a small apartment where he could carry on yet another affair, this one ending when he tried to strangle the young woman and was confined to a locked ward. Hardwick's response—so unlike her earlier thoughts of divorce—was to tell him that she would make "a superhuman effort to improve as a wife so that your home & daily life won't make you sick again."[17] No effort on her part could have prevented his manic episodes, which continued until the end of his life.

A View of My Own, a collection of 17 of Hardwick's essays, was published in fall 1962, and soon Hardwick's professional life changed dramatically. On December 8, the New York Typographical Union went on strike against several of the city's newspapers. No newspapers meant no book reviews leading into the all-important Christmas season, and publishers and authors were unhappy. Hardwick and Lowell were having dinner at the home of Jason Epstein, editorial director at Random House, and his wife, Barbara, a well-known book editor, when they hatched a plan to start a book review magazine, with Barbara and Robert Silvers, an editor at *Harper's*, as co-editors. They quickly found financial backers, publishers eager to advertise, and writers eager to review. The first issue of the *New York Review of Books (NYRB)* appeared in February, with nearly fifty reviews and an editorial statement promising to review *important* books rather than the purely commercial. For the first few months, Hardwick did everything from writing and soliciting reviews to sending out bills. As the magazine took off, she participated mostly as a writer. By June, she felt free to leave for Maine.

The *NYRB* proved that reviewing of the caliber that McCarthy and Hardwick had been promoting was both possible and commercially viable. Both of them could publish in nearly any magazine they wished, but they now had a place where they could write what they wanted, at the length they considered necessary, for the audience they valued most. For McCarthy, it became a place for political reportage; for Hardwick, it was home for her most important reviews and essays.

That August, Mary McCarthy's *The Group* was published and became an immediate and lasting bestseller in the United States and England, translated into 19 languages. The female characters, all members of the Vassar class of 1933, meet at the 1940 funeral of one of their roommates, where they catch up on one another's lives over the past seven years. McCarthy's Vassar classmates were scandalized by the frank descriptions of sex and the close resemblances to their own lives. It was reviewed in the *NYRB* by Norman Mailer, who savaged it. In September, a parody—"The Gang"—appeared in the *NYRB*. The byline was Xavier Rynne, but the unmistakable style was that of Elizabeth Hardwick. McCarthy was not amused, and Hardwick apologized: "It was meant as simply a little trick, nothing more.... I did not mean to hurt you and I hope you will forgive it."[18] No permanent damage was done to their friendship, and the negative critical reception did nothing to damage sales.

The Sixties

In 1960, the United States Information Agency sent McCarthy on a speaking tour of Eastern Europe. She, Broadwater, and Reuel were welcomed in Warsaw by James West, the public affairs officer for the U.S. embassy. McCarthy fell instantly and madly in love. West, married with three young children, felt the same way. For her, it was partly a physical attraction. She later wrote, "None of my other husbands was good-looking. Of course I've had affairs with good-looking men, but I've never married one—until now." Those other husbands suffered by comparison. She told a friend, "Reuel seems to be extremely attracted by Jim. I think he feels the lack of a virile and straightforward man in his family. Bowden is a child, and Edmund is an old woman."[19] After both divorces went through, they were married in Paris on April 15, 1961.

McCarthy and Hardwick began to write about political issues. McCarthy wrote in protest of the war in Vietnam, focusing on the impact of the war on civilians, and urging that American troops be withdrawn. Her essays were published in book form as *Vietnam* and *Hanoi*. She reported on the Watergate hearings for *The Observer* and the *NYRB*, with those articles published as *The Mask of State: Watergate Portraits*. She also worked on two novels during this period, *Birds of America* and *Cannibals and Missionaries*.

Perhaps because of her Southern roots, Hardwick focused on civil rights in her political writing, including "Selma, Alabama," "The Apotheosis of Martin Luther King," "Mr. America" (George Wallace), and "After Watts."[20] She covered the 1968 Democratic convention in Chicago, women's rights, and antiwar protests as well. In 1979, she returned to writing novels and published the semi-autobiographical *Sleepless Nights,* a critical and commercial success.

Maine and Paris

James West was made director of the Organisation for Economic Co-operation and Development, headquartered in Paris, where he and McCarthy bought an eight-room apartment on the fifth floor of a building on the rue de Rennes. They also needed a home base in the United States, and West suggested Maine, where he had been born. In 1967 Robert Lowell told them about a house that was available in Castine. The friends soon became close neighbors: McCarthy's house at 90 Main Street was right behind Hardwick's. Built in 1804, it is a Federal-style clapboard house that McCarthy painted yellow, defying the town's tradition of white houses. Its front door is unusually elegant, with a Palladian window, fanlight, sidelights, pediment, and columns. Inside, it has a graceful floating staircase.[21] Lowell may later have regretted making the suggestion, writing to Elizabeth Bishop: "The Wests are here…. The beautiful big house, the beautiful big meals, the beautiful big guests…. [N]othing seems addressed to me, and nothing I say is heard."[22] But the two women enjoyed each other's company and organized picnics and outings for the many mutual friends who visited each summer.

Hardwick began to write about Maine. On October 7, 1971, the *NYRB* published "In Maine," about the people as well as the scenery: "The fine house, the beautiful harbors and islands, yes. But Maine is a museum of another kind, a collection of the deserted and abandoned, a preservation of the feel of long, catatonic winters. Its exhibitions tell of no money and nothing to buy anyway, of nothing to do and no place to go. It preserves the face of lack, of minimum, the bottom—the pure, lost negative. Living in it your heart seems to stop sometimes, gripped by a fearfulness that is not altogether painful." In her descriptions of the beauty and the harshness of the landscape, the poverty and endurance of the people, and the contrasts and conflicts between year-round residents and summer visitors, her love of the place is clear. As she grew older, she told an interviewer, "Maine has taken the place of Kentucky in my life."[23]

Farewells

Robert Lowell met Lady Caroline Blackwood, the heiress to the Guinness brewery fortune, at a dinner party in London in 1970. They began an

5. Mary McCarthy and Elizabeth Hardwick

Mary McCarthy's house at 90 Main Street in Castine, Maine. Beginning in 1967, she divided her time between this house and an apartment in Paris. The Mercedes convertible in the driveway was a birthday gift from McCarthy to her fourth husband, James West. *Archives & Special Collections, Vassar College Library (McCarthy 285).*

affair and, unlike Lowell's other infidelities, this one lasted. In October 1972 he and Hardwick were divorced. The settlement gave Hardwick and their daughter Harriet an annual income, money for Harriet's education, the New York apartment and its contents, and the property in Castine.

What Hardwick lost in the divorce was her privacy. Lowell wrote *The Dolphin*, a sonnet sequence about his relationships with Hardwick and Blackwood, incorporating excerpts from Hardwick's letters and attributing words to her that she neither wrote nor spoke. The poet Adrienne Rich described his use of her letters as "one of the most vindictive and mean-spirited acts in the history of poetry." In 1974, Lowell won his second Pulitzer Prize, for *The Dolphin*.

Despite the hurt and public humiliation, Hardwick and Lowell continued to correspond frequently and to see each other. Hardwick told McCarthy in June 1977, "we are trying to work out a sort of survival for both of us," and that summer Lowell rented a place in Castine before returning to London. On September 15, he flew from London to New York and took a cab to Hardwick's apartment in the Hotel des Artistes. Summoned by the elevator operator, she found him dead in the taxi.[24]

As respected critics, McCarthy and Hardwick wielded a great deal of power in the literary world. They also made enemies. Both had alienated Simone de Beauvoir and Diana Trilling, but their really dangerous foe was Lillian Hellman. In 1967, Mike Nichols revived Hellman's *The Little Foxes* on Broadway. Hardwick demolished the play and the production in the *NYRB* on December 21, objecting especially to its uncritical view of the South. Hellman called on her friends to respond for her. The magazine published many of the letters, as well as Hardwick's response, on January 18 and February 1, 1968. New York's literary community took sides, and Hellman never forgave Hardwick.

That was a minor battle compared to the all-out war that McCarthy started on the *Dick Cavett Show* on October 18, 1979. Cavett asked her about overrated writers, and she named Hellman, "who I think is tremendously overrated, a bad writer, and *dishonest writer*." "What is dishonest about Lillian Hellman?" Cavett asked. *"Everything ... every word she writes is a lie,* including 'and' and 'the.'"[25] Two weeks later, Hellman sued McCarthy, Cavett, and the television channel for $2.25 million. As preparation for the case dragged on, Hellman's reputation suffered badly. The biographer Carol Brightman explains that opinion shifted, "thanks in part to the deconstruction of the Hellman legend by a small band of critics."[26] They used the evidence McCarthy's lawyers had gathered to demonstrate that many of Hellman's narratives were false, that she was stealing other people's stories and incorporating them into her memoirs. The case was scheduled to go to trial when Hellman died on June 30, 1984.

That year, Hardwick presented McCarthy with the Edward MacDowell Colony medal for outstanding contributions to American culture. McCarthy's acceptance speech was not optimistic: "As a person and a writer, I seem to have had little effect on improving the world I came into. I can see deterioration in every area of life. The belief in progress that animated my youth has vanished." When *Partisan Review* started, she said, "I felt at that time that we were fighting the literary battles, and we expected someone else would pick up the weapons. But no one did. We were trying to insist on artistic standards—trying to deflate what we considered false reputations—and we were pretty good at it. No one ever took our place."[27]

McCarthy spent the summer of 1989 in Castine, but that fall she was hospitalized with lung cancer and died on October 25. More than thirty years earlier, Hardwick had seen how unusual her friend was: "A career of candor and dissent is not an easy one for a woman; the license is jarring and the dare often forbidding. Such a person needs more than confidence and indignation. A great measure of personal attractiveness and a high degree of romantic singularity are necessary to step free of the mundane, the governessy, the threat of earnestness and dryness.... With Mary McCarthy the purity of style and the liniment of her wit, her gay summoning of the funny facts of everyday life, soften the scandal of the action or the courage of the opinion."²⁸

Elizabeth Hardwick had nearly twenty years of writing ahead of her when McCarthy died. She had sold the houses in Castine but kept the barn, which she remodeled and winterized. A visitor described her living room, with its "steel fireplace, open rafters, pumpkin-colored painted

Elizabeth Hardwick's cottage—a converted barn in Castine, Maine, where she lived and worked after Robert Lowell's death. *Harry Ransom Center, the University of Texas at Austin.*

floor, scatter rugs; goldenrod in jugs, hanging baskets of flowers; Japanese pictures, furniture of cane and bamboo, slipcovers in opaque motifs; a Winthrop desk; a pewter bowl ... full of smooth black stones."[29] She wrote the introduction to McCarthy's third memoir, *Intellectual Memoirs,* published in 1992, and continued to write reviews, essays, and short stories. In 2000, she published the biography *Herman Melville* in the Penguin Lives series.

Hardwick became a true resident of Castine. A neighbor wrote about her in the local newspaper, recalling that in the barn "she made a place to work: a small cramped bedroom with a card table for a desk. It was there she entertained—often large 'after-theater' parties following fund raising events. Writers, young and not so young, sought Lizzie out and would come to the barn with their manuscripts and hopes.... Lizzie had less interest in the 'gentry' than she did in the working people with their contributions of labor and character. Without them Castine would not have worked for her."[30]

In New York, with a cane and then a wheelchair, she needed help getting around—but she did get around, visiting museums, restaurants, and Central Park. Mostly, though, she wrote. Her last piece for the *NYRB,* on August 10, 2006, was a remembrance of Barbara Epstein, the magazine's original co-editor. Her last dinner at the Manhattan restaurant P.J. Clarke's, in November 2007, was white wine and oysters. She celebrated Thanksgiving with her daughter, and five days later she died in Roosevelt Hospital.

6

Edna St. Vincent Millay

Edna St. Vincent Millay's childhood was spent in poverty, and she was often left to care for her younger sisters while her divorced mother struggled to support the family. Yet by the time she was in her early thirties, she was a prize-winning poet, living in a mansion with a husband who adored her and ran the household so efficiently that she had nothing to do but write. Her brilliance, beauty, and dedication to poetry made her fame and fortune.

Vincent

Millay's middle name hints at aristocratic ancestry, but its origin is pedestrian. Shortly before her birth in 1892, her mother's brother Charles Buzzell nearly died after an accident at sea. He was saved by the doctors and nurses at New York's St. Vincent's Hospital, and Edna was named in their honor. She always preferred to be called Vincent. She was born in the north side of a newly built two-story duplex at 198/200 Broadway in Rockland, Maine. Her parents, Henry Tolman and Cora Buzzell Millay, had become the first tenants in 1892. They considered the house elegant, with its mahogany sliding doors between parlor and dining room. When Vincent was three months old, they moved to Union, Maine, where Henry's family lived. There two more daughters, Norma and Kathleen, were born, in 1893 and 1896.

It became an unhappy marriage. Money was always scarce, because Henry struggled to find and keep jobs, and he gambled. He abused Cora. Vincent wrote: "I remember a swamp, that made a short-cut to the railroad station when I was seven. It was down across that swamp my father went, when my mother told him to go & not to come back."[1] Cora filed for divorce in 1901, and the decree was granted in 1904, on the grounds of cruel and abusive treatment. Henry was ordered to pay five dollars a week for child support, but he never did, although he occasionally sent his daughters money. Nor did he visit the girls, despite promises in his letters. Vincent would not see him again until 1912, when he was thought to be dying. Cora supported her family by working as a nurse, usually living in patients' homes. The girls' uncle, Charles Buzzell, and his wife Jennie took them in so that Cora could continue to work. When the girls were old enough to be left alone, Vincent ran the household and took care of her sisters.

Cora and the girls moved back to Rockport, where they rented the second floor of an old house near the harbor. It was the first of many moves to barely habitable houses, spaces that the biographer Mark David Epstein describes as "spare rooms in farmhouses and town houses, [where] mother and daughters moved with their trunks of books and papers and homemade clothing and precious few other belongings dragging behind them." They lived with friends, uncles, cousins, and aunts. In 1904 they rented a house in fields outside Camden. The girls were 9, 11, and 12. The house, in poor repair, had four small rooms, and the only plumbing was a cold-water sink in the kitchen. Inadequate heat came from the kitchen stove and a coal stove upstairs in the living room, where they stored anything that could not survive being frozen. One frigid day the kitchen sink overflowed, and the girls used the floor as a skating rink. In the winter of 1904, they kept the house warm by burning shingles from a dilapidated house nearby. In "The Ballad of the Harp-Weaver," Millay wrote: "A wind with a wolf's head / Howled about our door, / And we burned up the chairs / And sat on the floor."[2]

She later wrote "To live alone like that, sleep alone in that house set back in the field on the very edge of Millville, the bad section of town where the itinerant mill-workers lived—this was the only way they could live at all.... But they were afraid of nothing—not afraid of the river which flowed behind the house, in which they taught themselves to swim; not afraid of that other river, which flowed past the front of the house and which on Saturday nights was often very quarrelsome and noisy, the restless stream of mill workers.... Once it took all three of the children, flinging themselves against the front door, to close it and bolt it, and just in time. And after that, for what seemed like hours, there was stumbling about outside, and soft cursing."[3]

Despite the hard times, the Maine landscape was an important element in Millay's poems. In "Inland," she wondered what people who lived far from the coast longed for, "as I long for / One salt smell of the sea once more?" Later, living inland herself, she bought an island in Casco Bay—the subject of her poem "Ragged Island" : "Where the wide, quiet evening darkens without haste / Over a sea with death acquainted, yet forever chaste."[4]

Cora made sure her daughters were educated and well read. As they traveled from place to place, they lugged trunks filled with books—Shakespeare and Milton, Tennyson and Wordsworth, Keats and Shelley—and she read aloud in a voice honed in amateur drama. No matter how ramshackle the house, there were musical instruments—a pump organ, piano, harp, and cornet. Cora defended her daughters fiercely—especially Vincent, whose precocity and outspokenness did not sit well with the head of her school. When he lost his temper and shoved Vincent out of his office, Cora convinced the principal of the Camden high school to allow her to enroll early.

In high school, Vincent began to act in plays. By 1908, the family had moved to an apartment on Chestnut Street, near the Camden Opera House, where she often performed. The pretty little girl had become a stunning young woman. She was just over five feet tall, weighed only a hundred pounds, and had a surprisingly deep voice. With her floor-length red hair and large green eyes, she dominated the stage and easily won starring roles. Memorization was second nature to her. She hoped one day to write plays.

Somehow—despite the onerous household responsibilities, school, performances and nightly rehearsals, outings with friends, piano lessons and daily practice—Vincent did a great deal of writing. By the time she entered high school, she was already a published poet. "The Land of Romance" won first prize in *St. Nicholas Magazine*'s 1906 competition, and the magazine published "Forest Trees" in the same year. She also kept two diaries. One is a record of everyday events; the second, private, was hidden under a loose floorboard or her mattress. It reveals the physical and emotional toll that she hid from others. She wrote often of being exhausted. Her 1908 diary addressed an imaginary "Mammy": "You'll have to take the place of Mama when she's gone.... I love my mama, more than I can ever think of loving you, and you mustn't be jealous a bit. You are very like her, so I love you in something of the way I love her, though not one-millionth part as much."[5]

By 1911, a mother was no longer the solution to her exhaustion and loneliness. Now her secret diaries were addressing an imaginary lover, with whom she engaged in a monthly candlelight ritual. "I am very lonely. I wish I might go to sleep tonight with my head on your arm.... You have been everything to me for half a year.... But I am so tired! But when you come I shall rest.... I am wearing a fluffy lavendar thing over my nightdress. It is very soft and long and trails on the rug behind me. My bare feet sink into the rug. My hair is in two wavy red braids over my shoulders. My eyes are very sweet and serious. My mouth is wistful."[6] At 19, Millay seemed to be seeking Prince Charming. In reality, she would escape from the scullery through poetry, and she would fascinate and reject countless suitors. Marriage would come only after literary success.

Rebirth

In 1911 the publisher Mitchell Kennerley held a poetry competition with a $1,000 prize. Millay spent the first months of the year writing her entry. She did not win, but "Renascence" was published in *The Lyric Year* anthology of 1912 and attracted critical and popular praise. She had signed it "E. Vincent Millay," and everyone assumed it had been written by a man. Arthur Ficke, another contributor, believed that "no sweet young thing of twenty ever ended a poem precisely where this one ends: it takes a brawny male of forty-five to do that." Beginning a lifelong correspondence and friendship, Millay sent a good-natured response and enclosed a photo to assure him that she was not a brawny male.[7]

The poem begins where Millay began, in Maine:

> All I could see from where I stood
> Was three long mountains and a wood;
> I turned and looked another way,
> And saw three islands in a bay.
> So with my eyes I traced the line
> Of the horizon, thin and fine,
> Straight around till I was come
> Back to where I'd started from;
> And all I saw from where I stood
> Was three long mountains and a wood.[8]

The poem moves from Maine to sky, eternity, infinity in a deeply personal exploration of spirit, faith, and nature. And the poem moved Millay from Maine to Vassar, Greenwich Village, and fame.

That summer, Norma Millay was working at Camden's Whitehall Inn, where Vincent attended a party. Norma urged her to recite from "Renascence." Her reading displayed her beauty, literary accomplishment, and talent for drama, and the guests were astonished. One visitor, Caroline B. Dow, offered to sponsor her education at Vassar. After spending a semester at Barnard to make up academic deficiencies, she joined the class of 1917. She was four years older than her classmates, and years of independence made her unwilling to follow college rules. She was frequently in trouble, but her intelligence and talent protected her. The president of the college told her that he would never expel her "because he didn't want another 'banished Shelley' on his hands." Just before graduating, though, she was forbidden to participate in any of the commencement activities beyond the granting of degrees. She couldn't join in singing the hymn she had composed for the ceremony.⁹

At Vassar, Millay began her sex life in earnest—with men when in New York City and with women when on campus, where "a man is forbidden as if he were an apple." According to Epstein, graduation was the beginning of a "four-year bacchanal."¹⁰ This was no search for Prince Charming, but a campaign for conquests, and her lovers had been forewarned:

> I shall forget you presently, my dear,
> So make the most of this, your little day,
> Your little month, your little half a year....¹¹

She remained close friends with a few of the men, including the poet and playwright Arthur Ficke and the critic Edmund Wilson. Another lover, the writer John Peale Bishop, writing thirty years later, said that "Edna ignited for me both my intellectual passion and my unsatisfied desire, which went up together in a blaze of ecstasy that remains for me one of the high points in my life." Floyd Dell's relationship with Millay was typical of the more serious liaisons: "There began for us a romance that was haunted by her sense of the inevitable impermanence of love. She refused to marry me. We parted several times. She fell in love with other men and then came back to me. We always forgave each other the hurts of love." Most of the relationships in these years, though, lasted only a little day, month, or half a year.¹²

She nevertheless had time for acting and writing. The fall after graduation, Millay's first book, *Renascence and Other Poems,* was published. She was already seeing poetry as a way to earn a living. In a letter to her mother and sister Norma, she wrote, "It's so funny for me to think of the business end of it—but I want it to be read—it's that more than the disgusting money—the dirty necessary money!"¹³ She would later change publishers when she felt her work wasn't being designed or marketed to her standards.

Millay moved to Greenwich Village, where she acted with the Provincetown Players, and a second volume, *A Few Figs from Thistles,* appeared. She was also writing short stories (as "Nancy Boyd"), which paid better than poetry, and an antiwar play, *Aria da Capo,* which opened in December 1919 at the Provincetown Playhouse, breaking box office records. By the fall of 1920, she told a friend, "I am becoming very famous. The current Vanity Fair has a whole page of my poems, and a photograph of me.... And there have been three reviews of something I wrote, in New York newspapers, in the last week alone. I am so incorrigibly ingenuous that these things mean just as much to me as ever."¹⁴

In 1921 Millay traveled to Europe as a correspondent for *Vanity Fair*, and a third poetry collection (*Second April*) and two plays appeared. She wrote poems under her own name, and prose as Nancy Boyd, and sent long letters about her travels to her sisters and mother. Her mother joined her, and they traveled throughout the Continent together. By the end of the trip, Cora was nursing her daughter. As Millay wrote to a friend, "I have been very sick, but I am better now. I have been quite respectably, but very unromantically ill,—trouble arising from an improper diet, unfamiliar queer foods in Hungary & Albania, etc., which have played the devil with me.—Thank heaven mother has been with me, & has been getting me straightened out.—But I came within an ace of having peritonitis, which is not a tidy thing to have." She was not "straightened out," and she returned to New York in December 1922 frail and exhausted. Yet she completed another volume of poetry, *The Harp Weaver and Other Poems*, which won the Pulitzer Prize for poetry in 1923.[15]

She was also in love, and for more than a little day. At a party, she had met Eugen Boissevain, a wealthy Dutch American widower 12 years her senior, and they almost immediately planned to marry. First, Boissevain insisted, she must see the best doctors available to figure out what underlay her illness. X-rays and other tests uncovered intestinal blockages resulting from what is now called Crohn's disease, and immediate surgery was recommended. At noon on July 18, 1923, the couple were married in Croton, New York, and drove from there directly to the hospital for her surgery the next day. They returned to Boissevain's country home for Millay to recover.

Marriage and Home

Boissevain was Prince Charming: wealthy, devoted, and madly in love. He took care of Millay as she recovered from surgery and throughout his life handled all household duties so that she could write. "If I let her struggle with problems of order ... she doesn't write," he explained, so "I look after everything." He paid off her debts and her mother's. He gave her extravagant gifts, including a ring whose large emerald matched her eyes.[16]

As befits a princely couple, they purchased a castle—or the nearest thing: Steepletop, a 635-acre blueberry farm near Austerlitz, New York, in the Berkshires. After they bought the property in 1925, they renovated the white clapboard farmhouse and added gardens of wildflowers, roses, and iris; a swimming pool and clay tennis court; groves of maples and pine; and a writing cabin. An ice house, potting shed, chicken coop, and guest house nestle nearby. The parlor was large enough for two pianos, and a long room on the second floor became a library for more than three thousand volumes, including every book that Millay and her mother owned. Millay's study, bedroom, and bath were adjacent to the library. Boissevain's bedroom was on the other side of the stairway.[17]

Much of the renovation was financed by income from a national tour on which Millay read her poetry to enthusiastic audiences. The tour was profitable, and she was flattered by the adulation she received, but she was not comfortable in the role of entertainer. After a reading in a private home, at which "a bunch of wealthy people come together to see what I looked like, & bet with each other as to how many of my naughty poems I would dare to read," she told Boissevain, "If ever I felt like a prostitute it was last night.—I kept saying over & over to myself while I was reading to them, 'Never mind—it's a hundred & fifty dollars.'—I hope I shall never write a poem again that more than five people will like."[18]

Edna St. Vincent Millay and her husband, Eugen Boissevain, at Steepletop, 1948. They bought the farmhouse in 1925 and remodeled the house and grounds extensively. *Archives & Special Collections, Vassar College Library (Millay 18.10).*

Boissevain devoted himself to farming, which in some years provided additional income, and to making life at Steepletop comfortable—even luxurious. Epstein describes him as "bursting with energy," a "master chef and connoisseur of wines (he published articles on cooking), sportsman, gardener, breeder of dogs and horses," who "lived for pleasure"—his wife's as well as his own. The couple entertained in the summer, but Steepletop was mostly a place of comfort and seclusion where Millay could work. In winter they were isolated, and Boissevain boasted of his measures to make them self-sufficient: "We have 12 tons of coal in the cellar and 15 cords of wood in the shed, three fireplaces, two stoves, a furnace, a hot-water heater and plenty of matches. We have thousands of tins of everything, a huge bag of potatoes, 100 lbs. of sugar, flour, beans, peas, rice."[19]

At Steepletop Millay completed three more poetry collections—*The Buck in the Snow* (1928), *Fatal Interview* (1931), and *Wine from These Grapes* (1934)—as well as the libretto for Deems Taylor's opera, *The King's Henchman*. The house was not, however, an escape from the world. Millay became politically active—as she had not been since 1919. She was arrested in a 1927 protest of the execution of the anarchists Nicola Sacco and Bartolomeo Vanzetti, whose murder conviction was widely believed unjust, and she wrote poetry supporting the Allied cause in World War II. In 1942 the actor Paul Muni read "The Murder of Lidice," her most famous political poem, on NBC radio, and it was aired throughout Europe.

Their marriage was happy, but financially and sexually complicated. After the 1929 stock market crash, Millay's income from writing became essential. Throughout the 1930s, she earned around $20,000 a year from her writing, just as Boissevain's business became less and less profitable. After the first five years, both had other sexual partners, though only one of these relationships was serious. In 1928 Millay became infatuated with George Dillon, a 22-year-old poet who is the subject of her *Fatal Interview* (1931), a bestseller in part because of the scandal. The on-and-off affair continued for more than a year. The two poets spent enough time together in Paris to collaborate on a translation of Baudelaire's *Fleurs du Mal*. Epstein claims that "Boissevain was no more threatened by this charming poet than he would have been by a puppy that his wife had gone mad about for a fortnight."[20]

Millay saw the risk differently:

> I think however that of all alive
> I only in such utter, ancient way
> Do suffer love; in me alone survive
> The unregenerate passions of a day
> When treacherous queens, with death upon the tread,
> Heedless and wilful, took their knights to bed.

Dillon ended the affair, and Millay conceded, "Well, I have lost you; and I lost you fairly; / In my own way, and with my full consent."[21]

The Candle

Millay's most quoted poem, "First Fig," written soon after she graduated from Vassar, became an even more accurate reflection of her mature life: "My candle burns at both ends; / It will not last the night...."[22] Now the candle was truly burning down. Throughout the 1930s, when her productivity and popularity were at their height, she drank heavily. In 1936 she was injured in a car accident. As she explained to a friend four years later: "for something over a year now I have been very sick,—or rather, not sick, simply in constant pain due to an injury to certain nerves in my back.... The nerve injury is the result, it seems probable, of my having been thrown out of the station-wagon one night—not by the driver, as you are probably thinking, but by the sudden swinging open of the door against which I was leaning. I was hurled out into the pitch-darkness—a very strange sensation it was, too—and rolled for some distance down a rocky gully." She began using morphine to control the pain, and by 1939 she had become addicted. Between 1940 and 1945, Boissevain was buying her enormous quantities of narcotics and barbiturates; syringes and needles; and hundreds of doses of injectable morphine per month. Their bills for gin, vermouth, scotch, and rum were astronomical. Millay entered rehabilitation programs in 1944 and 1946. She had published little since 1939, when *Huntsman, What Quarry?* had appeared, selling 60,000 copies in its first month.[23]

Millay and Boissevain had been extravagant, and in 1941 she wrote to Eugene Saxton, her editor at Harper's, asking for an advance on royalties: "Once again I must ask my publishers to come—come running—to my aid.... Eugen has lost everything he had. At least, for the present. There is not a penny he can get at. So for the time being it's up to me." After Saxton's death in 1943, she wrote to his assistant: "If I don't get some money I can't go on writing, can't go on doing anything.... I'm stone-broke. Can Harper's help me?" By spring of 1946, Cass Canfield, now her Harper's editor, had arranged for her to receive monthly payments. Millay thanked him: "I was deeply touched, and very grateful, and I still am. I admire you, too, for the easy manner in which you led me round that really muddy puddle, without letting me get splashed at all: it was chic, what you did." Canfield insisted that he was doing nothing extraordinary: "The continuing sales of your books make these payments possible without your being in debt to us. In other words, we are merely providing you with an accommodation and should not be given the credit for doing you any special favor!" Millay, no longer using drugs, was writing again. In June 1949 she told Canfield: "I have been working very hard, all day and during a great portion of the night also, for, I think, about seven months. A few poems are finished to my satisfaction, but on others I am still at work. I cannot give you a date line."[24]

In August 1949, Boissevain died suddenly of a stroke after surgery for lung cancer. Millay was for a while unable to write. Living alone at Steepletop, she survived by being both nurse and patient. "The nurse, now, cooks my meals, and sees to it that they are not only nutritious, but also appetizing and attractive. And she prepares my medicines with no repugnance, just as a matter of routine, almost automatically.... As for the patient, she obediently, and also absent-mindedly, swallows and swallows and swallows," all the while thinking about poetry. "To pretend that it is not agony, would be silly. But I can cope."[25]

On October 19, 1950, Millay left a note for the neighbor who helped with the housekeeping:

Dear Lena:

This iron is set too high. Don't put it on where it says "Linen"—or it will scorch the linen. Try it on "Rayon"—and then, perhaps on "Woollen." And be careful not to *burn your fingers* when you shift it from one heat to another.
It is 5:30, and I have been working all night. I am going to bed.

Goodmorning—
E. St. V. M.[26]

When Lena arrived, she found Millay's body. She had fallen down the stairs and broken her neck. Her last poetry collection, *Mine the Harvest*, was published after her death.

To Visit

Restoration of the birthplace, 198–200 Broadway, Rockland, Maine, is nearly complete. Consult the website, History and Restoration—Millay House Rockland, for current information.

Steepletop, 440 East Hill Road, Austerlitz, New York, is just over the border from West Stockbridge, Massachusetts. Consult the website, millay.org, for information on tours.

7

Celia Thaxter

Few writers are as closely linked to a single spot on the globe as Celia Thaxter. From the age of four, she spent at least part of every year on the Isles of Shoals, an archipelago of small islands off the coasts of Maine and New Hampshire. Her prose and poetry grew on those islands as surely as her garden, the subject of her last book.

Lighthouse

Celia was born in Portsmouth, New Hampshire, on June 30, 1835. Her father, Thomas Laighton, was a customs house clerk looking for a new venture. In April 1839, he and his brother Joseph bought Hog, Smutty Nose, and Malaga—three of the islands that compose the Isles of Shoals. Celia's mother, Eliza, gave birth to Oscar two months later. That fall, Thomas was appointed keeper of the lighthouse on White Island, the most westerly of the Isles. Celia was four years old, but she always remembered the adventure of sailing and the moment she first saw her new home: "It was at sunset in autumn that we were set ashore on that loneliest, lovely rock, where the lighthouse looked down on us like some tall, black-capped giant, and filled me with awe and wonder.... Some one began to light the lamps in the tower. Rich red and golden, they swung round in mid-air; everything was strange and fascinating and new." She later described the light in a poem, "The Wreck of the Pocahontas":

> I lit the lamps in the lighthouse tower,
> For the sun dropped down and the day was dead;
> They shone like a glorious clustered flower,—
> Ten golden and five red.

They were to live in an old stone cottage with "low whitewashed ceilings and deep window-seats, showing the great thickness of the walls made to withstand the breakers."[1]

It was an unusual but delightful childhood. Eliza and Thomas used the long, harsh winters to teach the children. In the evenings, Thomas read aloud to Eliza while she knitted, and the children listened. Poetry was a special favorite. In the spring and summer, the children explored their very small island, playing in the tide pools. Celia learned a great deal about birds, though in a grim way. Birds of all kinds crashed into the light and fell dead to the ground, where she could examine their corpses. She also began to learn about plants and flowers, though the rocky ground didn't encourage vegetation.

In 1841 Thomas was elected to the New Hampshire Legislature, and for the next two years, he spent the spring and fall sessions on the mainland, while a substitute keeper tended the light and the family moved to the Haley House on Smutty Nose Island.

Hotels

In the summer, Eliza ran the Haley House, built from the timbers of a wrecked ship, as an inn, the "Mid-Ocean House of Entertainment." The couple's third child, Cedric, was born there in 1846. The hotel's distinguished guests included the writer and editor Thomas Wentworth Higginson, and Richard Henry Dana, author of *Two Years Before the Mast*. Others would become lifelong friends of Celia's, including John Weiss, a Unitarian minister, and Levi Lincoln Thaxter, who became the children's tutor. For the first time, Celia spent time with girls her own age, the daughters of visitors.

Thomas saw an opportunity to expand the islands' tourism. He resigned as lighthouse keeper and in 1847 used his share of the money from the sale of family property in Portsmouth to build a house on Hog Island. It was the most promising of the islands—a mile long, with beaches, caves and ruins of earlier settlements to explore, and attractive vegetation. He promptly renamed the island Appledore—a far more appealing name. Levi Thaxter loaned him money to build a hotel, and construction began. Levi also built a house near the site of the hotel. The Appledore House Hotel grew to four stories plus a tower. The first floor housed the office, kitchen, parlors, and dining rooms, with guest rooms above that could accommodate more than a hundred guests. A blacksmith shop and forge, vegetable garden, and a cow provided needed services and supplies. The ocean provided plentiful fish for dinners.

When the hotel opened on June 15, 1848, the first guests arrived from Newburyport, Massachusetts, and Portsmouth. Levi Thaxter's parents, sisters, and brother spent the season there. Celia and Lucy Thaxter became close friends, and the two girls attended the Mount Washington Female Seminary in Boston together for a single term.

The Appledore Hotel, Isles of Shoals, Maine, ca. 1901. The cottage where Celia Thaxter lived is to the left of the main hotel. *Detroit Publishing Company Photograph Collection, Prints and Photographs Division, Library of Congress.*

The hotel quickly became fashionable, and Thomas Laighton bought out Levi Thaxter's share. Thaxter's interest in the island had shifted from the financial to the personal: He was in love with Celia. Levi was 26, and Celia—his student—was 15. Both fathers disapproved of the match, but the mothers favored it. According to Higginson, "Mrs. Thaxter senior was charmed with [Celia's] sagacity." In August 1850, Samuel Longfellow wrote to his sister-in-law Fannie, "Thaxter who lives in a house a stone's throw from the hotel, with a hedge of sweet peas and mignonette of marvelous fragrance before the door, is engaged to the daughter of him who once kept the lighthouse and now keeps the hotel—a simple, frank and pleasing girl of fifteen, who has grown up on the islands, the flower of the rock." On September 30, 1851, they were married in the front parlor of the hotel.[2]

Finding a Home

Although he was a Harvard-educated lawyer, Levi Thaxter had not yet found his vocation. His parents seemed willing to support him as he experimented. The young couple first lived in Watertown, Massachusetts, in a house owned by Levi's parents. By February 1852 Celia was pregnant, and their first child, Karl, was born in Levi's house on Appledore Island that summer. He was born with mild physical impairments that were immediately apparent and psychological problems that appeared later in his life. The young family went to live in the old parsonage on Star Island for a year, where Levi preached and taught school, and then moved to a house in Newburyport owned by family friends. Their son John was born there in November 1854.

The following summer they returned to Appledore. Levi and Celia's brother Oscar went sailing and were shipwrecked in a sudden storm. They both survived, but Levi became terrified of the sea. He vowed never to return to the Isles and sold Thomas Laighton his house and land. His decision meant that Levi and Celia would spend large stretches of time apart. Just as he could not bear to live on an island, she could not bear to be separated from the sea and her family. The house Levi had built became Celia's cottage, where she would live for part of every year for the rest of her life.

Newtonville

In 1856, Celia, Levi, Karl, and John moved into a house purchased for them by his parents at the corner of Nevada and California Streets in Newtonville, Massachusetts. The large house, with a wraparound porch, has ornately carved woodwork, fireplaces with overmantels and tile surrounds, and windows framed by small square panes.[3] Celia's upbringing in an isolated household had included all the homemaking skills. At 21, she could sew, do laundry, cook, keep the house clean, and care for her children. But she had always wanted more than that. The summers at the hotel, with its distinguished literary visitors, had provided intellectual stimulation. Now, she noted, "sometimes it's a great bore being exemplary."[4] She was not unhappy: she loved Levi and her boys, and they were close enough to Boston to find company and friendship. But this was the first time she had been away from the Isles for an entire year. She missed her mother and the sea. And she was soon pregnant again: Roland was born on August 28, 1858.

Celia began to express her homesickness for the sea in poetry. She sent a few verses to her brother Cedric, who encouraged her to continue writing. She was pleased enough with one poem, "Land-locked," to show it to her husband. It ended: "I but crave / The sad, caressing murmur of the wave / That breaks in tender music on the shore." Levi praised the poem and put it into his coat pocket. When she opened the March 1860 issue of the *Atlantic Monthly*, Celia was amazed to find her poem. Levi had sent it to the editor, James Russell Lowell. For a writer to succeed with a first submission to the *Atlantic* was unheard of, and Levi's literary friends now recognized his young wife as a talented poet.

The most important of these friends were James and Annie Fields.

The Thaxters' house in Newtonville, Massachusetts, where Celia lived part of the year from 1856 to 1879. *Portsmouth Athenaeum.*

James was a partner in the publishing house of Ticknor and Fields and would soon become the editor of the *Atlantic*. Annie had made their home a salon for James's authors and others whom he hoped to publish. At the Fields' house, Celia met Charles Dickens, Henry Wadsworth Longfellow, Ralph Waldo Emerson, and Oliver Wendell Holmes. Their company did not intimidate her but inspired her to keep writing. She was confident enough to resist editorial suggestions. A year after first being published, she told James Fields: "I thank you very much for the kind things you said about my little poem, and am grateful for the trouble you took in looking it over and making suggestions. I am sorry I could not act upon them all. I am not good at making alterations. The only merit of my small productions lies in their straightforward simplicity, and when that bloom is rubbed off by the effort to better them, they lose what little good they originally possessed."[5] The only limitations she placed on her work related to the subject matter. She tried once to write a poem about the Civil War but found she could not write about things outside her direct experience and observation. The sea, ships and wrecks, flowers, and birds were her subjects, and her poems were immediately popular. She sold her work to the *Atlantic, Harper's, Scribner's, Victoria, Youth's Companion,* and *St. Nicholas,* earning between five and fifteen dollars per poem—enough to hire a maid and to buy a sewing machine.

Back and Forth

Appledore House was prospering. Thomas and his sons had twice enlarged the hotel and added a much-needed landing pier. A competing hotel, the Oceanic, had been built on Star Island, and the Thaxters bought it in 1875. A new steamship, *The Appledore,* was launched in 1872 and made two round trips daily between Boston and the islands. The family welcomed hundreds of guests every summer and were chronically short-staffed. Celia handled reservations and, when she visited, helped out wherever she was needed. In the 1860s her father had several strokes, and her mother suffered from neuralgia, so her presence was frequently necessary. After her father died in 1866, her mother was even more in need of company. Levi's health, too, was precarious, and he had been advised to spend the winter in a warmer climate. Beginning in 1869, he and the younger boys went to Florida each winter, while Celia and Karl went to Appledore. Karl was increasingly in need of attention, veering between depression and anger. Traveling back and forth between Newtonville and Appledore, with family obligations in both places, left Celia little time or energy for writing.

In both places, though, she found intellectual stimulation. From Newtonville she could attend the theater, concerts, opera, and lectures in Boston, and spend time at Annie Fields's salon. In the summer, Appledore was full of guests, many attracted to the island by reading Celia's poems. John Greenleaf Whittier spent several summers, and he and Celia became lifelong friends and correspondents.

Her favorite and most productive times were spring and fall at Appledore, with few if any guests, when she could be alone with the island. On September 1, 1863, she wrote to Elizabeth Whittier: "I am almost alone here, the crowd has thinned to two tables full of people, all my immediate family are gone ... and it is so lovely to be alone.... I've had such a long siege of people, I almost grow to dislike the aspect of the human shape divine in a perfectly wholesale manner." The next week she wrote to Lucy Larcom of the joys of simply watching the sea and birds, "gathering driftwood and sketching and picking up shells and seaweed and things, and hunting mushrooms and being deliciously lazy and carefree generally."[6]

In the fall of 1871, the Thaxter family lived together in Newtonville for the first time in years. They redecorated the house, the younger boys took music lessons, and Levi helped Celia with publishing details, correcting proofs and registering copyrights. A year later, though, Celia's mother was ill, and she was needed at Appledore. Levi, too, was ill and did not want to spend another winter in the cold. In 1873, he rented out the Newtonville house. Annie Fields found the place empty. Her reaction may reflect confidences that Celia had shared: "Ah! Poor Celia! This was her first home when she was brought away from her islands to begin their married life. She has suffered much under the roof, yet all her married joys have been here too, and I know she must suffer to see this forlorn shell—only too emblematic of their love." Annie later commented thoughtfully on the Thaxters' marriage: "Their natures were strongly contrasted, but perhaps not too strongly to complement each other, if he had fallen in love with her as a woman, and not as a child."[7] Annie did not comment on Levi's failure to support the family or to provide household help, but that undoubtedly added to strains in the marriage.

In 1872, Celia's first volume of poetry, *Poems*, was published by Hurd and Houghton. It was an immediate success and went through several printings. At the same time, James Fields was urging Celia to try her hand at prose. Whittier added his encouragement: "Write thou must. It is thy Kismet."[8] She began work on a series of essays for the *Atlantic* that were then combined as a book, *Among the Isles of Shoals*, published by James R. Osgood in 1873 and later reprinted in an inexpensive edition sold at train stations as a guidebook. Although it was first published serially, the book is not divided into chapters. Reading it is like sitting on the porch of the hotel listening to her talk about her islands as she weaves together history, geology, myth, landscape, humor, and nature. She explains the charm of the islands for visitors: "the wonderful sound of the sea dulls the memory of all past impressions, and seems to fulfil and satisfy all present needs." Those who have been brought up there "find it almost as difficult to tear themselves away from the Islands as do the Swiss to leave their mountains.... No other place is able to furnish the inhabitants of the Shoals with sufficient air for their capacious lungs; there is never scope enough elsewhere, there is no horizon."[9]

In 1875 she wrote a very different sort of story, "A Memorable Murder." Smutty Nose Island had recently become home to Norwegian immigrants whom the Islanders regarded as gentle people with close-knit families who worked hard on their land and boats. The men fished, and the women stayed home on their small plots. Celia Thaxter knew most of the women, some of whom worked in the hotel, and she was at Appledore when the crime occurred.

Early on a March morning, two children playing in their yard on Appledore heard a woman crying for help across the harbor. Their father, Jorge Ingebertsen, came out to see a young woman, Maren Hontvet, bloodied and freezing. He rowed across and brought her to his house. He and some neighbors, armed with guns, when over to Smutty Nose, where they found the bodies of Maren's sister and another young woman. One had been strangled, the other hacked to death. Their husbands returned from their fishing trip to this horrific scene. Maren named their attacker—Louis Wagner, a hired man whom their families had befriended. Newspapers across the country reported on the crime and the subsequent trial, in which Wagner was found guilty. He was hanged at the Maine State Prison on June 30, 1875. Celia knew all three women, and she wanted to "tell the story of their sorrow as simply as may be."[10]

Worried that she might have "offended against the good taste" or "proprieties of existence," she first sent her manuscript to James and Annie Fields. "The subject," she wrote, "was a delicate one to handle, so notorious, so ghastly and dreadful! I would not dare send it to Howells without asking Mr. Fields first." They recommended sending it to William Dean Howells, editor of the *Atlantic,* and he published it in the May 1875 issue. She left out no bloody details yet told the story with restraint and with sympathy for the victims. She emphasized their innocence, the kindness they had shown Wagner, his cruelty, and the pointlessness of the crime. She also tied the murders to their island setting, with the winds and tides playing a fateful role. The readers of her poetry must have been astonished to find that she was the author.

Celia stayed on Appledore until 1877, when she moved with her mother to Portsmouth. In her last winter on the island, 1876–1877, she began painting. In that winter alone, she painted more than a hundred tiles, plates, cups, and bowls as well as two Japanese screens for which she was paid $100. Her subjects for painting were those of her poems—birds, butterflies, and flowers—and painting became a significant source of income. She wrote to Annie Fields about her mornings, which began at six with her hotel responsibilities. Then, she wrote, "I sit down at my desk with a student lamp to write till the winter sun rises. I write as fast as I can, not to take sunshine from my painting. We have breakfast at eight."[11]

After her mother's death, in 1877, the family made one last try at living in Newtonville. Karl and John were grown and away from home, but Roland—about to go off to Harvard—wanted to spend time together. He told Celia, "Everyone has had more of you than I, who feel as if I had never had a mother!"[12] Although Celia was working and earning money, Levi expected her to do all the housework. Her Boston friends invited her to concerts, plays, lectures, and the opera. Somehow she completed another volume of poetry, *Drift-weed,* published by Houghton, Osgood and Company in 1878, and illustrated with small drawings of her own. The volume was well received, and she took orders for customized copies to which she added watercolor sketches. She sold these for 25 dollars.[13]

Farm

In 1879, they finally sold the Newtonville house. Their son John had been working as a farmer, and they bought Cutts Farm at Brave Boat

Harbor, Kittery Point, Maine, for him. They built a roomy, comfortable house with a mansard roof, dormer windows, and six fireplaces. The house had views of pastures, woods, and seashore. It could be seen from Appledore. Before settling in at Kittery Point, though, Celia accompanied her brother Oscar on a five-month trip to Europe. They visited England, France, Belgium, Germany, Switzerland, and Italy. With a letter of introduction from Annie Fields, Celia met Robert Browning, and she called on Charles Dickens, whom she had already met.

Celia settled into a routine of sorts during the 1880s. She spent summers on Appledore, spring and fall in Kittery, and winters at the farm or in a Boston hotel, where she stayed with Karl. She had despaired of Karl's future, telling John, "I have never seen poor Karl so daft. I think he is going to lose what little mind he had poor unfortunate fellow."[14] Then, in the mid–1880s, Karl became interested in photography and hand printing and developed considerable skill. He had workshops in their rooms at the Hotel Clifford on Cortes Street in Boston, where Celia painted and wrote, and on the farm. Levi, too, finally created a career reading Browning's poetry to enthusiastic audiences. He continued until 1883, when he became ill. Roland took care of him, but he died in 1884 and was buried at Kittery Point.

It was the summers at Appledore that brought Celia her greatest happiness. The hotel had become a fashionable vacation spot. Guests dressed for dinner, and a band played Gilbert and Sullivan tunes. The women paraded around the grounds in long skirts and parasols and bathed in black outfits with puffy sleeves, baggy bloomers, and knee-length skirts. But Celia's life centered around her own cottage and garden. She enlarged the parlor, which was crowded from floor to ceiling with drawings, photographs, and paintings. She was surrounded by a circle of writers, musicians, and artists: Lowell, Emerson, Holmes, Hawthorne, Longfellow, Whittier, Annie and James Fields, Sarah Orne Jewett, Mark Twain, and Howells; pianists John Knowles Paine and William Mason; violinists Julius Eichberg and Ole Bull; and the artist Childe Hassam. She published three more books: *Poems for Children* (1884), *Idyls and Pastorals* (1886), and *The Cruise of the Mystery and Other Poems* (1886).

Garden

A source of joy and inspiration was her cottage garden at Appledore. She arrived in March with seedlings, prepared the soil, and spent the rest of the summer weeding, dealing with pests, but mostly enjoying the carefully designed garden plots that surrounded her. She began work on *An*

Island Garden, published in 1894. This beautiful book, bound in green cloth with gold stamping in a pattern of stylized flowers and stems, is illustrated with a dozen full-page watercolors by Childe Hassam and chapter headings decorated with his "illuminations" of flowers. It offers practical advice on choosing plants, planning and designing a garden, controlling weeds and insects, and arranging cut flowers. It includes the plan of her garden, with a list of the 57 varieties of flower it boasted.[15]

Thaxter wrote the book to answer admirers of the garden who asked, "What is your secret?" Anyone hoping for a magic formula would be disappointed: "I answered one word, 'Love.' For that includes all.—the patience that endures continual trial, the constancy that makes perseverance possible, the power of foregoing ease of mind and body to minister to the necessities of the thing beloved, and the subtle bond of sympathy which is as important, if not more so, than all the rest." The gardener's enemies—plant or insect—are "legion, and they must be fought early and late, day and night, without cessation." Her garden is small, but "it is wonderful how much work one can find to do in so tiny a plot of ground." And the reward for all this work? In the morning, "the fair face of every flower salutes me with a silent joy that fills me with infinite content; each gives me its color, its grace, its perfume, and enriches me with the consummation of its beauty. All the cares, perplexities, and griefs of existence, all the burdens of life slip from my shoulders and leave me with the heart of a little child that asks nothing beyond its present moment of innocent bliss."[16]

That summer, with her garden at its height, Celia Thaxter felt unwell. Roland and his two

Celia Thaxter in her garden on Appledore Island. In 1892, her friend Childe Hassam showed her in a similar pose in a painting now owned by the Smithsonian American Art Museum. *Portsmouth Athenaeum.*

children arrived at Appledore and were with her when she died during the night of August 25. She was buried on Appledore next to her parents.

Afterwards

The Thaxters' hotel on Appledore burned down in 1914, and the island is now the home of the Shoals Marine Laboratory. The only survivor of Celia Thaxter's story—besides her books—is her garden, which has been restored according to the plan in *An Island Garden* and with descendants of some of the plants she grew. It is tended by volunteers from the laboratory.

To Visit

The Shoals Marine Laboratory offers walking tours of Appledore Island and tours of the garden. For information, visit its website, https://www.shoalsmarinelaboratory.org/.

The Oceanic Hotel on Star Island remains and is open to guests in a limited fashion, mostly for conferences. See https://starisland.org/ for information.

The Newtonville house is a private residence.

Massachusetts

8

Louisa May Alcott

Louisa May Alcott became rich and famous because, confined to a house she did not like, she wrote a book she did not want to write. She had rarely had the luxury of living comfortably or writing as she wished, and she had learned from necessity to tailor her art to the market. *Little Women* was her most successful work, but it built on a lifetime of learning what readers—and editors—were looking for.

Sibling Rivalry

Louisa's father, Bronson, was a progressive educator and a brilliant thinker, but he was rarely able to support his wife and daughters. His first school, in Germantown, Pennsylvania, provided an ideal domestic arrangement. He and Abigail May had been married in May 1830. Abigail, who came from a distinguished Boston family, had been educated by a tutor and grew up among reformers and abolitionists. Bronson's educational philosophy appealed to her own ideas about childrearing and social responsibility. In 1833 the couple moved to a rent-free cottage that Abigail described as a "little paradise." Their first daughter, Anna, had been born in March 1831. Abigail was a loving mother, and Bronson was fascinated by the baby's development, so Anna had her parents' constant attention. In November 1832, though, Louisa was born. Anna became intensely jealous of the new baby, and neither parent had any idea how to handle her anger, which manifested itself in biting and scratching the baby and her mother.[1]

To add to their worries, the Germantown school failed, as did another attempt in Philadelphia. In July 1833 the family moved to Boston. They lived in boardinghouses, then with Abigail's father, and finally in a rented house that they shared with paying guests. In June 1835 a third daughter, Elizabeth, was born, and it was Louisa's turn to be jealous, once threatening to throw the baby out the window.

Despite domestic chaos, Bronson found support for a new school that he opened at the Tremont Masonic Temple. Funds were provided by influential Bostonians impressed by lectures and "conversations" he had presented. He borrowed heavily for elegant furnishings and an impressive library. The school opened in September 1834. Bronson's philosophy and the quality of teaching appealed to socially prominent parents, and for nearly three years his experiment thrived. In 1835 he published *Record of a School* to provide a model for other educators. It was well received, and he followed it with a sequel, *Conversations with Children on the Gospels,* in which he quoted his students' ideas. He included the children's first names and covered controversial topics like religion and sex. One student, "Josiah," explained where babies come from: "The spirit comes from heaven, and takes up the naughtiness out of other people.... And these naughtinesses, put together, make a body for the child."[2] Josiah was immediately recognizable as the grandson of Josiah Quincy, former mayor of Boston and now president of Harvard. Brahmin Boston was scandalized, and parents withdrew their children. The admission of a Black student sealed the school's fate.

Soon Bronson could not pay the rent on the school or his home. In 1837, the Alcotts moved to a small house on Cottage Place and then to a shared house on Beach Street. Bronson was $6,000 in debt. Abigail told her brother Samuel May, "We are as poor as rats."[3]

Concord: Dove Cottage

Ralph Waldo Emerson admired Bronson's lectures and conversations, and he encouraged him to move to Concord, where he would find intellectual companionship. Abigail's brother and father gave the family enough money to rent Dove Cottage, where in July 1840 a fourth daughter, May, was born. The family's finances remained precarious. Abigail wrote in her journal, "Mr. Alcott cannot bring himself to work for gain; but we have not yet learned to live without money or means." She asked her brother Samuel, "Must we too embrace some device to *get money* that we may live? ... We *must* or starve, freeze, go thirsty and naked."[4] Earning enough to survive fell to Abigail and the older girls, who took in sewing.

Fruitlands

A group of English educational reformers had started a school named Alcott House, based on Bronson's principles. They invited him to visit, and Emerson—always sympathetic and generous—paid for the voyage. While he was gone, Abigail's father died, leaving her a small legacy that enabled her to pay off some of their creditors.

Bronson stayed in England for six months, and he and two of his admirers decided to start a self-sufficient "consociate family" in New England. On October 20, 1842, Bronson, Henry Wright, Charles Lane, and Lane's son moved into Dove Cottage while they looked for a suitable property and, they hoped, a few others who shared their commitment. It was crowded, Abigail wrote: "Circumstances most cruelly drive me from the enjoyment of my domestic life. I am almost suffocated in this atmosphere of restriction and gloom … perhaps I feel it more after five months of liberty."[5]

In 1843, the men found a run-down farm in Harvard, Massachusetts. The money they needed came from Lane and a loan that Samuel May signed for. They moved in that spring and, rejoicing in the few scraggly apple trees on the property, named it Fruitlands.[6] They were committed to a strict vegan diet that also excluded coffee, tea, molasses, and root vegetables. They ate unleavened bread, perhaps because yeast is a living organism. They wore only linen (wool belonged to the sheep, silk to silkworms, and cotton was harvested by slaves). They could not read after dark because candles and oil lamps relied on animal fats. A nearby farmer offered the use of his team to plow, over the objections of the proprietors: the animals had not given their consent to either their labor or their manure. One of their recruits, Samuel Hecker, later wrote that "Mr. Alcott looked benign and talked philosophy, while Mrs. Alcott and the children did the work."[7]

The small, ramshackle house was drafty and uncomfortable. The three oldest girls slept in the windowless attic, with ceilings so low that they could not stand up. Bronson usually slept with the other men. Lane believed that the nuclear family was incompatible with community and advocated celibacy and breaking familial bonds. Abigail might have tolerated the hard work, the cramped living conditions, and the cold, but not Lane's attempt to break up the family. Lane wrote that Bronson's "constancy to his wife and inconstancy to the Spirit have blurred over his life forever." Abigail's interpretation was that "Mr. Alcott's conjugal and paternal instincts were too strong for him."[8] The girls, aware of the conflict, feared for the family's future.

After only six months, with winter approaching, Abigail decided to end the experiment. She asked her brother Sam not to pay the November 1843 installment on the loan, and she left, taking the furniture. Bronson chose Abigail and his daughters over his fellow dreamers. The family moved into a nearby farmhouse, living in three rooms. Abigail wrote in her journal: "The end I desire [is] to obtain by some concert of means and action a home for me and my family … a house and [a] few acres of land for us to occupy.... I ask but little—but that little I must have or perish."⁹ She would not achieve that end until the spring of 1845.

Concord: Hillside

When Abigail's father's estate was settled, there was enough money to pay Bronson's debts from the Boston school, leaving $2,000 in trust for Abigail. In 1845, the trust paid $850 for a house in Concord, and Emerson gave the family $500 to buy eight acres of nearby farm land. The house was more than a hundred years old and needed work, but Bronson was determined to make it a home. He enlarged the main structure by moving and attaching outbuildings, added a kitchen, and put in a new staircase. He planted a garden to feed the family. They named this house, the first they had owned, Hillside.¹⁰

Hillside and Concord were ideal for the family. Each of them, for the first time, enjoyed space and privacy. Bronson had the company of Emerson, Thoreau, and visiting thinkers. He had his own land, where he could plant trees and build terraces, walls, and arbors. Abigail had a real home for her family. The older girls, now teenagers, began to achieve independence. Emerson opened his library to Louisa as well as to Bronson.

"Hillside in 1845," drawing by A. Bronson Alcott. The house now looks very different: in 1852, Nathaniel Hawthorne made several additions, including a tower. He also renamed the house, which continues to be known as "The Wayside." *Published in* Bronson Alcott at Alcott House, England, and Fruitlands, New England (1842–1844) *by Franklin Benjamin Sanborn (Cedar Rapids, Iowa: The Torch Press, 1908).*

Louisa had once told her mother, "I have been thinking about my little room which I suppose I never shall have. I should want to be there about all the time and I should go there and sing and think." Settled at Hillside she wrote happily: "I have at last got the little room I have wanted so long, and am very happy about it. It does me good to be alone, and Mother has made it very pretty and neat for me. My work-basket and desk are by the window, and my closet is full of dried herbs that smell very nice. The door that opens into the garden will be very pretty in summer, and I can run off to the woods when I like."[11] She began to write in earnest—theatricals, poems, and stories. Anna, too, had her own room. This was the house where the family lived when the girls were the ages of the characters in *Little Women*, the house where they carried out their theatricals, explorations, and flirtations.

The family's financial worries continued. Bronson earned a little money by conducting conversations, but not enough for wood, clothing, and staples that they could not raise themselves. Abigail took charge. She wrote to her brother: "I have taken the ship into my own command, but whether I shall do better as Captain than I have as mate, the revenue and record of the year must decide. At least I think I shall keep better soundings, and ascertain oftener and more correctly whether I am sailing in deep waters or in shallows. We have been nearly wrecked twice."[12]

Boston and Walpole, New Hampshire

Their happiness lasted only three years. By 1848, it was clear that Abigail and the girls would have to find work, and they rented out Hillside and moved to Boston. In her journal, Louisa echoed Abigail's earlier appraisal that they were "poor as rats."[13] Abigail worked for charities among the city's poorest people; Anna took a position as a live-in governess and then as a teacher in Syracuse; Louisa taught, took in sewing, and continued to write. In 1852 they sold Hillside to Nathaniel Hawthorne for $1,500, which enabled them to rent a four-story house in Boston. Bronson earned some money from his conversations. Abigail, working in the city's impoverished neighborhoods, brought home the diseases that were rampant there. In 1850 the whole family contracted smallpox, and in 1856 Lizzie and May had scarlet fever.

In 1855, a cousin, Benjamin Willis, offered the family a home rent-free in Walpole, New Hampshire. Anna had been the governess of the Willis children, and she had liked the town. They lived in the west side of the large Greek Revival house on High Street, and the girls took part in amateur theatricals. Some of the scenes in *Little Women* are based on stories from the two years they spent there.[14]

Concord: Orchard House

In 1857, Bronson convinced Abigail and their daughters that they should move back to Concord. Right next to Hillside, he had found a lot with an antique, ramshackle house that could be bought for $950. "Let me be the central figure of the Group, and try our family fortunes so, for a little time," he begged. "Please give me my last chance of redeeming my good-sense and discretion."[15] It took him nearly a year to make the house livable. The writer Lydia Maria Child provided details of the way they turned the wreck into a home: "He let every odd rafter and beam stay in its place, changed old ovens and ash-holes into Saxon arched alcoves, and added a washerwoman's old shanty to the rear. The result is a house full of queer nooks and corners, with all manner of juttings in and out.... The capable Alcott daughters painted and papered the interior themselves. And gradually the artist-daughter filled up all the nooks and corners with panels on which she had painted birds and flowers; and over the open fireplaces she painted mottoes in ancient English characters. Owls blink at you, and faces peep from the most unexpected places."[16] Bronson was proud of the house; Louisa did not like it. His Orchard House was her "Apple Slump."

When Abigail and Bronson moved into Orchard House in the summer of 1858, they were alone. Elizabeth had died in March of heart disease, probably a result of the scarlet fever she had contracted in Walpole. Anna had become engaged to John Pratt and was living with his family. May was living in Boston and would soon move to Syracuse. Louisa was settled in Boston, where she was becoming a member of the literary community. She counted Henry Wadsworth Longfellow, Harriet Beecher Stowe, Oliver Wendell Holmes, Sr., and James and Annie Fields among her friends. In 1862, though, in the middle of the Civil War, she was forced to move in with her parents. She had volunteered as an army nurse but contracted a serious case of typhoid pneumonia. She wrote about her war experiences in a series of magazine stories that were collected in 1863 as *Hospital Sketches*.

Since the 1850s, Louisa had been writing for magazines. Between 1854 and 1856, she sold several stories to the *Saturday Evening Gazette*. By 1859, she was selling stories regularly. In 1860, she sold two stories to the *Atlantic Monthly*, and in 1854 her first book, *Flower Fables*, was published. Elves and fairies were the subjects of her early stories, but she soon learned that she could write profitably in other genres. During the Civil War, she had heard that James Fields wanted war stories for the *Atlantic*. She told a friend that she would "write 'Great Guns' Hail Columbia & Concord Fight, if he'll only take it for money is the staff of life & without one falls flat no matter how much genius he may carry."[17]

A stereograph image of "Orchard House," the home of Abigail and Bronson Alcott from 1857 until Abigail's death in 1877. Louisa May Alcott stayed in the house when her mother was ill and wrote *Little Women* there. *Prints and Photographs Division, Library of Congress.*

In 1862 Louisa submitted a "blood and thunder tale," "Pauline's Passion and Punishment," to a contest sponsored by *Frank Leslie's Illustrated Newspaper* and won the $100 prize. She did not, however, sign her name to it: When the story appeared on January 3 and 10, 1863, the author was identified as "a lady of Massachusetts." She wrote in her journal for February 1865 that such stories, which she called "rubbishy tales," "pay best & I cant afford to starve on praise, when sensation stories are written in half the time & keep the family cosy." She refused to be identified as the author of the stories she wrote purely for money. Her favorite pseudonyms were Tribulation Periwinkle and A.M. Barnard. When James Elliott, editor of *Flag of Our Union*, a weekly newspaper, offered to pay her more if she would let him print her name, she refused, continuing to use A.M. Barnard or "a well-known author." He nevertheless paid better than the *Atlantic*.[18]

Louisa signed her own name to a novel, *Moods*, and became editor of a children's magazine, *Merry's Museum*, a post that paid $500 a year. A Boston publisher, Thomas Niles, had offered her $500 to write a book for girls. She wrote in her September 1867 journal, "began at once on both new jobs but didn't like either."[19] The editorial salary was enough for her to rent an apartment in Boston. But in 1868, when Abigail was suffering from heart disease and needed her help, Louisa found herself back at Orchard House. She spent the time on the girls' book that Niles wanted. It took her nine weeks to write the first half of *Little Women*.

Niles offered Louisa the choice of a $1,000 payment or $300 plus a royalty on each copy sold. She had enough confidence in the book to choose the royalty arrangement. The first printing, 2,000 copies, sold out in two weeks. Louisa moved Abigail to Anna's house for the winter and was "so glad to be off out of C[oncord] that I worked like a beaver, and turned the key on Apple Slump with joy."[20] In the Boston apartment she shared with May, she began the sequel that became part two of the book we know today. She finished it in just a few weeks. When she dropped in at Niles's office, he greeted her with the news that her book was "the triumph of the century." Part two was not yet printed, but 3,000 copies had been sold in advance. With 40,000 copies in print, the book soon set a record. Louisa told her mother, "Hard times for the Alcotts are over forever."[21]

Louisa built on her success by publishing *An Old-Fashioned Girl* in 1870, and she and May traveled to Europe. In December they learned that Anna's husband, John Pratt, had died. To provide for Anna and her two sons, Louisa wrote *Little Men*. She negotiated a royalty of 10 percent of the wholesale price, a higher rate than other authors (including Harriet Beecher Stowe) had been given. The book was issued the day she returned from Europe, with 50,000 copies sold in advance.

Louisa was earning thousands of dollars in royalties each year. She helped May to return to Europe to continue studying art and helped Anna buy Henry David Thoreau's old house in Concord, less than a mile from Orchard House. Her generosity extended to relatives beyond her immediate family, for whom she paid college tuition, bought houses, and funded a new medical practice. Nevertheless, she continued to write for magazines and newspapers and to add to the *Little Women* empire by writing more books and by repackaging previous volumes. Her prosperity brought security but neither leisure nor an idle moment.

Louisa returned to Orchard House for the last time in the summer of 1877, again to care for her mother. She wrote *Under the Lilacs* in her mother's room. In November, Abigail moved to Anna's house, where she died two weeks later. Anna added a study to her house, and Bronson moved in with her. Louisa no longer had any reason to return to Orchard House. "The old house is to let, as it is no longer home without 'Marmee,'" she wrote. "I never go by without looking up at Marmee's window, where the dear face used to be."[22] The house was sold in 1882.

A New Generation

May was painting and studying art in Paris when she married Ernest Nieriker, a 21-year-old Swiss banker 16 years her junior. In November 1879 she gave birth to a daughter, Louisa May Nieriker. May became ill soon after the birth and died in December. Baby Lulu was brought to Boston, to be raised by her aunts, Louisa and Anna. Louisa purchased a house at 10 Louisburg Square, one of the most exclusive neighborhoods in the city. Even with servants, the two women had their hands full: they were caring for their infirm father, and May's sons were teenagers. But according to Anna, Louisa was "entirely absorbed in her baby whom she loves passionately & on whom she lavishes all the strength & affection of her generous nature."[23]

Louisa's health had not been robust since the Civil War. Both typhus pneumonia and the mercury used to treat it had lasting effects. In 1888 she moved to a nursing home, and Anna took over the household. Very much aware of the lasting value of her writing, Louisa drew up a new will. The copyright law allowed only descendants to renew copyrights, so Louisa adopted Anna's son John. He would hold her copyrights in trust, sharing the income equally with his brother, Lulu, and Anna. On March 4, Bronson died at home. Louisa died on March 6, the day of her father's funeral. Lulu returned to Switzerland, to be raised by her father.

To Visit

Fruitlands Museum, 102 Prospect Hill Rd, Harvard, Massachusetts, is open to the public. It includes the original house, somewhat altered, as well as another house (giftshop and cafe) and three other museums. It is owned by the Trustees of Reservations. For hours, see www.fruitlands.org.

Hillside, now known as The Wayside, 455 Lexington Road, Concord, is open to the public as part of Minute Man National Historical Park (www.nps.gov/mima/). It has been restored to its appearance when the Hawthornes lived there.

Orchard House, 399 Lexington Road, Concord, is open to the public. For hours, see the website, louisamayalcott.org.

9

Emily Dickinson

From the age of 25, Emily Dickinson had a room of her own, where she wrote nearly all her poetry. Her room was in a large house with a well-kept garden, in the center of a growing community in which her family played an active role. Her room gave her the peace, quiet, and privacy she needed to write, but her poems arose from the interaction of her imagination with a larger world: her garden, family, friends, and books.

The Homestead

In 1813, Samuel Fowler Dickinson built Amherst's first brick house, on Main Street. Fowler, as he was known, was a lawyer and politician. He helped found the pre-collegiate Amherst Academy, open to young men and women, and Amherst College. His law practice and bank account suffered because he was so generous with his time and money, and he was forced to sell the house. His oldest son, Edward, bought the western half in 1830, and the rest was sold out of the family three years later.

Emily was born to Edward and his wife, Emily Norcross, in the Homestead in 1830. Her brother, William Austin—always known as Austin—was a year older, and Lavinia was born in 1833. As the children grew, the house became crowded. Edward sold his half and moved the family to North Pleasant Street in 1840. Emily was fond of the house, especially the garden and the kitchen with its large hearth. Emily and Vinnie shared a bedroom.[1]

The two girls also shared a lively social life. Each had her own friends among their classmates at Amherst Academy. Their evening reading club might end with a dance, and the faculty of the academy entertained students in their homes. Emily told an uncle one winter, "Sleigh rides are as plenty as people—which conveys to mind the idea of very plentiful plenty.... Parties can't find fun enough—because all the best ones are engaged to attend balls a week beforehand—beaus can be had for the taking."[2]

The sisters remained close throughout their lives, and over the years Emily became dependent on Vinnie. They were separated only when each of them spent a year at boarding school: the Ipswich Academy for Vinnie and the Mount Holyoke Female Seminary for Emily. Once Vinnie went off on a visit, and Emily (then 29 years old) told a friend, "I would like more sisters, that the taking out of one, might not leave such stillness. Vinnie has been all, so long, I feel the oddest fright at parting with her for an hour, lest a storm arise, and I go unsheltered."[3]

In 1850, a candidate for a second sister arrived when Susan and Martha Gilbert moved to Amherst. Emily and Vinnie became close friends with the two young women, who were in and out of the Dickinson house. When Sue left to teach in Baltimore in 1851, Emily missed her terribly and wrote frequent impassioned letters. She had begun to think of Sue as a member of the family: "My father will be your father, and my home will be your home, and where you go, I will go, and we will lie side by side in the kirkyard." She would later express the relationship in a poem: "One sister have I in our house, / And one, a hedge away."[4]

Austin, too, had noticed Susan Gilbert and began courting her. Emily and Vinnie adored their brother. When he was away at Harvard Law School, Emily wrote to him often: "We think about you the whole of the livelong day, and talk of you when we're together."[5] Edward Dickinson waited eagerly for Austin's letters and read them at the post office, reread them at his own office, and then had Emily read them aloud at the supper table. The prospect of a marriage pleased the entire family.

Austin proposed to Sue in 1850, but their engagement lasted six years, apparently because of hesitation on Sue's part. When they were finally married, in 1856, they moved to a new house, the Evergreens, built for them by Edward Dickinson. In April 1855, he had bought back the Homestead, made extensive renovations, and built the Evergreens next door. Emily would have her beloved brother and second sister just footsteps away.

Moving

Emily had been happy in the North Pleasant Street house for fifteen years, and she hated change. She described the day to a friend: "I cannot tell you how we moved. I had rather not remember. I believe my 'effects' were brought in a bandbox, and the 'deathless me,' on foot.... They say that 'home is where the heart is.' I think it is where the *house* is, and the adjacent buildings."[6]

Despite her misgivings, Emily found the Homestead ideal. She had

9. Emily Dickinson

Detail, "Residence of Hon. Edward Dickinson," from the lithograph, "View of Amherst, Mass., 1858," by John Bachelder. This shows the Dickinson Homestead on Main Street shortly after the house was reacquired by Emily's father, Edward. The tower was the most visible alteration made when the house was renovated. Emily's bedroom was on the second floor, at the left. *Courtesy of the Jones Library, Inc., Amherst, Massachusetts.*

her own room, where she could write letters and poems late into the night without disturbing anyone. Edward had added a conservatory, where she and Vinnie could grow exotic plants even in the New England winter. New porches on the east and west sides of the house offered comfortable access to fresh air and the scent of flowers. A cupola—a feature of the newly stylish Italianate architecture—improved the circulation of air. The first floor had two parlors on the west side, and a library, dining room, and pantry on the other side. A new two-story wing housed the kitchen and laundry on the first floor with servants' quarters above. Upstairs, each corner of the main house was a bedroom. Emily's was in the southwest corner, over the front parlor, giving her views of Main Street and the Evergreens. When Emily did not wish to join visitors, she could hear music and conversation in the parlor rising up the staircase to the hall outside her room.[7]

A short footpath connected the two houses. The Evergreens, designed by the architect William Fenno Pratt, is an impressive wooden structure with a square tower. Granite steps lead to an arched front door with a balcony above. Like the Homestead, it has porches on the east and west sides. A large central hall opens into the parlor, dining room, library, kitchen and pantry, and Austin and Sue's bedroom. The couple bought furniture from Boston and over the years accumulated a large art collection. Austin was treasurer of the college and, like his father, a prominent citizen of the town. The Evergreens was well suited to entertaining Amherst's elite and visiting dignitaries. An Amherst professor wrote that "the social leader of the town was Mrs. Austin Dickinson, a really brilliant and highly cultivated woman of great taste and refinement, perhaps a little too aggressive, a little too sharp in wit and repartee, and a little too ambitious for social prestige, but, withal, a woman of the world in the best sense, having a very keen and correct appreciation of what was fine and admirable."[8]

Emily and Lavinia paid casual visits to the Evergreens during the day, or joined Austin and Sue at dinner. They were invited to evening events, including parties and receptions for distinguished visitors. Emily sometimes brought her dog Carlo, played the piano, and had a good time, with her father fetching her home at midnight. When Ned, the couple's first son, was born in 1861, his aunts doted on him, and they were also pleased when a daughter, Mattie, was born in 1866. In 1875, Thomas Gilbert, "Gib," was born and became Emily's favorite.

Emily spent time in Boston in 1864 and 1865 to receive treatment for an eye disease but never again left the houses in Amherst. As she explained

Emily Dickinson's bedroom, with her writing desk at the window overlooking The Evergreens. *Courtesy of Emily Dickinson Museum.*

9. *Emily Dickinson* 103

"Residence of W.A. Dickinson, Esq., Amherst, Mass.," by Charles Prouty, from *Photographic Sketchbook: Views in the Valley of the Connecticut, 1870*. The house, known as The Evergreens, was the home of Emily's brother Austin and his wife, Susan. Emily could walk from the Homestead, next door on the right, by a path through the gardens. *Courtesy of the Jones Library, Inc., Amherst, Massachusetts.*

to her friend and mentor Thomas Wentworth Higginson in 1869, "I do not cross my Father's ground to any House or Town." She did receive visitors, although she believed her friends "are a very few. I can count them on my fingers—and besides have fingers to spare."[9] She welcomed Higginson, the newspaper editor Samuel Bowles, Judge Otis Lord, her childhood friend Abby Wood Bliss, the poet Helen Hunt Jackson and her husband, and Rebecca Mack (a former family servant). Generally, though, conversation was limited to the family circle.

That conversation ranged far and wide, because the family subscribed to newspapers, read them aloud to one another, and discussed their content. Although they did read national and international news, their favorite articles were accounts of local events—the more calamitous or bizarre, the better. "Who writes these funny accidents, where railroads meet each other unexpectedly, and gentlemen in factories get their heads cut off quite informally? The author, too, relates them in such a sprightly way, that they are quite attractive. Vinnie was disappointed tonight, that there were not more accidents—I read the news aloud, while Vinnie was sewing."[10]

Emily's poetry, of course, travels far beyond the Homestead. Her imagination was fired by her reading: The family owned many books, and she had access to the college library. She also had an extensive correspondence, receiving letters from friends who described their travels. Higginson led the First South Carolina Volunteers during the Civil War and wrote to her about the South. Samuel Bowles wrote about his travels in the American West, several friends wrote from Europe, and her friend Abby Bliss wrote from Syria, where she lived with her missionary husband. She enjoyed their adventures vicariously but did not envy them. She told her friend Elizabeth Holland that she "saw the sunrise on the Alps since I saw you. Travel why to Nature, when she dwells with us?" With her conservatory at hand, she wrote, "I have but to cross the floor to stand in the Spice Isles."[11] Emily's correspondence kept her in touch with the lives of people who were important to her, just as newspapers reported world events. But the Homestead and the Evergreens were becoming scenes of drama as well.

Family Tensions

Edward Dickinson died in 1874, leaving no will, and it took Austin some time to sort out his estate. Emily Norcross Dickinson had a stroke in 1875, and she and her daughters depended on Austin for support. There were rumors of financial difficulty. Sue continued to entertain and add to their art collection (which may have contributed to money problems), but Austin was now focused on his law practice and town affairs. A friend wrote that without Austin's help, "nobody in the town could be born or married or buried, or make an investment, or buy a house-lot, or a cemetery-lot, or sell a newspaper, or build a house, or choose a profession." He began to refer to Sue's entertaining as "my wife's tavern."[12]

Emily and Vinnie were aware of the strains in the marriage, and they sided unquestioningly with their brother. After 1868, Emily did not visit the Evergreens. She and Sue continued to correspond and to share books, but they did not meet. Emily still asked Sue's opinion of her poems and sometimes accepted her suggested changes. In 1877 Emily sent Susan a poem that begins "But Susan is a Stranger yet," but there was never a complete break because, as Emily explained, "The tie between us is very fine, but a Hair never dissolves."[13] Vinnie, too, grew distant from Sue, if only because she was protective of Emily and unhappy when anyone caused her distress. But the greatest strain arose in 1881, when Amherst College hired a new astronomy professor with a talented and beautiful wife.

David and Mabel Loomis Todd arrived in Amherst on August 31, 1881. Mabel was a pianist trained at the New England Conservatory and an amateur painter. Austin and Sue called on them in October, and Mabel was impressed. Writing to her mother, she described Sue as "the most of a real society person here, and her presence filled the room with an ineffable grace and elegance.... I liked her *so* much. She is said to give elegant little entertainments and musicales." After attending one of those entertainments, she wrote, "I am thoroughly captivated with her now. She does, as I supposed, live very handsomely, & she is so easy and charming, & sincere—and she understands me completely." She was also impressed by Austin: "He is fine (& very remarkable) looking—& very dignified & strong and a little odd."[14]

Mabel soon visited both Dickinson houses. Vinnie extended an invitation, and Mabel played the piano for her, with Emily listening in the hall. Emily and Mabel began corresponding: Emily sent poems, and Mabel sent drawings. Their correspondence continued, but they never met. At the Evergreens, Mabel gave Mattie piano lessons and often joined the family for tea or dinner. When David Todd was out of town, Ned escorted Mabel to social events. And sometimes Austin escorted her home from the Evergreens. Before long, Mabel and Austin were in love. By November 1882, they were exchanging passionate letters. Sue became aware of their liaison, which did not go beyond letters for a little more than a year.

In the autumn of 1883, the Dickinsons' younger son, Gib, became ill. For the first time in fifteen years, Emily walked along the path to the Evergreens, to sit by his side. The little boy, eight years old, died on October 5. Sue was overwhelmed, unable even to go to the cemetery. Emily was sent to bed with what the doctor called nervous prostration. Austin sought comfort from Mabel. Their affair was consummated on December 13, at the Homestead. According to Mabel, Austin "told me over and over again that I kept him alive through the dreadful period of Gilbert's sickness and death. He could not bear the atmosphere of his own house, & used to go to his sisters', & then he or Lavinia would send for me."[15]

Emily and Vinnie were complicit in Austin's infidelity. In addition to providing a convenient place for the lovers to meet, Vinnie received Mabel's letters and re-sent them in envelopes addressed in her handwriting so that Sue would not know their source. Austin gave Mabel's letters to Vinnie for safekeeping. Despite the couple's attempts at secrecy, Sue became aware of what was happening and was furious. Ned later described that time to a family friend: "There were weeks when Sue would not speak to Austin and when Austin would not speak to her." When Sue wanted to redecorate the central hall, "Father positively forbid anything being done.... Whereupon mother began to pull off the paper."[16]

Mabel's marriage was not affected. She and David had always accepted each other's frequent infidelities. But all the children were hurt badly. Ned and Mattie took their mother's side, creating a permanent distance from their father. When Austin and Mabel met at the Todds' house,

Mabel's daughter, Millicent, was often at home. She remembered: "There was but one repugnant thing which did positively unnerve me. It was a sore which never healed and which got me in the middle like solar plexus nausea each time I looked at it. That was a diamond engagement ring and wedding ring which mamma wore on her left hand—her others, almost identical, which had preceded the union resulting in my birth, were now worn upon her right.... I felt numbly degraded by the sight of those rings, and in a way disinherited."[17]

The affair lasted thirteen years, until Austin died in 1895. Millicent Todd remembered that both her parents cried all day. On the day of Austin's funeral, while the family was at lunch, Ned admitted Mabel to the house through a side door so that she could say good-bye privately.

Emily's Death and Legacy

When Emily became ill after Gib's death, the cause was nephritis, inflammation of the kidneys. Despite her illness, she continued to write poems until shortly before her death on May 15, 1886. Sue wrote a heartfelt and moving obituary. In Emily's room, Vinnie found hundreds of poems, which she turned over to Sue, who had hundreds more that she had kept, to prepare them for publication. When Sue made little progress, Vinnie took back the poems she had found and gave them to Mabel Todd. It took Mabel two years to transcribe a selection of the poems, which she sent to Thomas Wentworth Higginson. He convinced Roberts Brothers, a Boston publisher, to issue a small volume in 1890. It sold far better than expected and went into five printings. Additional volumes appeared in 1891 and 1896. The covers of the early printings were decorated with one of Mabel's drawings. Vinnie was delighted at seeing Emily's poems in print, but Sue was angry that Mabel had usurped yet another of her roles. Vinnie and Sue stopped speaking.

Mabel also decided to publish a volume of Emily's letters. She wrote to Emily's correspondents and asked them to send any letters they had kept. Austin insisted that Sue's name be omitted, and the expurgated volume appeared in 1894. After Mabel's death in 1932, her daughter Millicent prepared a revised edition without the omissions. She delayed publication until 1945, after Mattie Dickinson had died, to avoid hurting her.

When Austin died in 1895, he left almost everything to Sue, but a small legacy was left to Vinnie with the understanding that she would privately pass it on to the Todds. Vinnie decided not to do so, and the matter ended up in court. The people of Amherst had always turned a blind eye to Austin and Mabel's affair out of respect for the Dickinsons. But when the matter was discussed in open court, there was no keeping silence. In May 1898, final judgment was delivered in favor of Vinnie, and all relations between the Dickinsons and the Todds ceased. Mabel locked the poems and letters in a camphorwood chest.

Publication of most of Emily's poems was left to the next generation. Martha Dickinson Bianchi, Austin and Sue's daughter, arranged the publication of the poems in Sue's possession after her mother's death. She sold the manuscripts to Harvard University in 1950. The unpublished poems in the camphorwood chest were edited by Millicent Todd Bingham and published in 1945. She donated the manuscripts to Amherst College in 1956. The first definitive edition of all the poems was published in 1955, and a scholarly edition followed in 1958. The most recent complete edition was published in 1998.

The houses were brought together as a single museum in 2003. The Homestead was completely restored in 2021 and 2022, and restoration of the Evergreens is under way. The museum has been a mecca for those who love Dickinson's poetry as well as those who have been introduced to her life through television and film.

To Visit

The Emily Dickinson Museum, which includes the Homestead and the Evergreens, is located at 280 Main Street, Amherst MA 01002. It is open to visitors. For information on hours and tickets, see info@EmilyDickinsonMuseum.org, or call (413) 542-8161.

10

Sojourner Truth

Sojourner Truth's story of her first twenty-five years brings to life the cruelty of Northern slavery. She was sold, abused, separated from her family, and kept illiterate. In their old age, her mother died in an unheated cabin and her father, without his wife to care for him, froze to death. With great courage and charisma, she became a celebrated evangelist and orator, speaking eloquently for the rights of women, the enslaved, and the impoverished. We learn about her life from her two books. She never learned to write, so she needed the help of collaborators, but the books nevertheless allow us to hear Truth's voice.

Slavery

In 1797, a daughter was born to James and Elizabeth, who were enslaved on the Hurley, New York, farm of Colonel Johannes Hardenbergh. The Hardenberghs spoke Dutch to their slaves, isolating them from English-speaking neighbors. Hardenbergh's large stone house, very plain on the outside, was large, with many rooms, fireplaces, and elegant woodwork.[1] James and Elizabeth lived in the basement slave quarters. The two had at least ten children, but all were sold except one daughter, Isabella, and a son. At a very young age, Isabella joined her mother in doing laundry, sewing, cooking, making butter and cheese, gardening, and tending chickens.

After Johannes Hardenbergh died, his son Charles moved James's family to his hotel. Isabella was only five or six years old, but she spent her days cleaning guest rooms, doing laundry, cooking, and baking. When Charles died, in 1808, Isabella was sold to John Neely. He mistreated her badly, leaving her without shoes or adequate clothing. He gave orders in English, which she did not understand, and then beat her for disobedience. Decades later, speaking to college students, she asked, "Well, children, when you go to heaven and God asks you what made you hate the

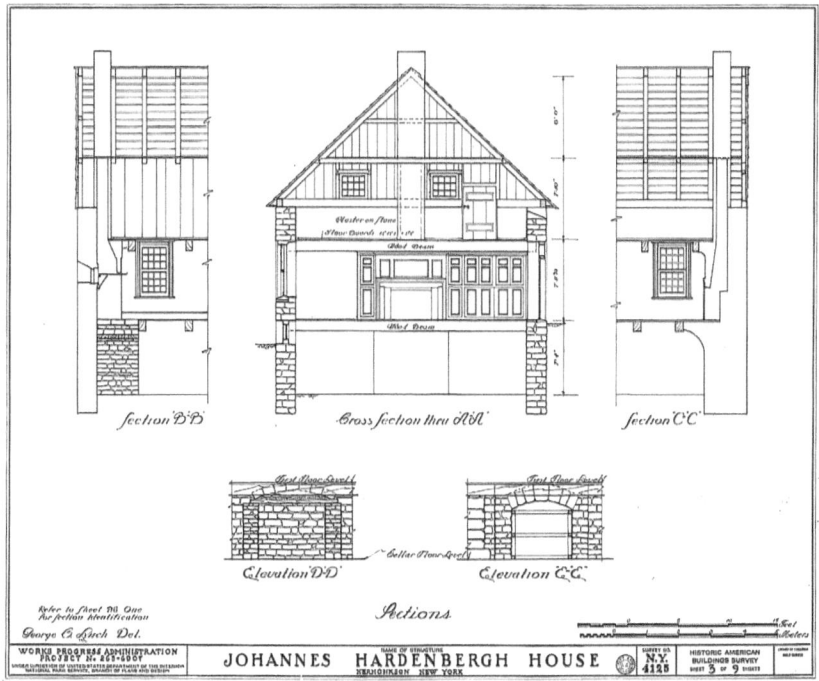

Plan of the Hardenburgh house, in Ulster County, New York. Isabella—who became Sojourner Truth—was born in the basement slave quarters. This plan was drawn for the Historic American Buildings Survey conducted by the National Park Service during the Great Depression. *Prints and Photographs Division, Library of Congress.*

colored people, have you got your answer ready?" She paused before continuing, "When I go before the throne of God, and God says, 'Sojourner, what made you hate the white people?' I have got my answer ready." Then she pulled down the shoulder of her dress to show the pattern of deep scars left by Neely's beatings.[2] Her father learned of the abuse and asked a local merchant, Martimus Schryver, to buy Isabella from Neely. He did so, even though he had never owned a slave. Schryver brewed beer and cider, and Isabella found the work relatively easy. She also began to learn English. Schryver then sold Isabella to John Dumont—her third owner in one year.

At the Dumonts, her work combined that of a domestic servant with field work: making breakfast, gathering eggs, milking cows, and doing household chores, but also working alongside men in the field. The fieldwork was hard and dangerous, and she lost a finger. Dumont's wife, Elizabeth, grew to hate Isabella and did her best to make her life difficult, perhaps out of jealousy: The biographer Margaret Washington argues convincingly that John and Isabella may have had a sexual relationship and that Isabella's daughter Diana, born around 1815, may have been his child.[3]

In 1817, New York passed a gradual emancipation law, updating a law passed in 1799, under which enslaved adults would be freed on July 4, 1827. Those born after 1799 would remain enslaved until adulthood, and slaves could not be sold out of state. Around 1820, Isabella married Thomas, also enslaved in the Dumont household. They had three children together: Peter (born in 1821), Elizabeth (born around 1824), and Sophia (born in 1826). Isabella had had two children with another man: James, who died in infancy, and Diana. Her children could look forward to freedom only as adults.

Dumont told Isabella that if she worked hard, he would free her a year before the deadline. When 1826 dawned, Isabella reminded Dumont of his promise, but he said she hadn't worked hard enough. Leaving her older children behind, she fled with Sophia to the home of Isaac D. Van Wagenen and his wife, Maria Schoonmacher. The Von Wagenens had no desire to own slaves, but they paid Dumont 25 dollars for Isabella and Sophia and then emancipated them. In Isabella's recounting of the moment, "the sum was paid, and her master Dumont departed; but not till he had heard Mr. Van Wagener tell her not to call him master—adding, 'there is but *one* master; and he who is *your* master is *my* master.'"[4] She lived with the Von Wagenens for a year and took their name.

Isabella had left her children with their owner, John Dumont. Violating New York law, Dumont sold Peter (who was five years old) to a relative who in turn sold him to John Fowler, a planter in Alabama. Isabella immediately set out to get her son back. She walked to the county seat and, with the help of sympathetic Quakers, filed the necessary papers. The writ was misdelivered, the first of many delays. When the New York Manumission Society became involved, Peter was finally brought back from Alabama. It was a difficult reunion, as Isabella recounted:

> When the pleading was at an end, Isabella understood the Judge to declare, as the sentence of the Court, that the "boy be delivered into the hands of the mother—having no other master, no other controller, no other conductor, but his mother." This sentence was obeyed; he was delivered into her hands, the boy meanwhile begging, most piteously, *not* to be taken from his dear master, saying she was not his mother, and that his mother did not live in such a place as that. And it was some time before lawyer Demain, the clerks, and Isabella, could collectively succeed in calming the child's fears, and in convincing him that Isabella was not some terrible monster, as he had for the last months, probably, been trained to believe; and who, in taking him away from his master, was taking him from all good, and consigning him to all evil.

When at last kind words and *bon-bons* had quieted his fears, and he could listen to their explanations, he said to Isabella–"Well, you *do* look like my mother *used* to"; and she was soon able to make him comprehend some of the obligations he was under, and the relation he stood in, both to herself and his master. She commenced as soon as practicable to examine the boy, and found, to her utter astonishment, that from the crown of his head to the sole of his foot, the callosities and indurations on his entire body were most frightful to behold.[5]

In horror and anger, Isabella cursed John Fowler and his family: "Oh Lord, 'render unto them double' for all this!" Soon she learned that Fowler had murdered his wife, and although God had apparently answered her request, she spoke to Him again: "Oh, my God! that's too much—I did not mean quite so much, God!"[6]

Freedom, Church and Scandal

Isabella and the Van Wagenens attended Methodist camp meetings, which were a source of joy, with the freedom of the outdoors and the large tents, the spontaneity of worship and song. Isabella recalled falling into a trance at one of these meetings as the moment of her conversion. She joined St. James Methodist Episcopal Church in Kingston and began her public ministry. Margaret Washington describes the beginnings of Isabella's evangelism: "She possessed a natural spirituality and confidence. She found a religious denomination that accepted her voice, despite her color, sex, condition, and lack of education. She formed positive relationships with white women for the first time, and they encouraged her to seek broader horizons."[7] Eager to learn Scripture, but unable to read, she relied on others to read to her and committed to memory what she heard.

In 1828, to further her ministry, Isabella moved to New York City. She quickly found housekeeping and childcare work with Methodist families. For two years she worked for James and Cornelia La Tourette. Isabella had her own living quarters in their home, which she furnished with savings from her salary. La Tourette was a merchant and unordained preacher, and Isabella was welcomed into the John Street Methodist Church. She attended Bible classes, improved her English, and learned her way around the city. Soon, with La Tourette's encouragement, she began preaching. By 1831 she had joined the African Methodist Episcopal Zion Church at Leonard and Church Streets. In addition to religious services, the church sponsored debates and lectures on issues affecting Black people.

Isabella's evangelism took her to Five Points, a crowded neighborhood notorious for disease, crime, prostitution, and poverty. She preached to prostitutes, encouraging them to get in touch with the Magdalen Society, dedicated to their reform. She conducted prayer meetings and catechism classes, visited the sick and dying, taught Sabbath schools, and worked tirelessly to bring people to Christ. Isabella was nearly six feet tall, with a remarkable physical presence. She was highly visible, and was constantly taunted and harassed, but day after day she continued her efforts.

She began working in the home of Elijah Pierson, a preacher and abolitionist, in 1831. In his circle, men and women, Black and white, the poor and the wealthy worshiped together. Egalitarianism and communal worship appealed to Isabella, and she became his "preaching associate" in what promised to be a productive relationship. She could not have foreseen that Pierson would involve her in one of the most notorious scandals of the era.

In 1832, a man with long hair and a full beard appeared at Pierson's door. Robert Mathews, who called himself Matthias, claimed to be the lost apostle. Pierson and Isabella became his followers, accepting him as the "Spirit of Truth," even though his doctrines forbade praying, reform efforts, and Sabbath schools. Pierson began recruiting converts, and Isabella moved with Matthias to the home of Sylvester Mills. The new household became Matthias's "kingdom."

Sylvester Mills' family brought the police to the house and attacked Matthias. Isabella tried to protect him but was violently restrained. Washington describes the family's actions: "Some men held Isabella while others shaved Matthias clean, cut his hair, took his money and his watch, stripped off most of his clothing, and generally humiliated him. While the 'Christians' restrained Isabella, they also lectured her. When satisfied that the prophet was sufficiently ridiculed, they and the police took Matthias to the 'apartment for the insane' at Bellevue Hospital, as he reportedly screamed he was 'God Almighty.'" Mills was confined at the Bloomingdale Lunatic Asylum.[8]

Isabella and Elijah Pierson secured Matthias's release and had the charges dismissed. New benefactors then entered the picture: Benjamin Folger, a wealthy merchant, and his wife Ann owned a mansion on the Hudson River near the village of Sing Sing. In the fall of 1833, Pierson and Matthias moved in and convinced Isabella to join them. She was to manage the household and do the heavy work (white women would do the lighter work), but she would not be paid. The estate was renamed Zion Hill. Over the next year, Zion Hill became the site of sexual intrigues revolving around Ann Folger, who convinced her husband to "offer" her to Matthias, her "spirit match," as his wife. When Ann discovered she was pregnant, she declared it a virgin conception that would result in a holy child. Meanwhile Pierson was ill, having seizures that became increasingly violent and frightening. The kingdom was strained by other liaisons, jealousies, and suspicions as well. In the nearby village, hostility was growing. Once a young man from Sing Sing broke into the house and, on a bet, cut off Matthias's beard.

Where was Isabella in all of this? She had become simply the Black domestic servant. She stayed out of the intrigues, did the housework, and cared for Pierson. In the background, usually unnoticed, she observed, analyzed, and remembered everything. She saw through Ann Folger and pitied her husband. This was not the egalitarian community she had hoped for, and she was doubly subservient for both her race and her gender. Nevertheless, she remained loyal.

The kingdom came to an end in the summer of 1834. Pierson died on August 4, and his financial affairs and those of the community came under scrutiny. The Folgers raised suspicions about Pierson's death, claiming that Matthias and Isabella had poisoned him. This was the sort of story that sold newspapers: sex, religious fanaticism, money, race, and murder. Unsurprisingly, the strange religious man and the Black woman were to be the scapegoats. The Folgers wrote a book about the kingdom that repeated the accusations.

Still loyal to Matthias and knowing that he had not poisoned anyone, Isabella found a lawyer to represent them. For her own defense, she solicited letters from former employers and associates testifying to her good character. She sued the Folgers for slander and won a judgment of $125 plus costs. Matthias's trial for murder began on April 16, 1835, and lasted four days. Truth was never called to testify. When the coroner attested that no poison had been found at the several autopsies performed on Pierson's body, the judge, prosecutor, and defense agreed to dismiss the charges.

Isabella was relieved, but "grievously disappointed in not getting her unsophisticated narrative in the court." When an editor named Gilbert Vale approached her, suggesting that with his help she could write her own book, she agreed. The result was *Fanaticism; its source and influence, illustrated by The Simple Narrative of Isabella*, published in 1835. The story is Isabella's, though most of the words are Vale's. Her co-author, though, included her own words to give a sense of her personality. He was also careful to reassure readers of her credibility. He found her version to agree with other testimony, including what he called "white evidence."[9]

The text gives the flavor of their interviews. In describing Ann Folger's seduction of Matthias, Isabella told Vale: "When he appeared, in the kindest accents she would ask his wishes, thus: '*Father*, would you like this? *Father*, will you have that? *Father*, shall we do this?' ... We have been amused at Isabella's attempt to imitate the soft manner of Mrs. B. Folger, which was certainly clumsily done, and generally terminated in the expression, 'O, I can't do it,' heartily expressed. Indeed, Isabella's manners are what we think the reverse of Mrs. B. Folger's; she has shrewd, common sense, energetic manners, and apparently despises artifice."[10]

The Folgers' lies made Isabella angry: "She is really very energetic and not very timid," Vale explained. "She said 'I have got the *truth,* and I know it, and I will *crush* them with the *truth.*" According to Vale, Isabella's "moral principles were awakened in favour of Matthias when his life was sought by those who had nourished his delusions."[11] Both the courts and historians have accepted her version over that of the Folgers and the press.

The book also provides a description of Isabella's beliefs at this time: "Her ancient faith is shaken; she is not a believer in the supernatural character of Matthias, but still regards most of his interpretations as more rational, and probably true, than that of any other teacher of religion.... Her moral principles are the same as formerly; she is still faithful, attached to truth, industrious, and consequently independent; with a ready perception of right and wrong, and with an uprightness and energy of character."[12]

Sojourner Truth

Isabella stayed in New York City, working for Perez and Lucy Whiting, until 1843. After preaching an antislavery sermon on May 11, 1843, at the Sixth Street Methodist Church, she heard a call to devote her life to a larger cause, in another place. She explained, "having made what preparations for leaving she deemed necessary,—which was, to put up a few articles of clothing in a pillow-case, all else being deemed an unnecessary incumbrance,—about an hour before she left, she informed Mrs. Whiting, the woman of the house where she was stopping, that her name was no longer Isabella, but SOJOURNER; and that she was going east. And to her inquiry, 'What are you going east for?' her answer was, 'The Spirit calls me there, and I must go.'" She added "Truth" because people generally had two names, and truth was what she sought to convey.[13]

She walked to Brooklyn, then on to Long Island, where she spent a month preaching about religion, temperance, and abolition at outdoor meetings. She crossed the Long Island Sound to Connecticut, preaching in churches and at tent meetings. By 1844, she had found her way to Springfield, Massachusetts, where a Black church had recently been established. Some Springfield friends recommended that she join their relatives at the Northampton Association of Education and Industry, a few miles to the north. Known as the Community, it was a commune that had been founded two years earlier. Set on 420 acres, it included mulberry trees where silkworms were raised, a silk factory, and workshops for lumber, farming, and other activities. One building was set aside for education. The main building, four stories tall, provided housing, a kitchen, dining room, reading room, laundry, and a store that offered goods at reasonable prices. Men and women, Black and white, worked side by side. All shared a commitment to abolition, communal living, and the dietary principles of Sylvester Graham.

Sojourner Truth was welcomed immediately and became director of the laundry. With her commitment to hard work, she set an example for the younger members and was quick to note any slacking. The Community was dedicated to equality between men and women, and she soon added gender issues to her preaching. When the Community met, she spoke of her years as a slave, her persecution in the Matthias scandal, her beliefs, and her understanding of Scripture. Her daughters Elizabeth and Sophia arrived in July 1844. She later recalled, "What good times we had. If any were infidels, I wish all the world were full of such infidels."[14]

Truth began traveling to preach wherever she could find an audience. She borrowed a horse from the Community and set out. She frequently encountered threats from drunks, rowdy young men, and others hostile to Black people and abolitionists, but she learned how to calm a crowd and sometimes even win them over.

Truth's stay at the Community ended when the group ran out of money and had to close in November 1846. She was now nearly fifty, and although she had no thought of giving up her "sojourning," she needed a home. With the help of friends, she managed to buy a house. For the first time, she would have a place to live where she was neither a servant nor a guest. To pay for it, she would tell the story of her life.

A Home of Her Own

When the Community closed, Samuel Hill, one of the original investors, divided his share of the land into building lots, with the proceeds going to pay off the Association's debts. He sold one of the lots to Truth, built a house on it for her, and gave her a mortgage. The white clapboard house, which still stands at 35 Park Street, is two stories plus an attic under its peaked roof. The only ornament is a wide front porch supported by slender columns. Truth was helping to care for Sarah Benson, who had breast cancer. Another caregiver was Olive Gilbert, an active abolitionist. They had several friends in common, including Gilbert's pastor, the abolitionist Samuel May, uncle of Louisa May Alcott. Truth knew that

Frederick Douglass had had great success with his autobiography, and she agreed with her friends' suggestion that she let Gilbert help her write hers.

As with *Fanaticism*, we have a story told—at least in part—in someone else's words. The *Narrative*, though, has a lot more of Sojourner Truth in it than the earlier book. Even though it is written in the third person, we often hear Truth's voice. In her childhood memories, we can imagine the little girl, sleeping in the basement of Hardenbergh's hotel, with windows "through which she thinks the sun never shone ... and the space between the loose boards of the floor, and the uneven earth below, was often filled with mud and water."[15]

Her account of the years she spent with the Dumonts is clearly her own: no white collaborator would have used her language or subtle sarcasm, or expressed the same opinions. She understood that she was *property*: Mr. Dumont, "being naturally a man of kind feelings, treated his slaves with all the consideration he did his *other* animals, and *more*, perhaps." She worked extra hard for Dumont, and "these extra exertions to please, and the praises consequent upon them, brought upon her head the envy of her fellow slaves, and they taunted her with being the *'white folks' nigger.'*" Her continued loyalty to Dumont, despite beatings and his failure

Sojourner Truth's first house, at 35 Park Street, Florence, Massachusetts, which she built in 1846 and sold in 1857. Income from her autobiography and speaking tours paid off the mortgage. Photograph ca. 1900 by the Howes Brothers. *Howes Brothers Collection, Historic Northampton, Northampton, Massachusetts.*

to keep his promise to her, was a source of pride, which might have puzzled Olive Gilbert.[16]

The *Narrative* is also remarkable because Truth was so thoughtful and forthright about the evolution of her views. She admits that, up until her emancipation, "she then firmly believed that slavery was right and honorable." She describes in detail the ways her religious understanding developed. The most moving passage about the way freedom changed her is about motherhood: "Isabella found herself the mother of five children, and she rejoiced in being permitted to be the instrument of increasing the property of her oppressors! ... But since that time, the subject of this narrative has made some advances from a state of chattelism towards that of a woman and a mother; and she now looks back upon her thoughts and feelings there, in her state of ignorance and degradation, as one does on the dark imagery of a fitful dream. One moment it seems but a frightful illusion; again, it appears a terrible reality. I would to God it *were* but a dreamy myth, and not, as it now stands, a horrid reality to some three million of chattelized human beings."[17]

When the manuscript was complete, James M. Yerrinton, the printer of William Lloyd Garrison's *Liberator,* printed it on credit. Garrison wrote a preface, and other well-known abolitionists provided endorsements. Publicity for the book began in 1850 in *The Liberator.* From then on, every speaking engagement was an opportunity for Sojourner Truth to promote abolition, women's rights, and the *Narrative*. She carried copies in a carpetbag. Having heard her speak, audiences were eager to learn more. She would tell them, "Read my little book. It's all there."[18] By 1854, enough people had bought her book that she was able to pay off her mortgage and pay the bill for the first printing. She sang along with her speeches, and Garrison printed up some of her songs, which she sold for five cents apiece.

Fame

The Fugitive Slave Act of 1850, which required citizens of free states to return fugitives to their owners, had turned many more Northerners into abolitionists. Truth became one of the most sought-after orators on the abolitionist and women's rights speaking circuits, regularly addressing audiences of hundreds. In 1850 she traveled throughout New England, and that fall she was the only Black woman to speak at the women's rights convention in Worcester. Not all newspaper coverage was favorable, but Horace Greeley's influential *New-York Tribune* offered praise, albeit tinged with racism: "Sojourner Truth, a colored woman, once a slave, spoke, and gratified the audience highly. She showed that beneath her dark skin, and uncomely exterior, there was a true, womanly heart. She uttered some truths that told well. She said woman set the world wrong by eating the forbidden fruit, and now she was going to set it right."[19] The *Tribune* regularly announced Truth's appearances.

In the summer of 1851 Truth spoke to large crowds at abolitionist and women's meetings in Ohio, western New York, New York City, Pennsylvania, New Jersey, and throughout New England. Protesters infiltrated even the most receptive audiences, and Truth became proficient at dealing with hecklers. An audience member in Springfield interrupted a fellow speaker, Stephen Foster, with a long rant, ending with "Your statements are too sweeping." Truth came to his rescue. She "drew a picture which every one present both saw and felt, of what slavery is to its victims, and of the guilt of those who inflict it and of those who uphold it. With the tone of one of the old prophets, turning to Mr. Foster, she said: 'Sweep away, Stephen, sweep away.'"[20]

Truth traveled to Michigan and moved into the Harmonia commune, near Battle Creek. Harmonia was part of the Underground Railroad, a biracial community of people from varying economic and educational backgrounds. It had a Methodist church and a well-known academy that charged affordable tuition. In 1857 she sold her Northampton property and bought a lot in the commune next to the academy, where she lived until 1867. From her Michigan base, she traveled to Indiana, Illinois, Iowa, Missouri, Wisconsin, and Kansas, often facing violent mobs and police harassment. In Indiana, she was arrested and tried six times, always winning in court.

Truth continued traveling and speaking continuously until late in 1862, when she became seriously ill. She had little confidence in Lincoln's commitment to emancipation, and was afraid she would die before her people were free. In late December she began to believe she had been too pessimistic, and she let people know that she would like to celebrate Lincoln's announcement with friends. On January 1, 1863, Black celebrants gathered in Battle Creek, as Truth's other friends met happily in New York, Boston, and Washington.

By spring of 1863 she was sufficiently recovered to have photographs taken that she could sell at meetings and by mail. She explained that she "used to be sold for other people's benefit, but now she sold herself for her own." She had the motto "I sell the shadow to support the substance" printed below her portrait and took the unusual step of copyrighting her image. She told her friend, Mary Gale: "Please tell any friends who may want my pictures that they can have them by writing to me in this place.... I sell the three for $1 or a single one for 35 cents."[21]

Of course, emancipation did not end racism, and Truth's speeches now addressed that issue directly. On a practical level, the Black soldiers who had joined the Union Army needed food and clothing, and she worked to raise money and donations for them. This was a personal crusade: her grandson James Caldwell had joined the Massachusetts 54th Regiment and had been wounded and taken prisoner. Truth joined the Michigan branch of the Ladies Freedmen's Aid Society, working to raise money and donations of clothing and other necessities for the many Southerners freed from slavery who were homeless and starving.

Truth decided in 1864 that she should travel to Washington to thank Abraham Lincoln and to help the freedmen who had sought refuge in the capital. With her grandson Sammy, she set out in July. Staying with friends, holding meetings, selling her book and photographs, she traveled through Ohio to Rochester (where she shared a platform with Frederick Douglass), New York City, New Jersey, and finally to Washington.

At last, she visited the White House. In an account a month later, she said, "I am proud to say that I never was treated by any one with more kindness and cordiality than was shown to me by that great and good man, Abraham Lincoln, by the grace of God President of the United States for five more years." Truth had brought with

Sojourner Truth's carte de visite, 1864. The caption, "I sell the shadow to support the substance," reflects the fact that sales of her photograph were a significant source of income for her. *Unidentified artist, Sojourner Truth (c. 1797–1883), Harvard Art Museums/Fogg Museum, transfer from Special Collections, Fine Arts Library, Harvard College Library, bequest of Evert Jansen Wendell. Photo ©President and Fellows of Harvard College, 2010.69.*

her a scrapbook that she called her *Book of Life*. In it, she kept newspaper clippings, messages from friends, and autographs of people she respected. Lincoln, she reported, "took my little book, and with the same hand that signed the death-warrant of slavery, he wrote as follows: 'For Aunty Sojourner Truth, Oct. 29, 1864 A. Lincoln.' As I was taking my leave, he arose and took my hand, and said he would be pleased to have me call again. I felt that I was in the presence of a friend."[22]

And then she went to work. She spent six months at Freedmen's Village in Arlington, Virginia, as a counselor for the National Freedmen's Relief Association. Next she worked at the Freedmen's Hospital, nursing the sick. Finally, in 1867, she returned to Michigan and built a house in Battle Creek at 38 College Street that was not too different from her house in Northampton: two stories, a peaked roof over an attic, but with a wraparound porch. It was a bit larger, perhaps to accommodate family members: Diana and her son Sammy were living there. It had large windows, hardwood floors, and pocket doors between some of the rooms.[23] With the money that the government paid her for her work at the Freedmen's Relief Association, she furnished it and paid off the mortgage. She resumed her speaking career, navigating the fraught politics of the suffrage movement. As late as 1877, she was lecturing and selling books in Ohio, Michigan, Rochester, and New York City.

By the fall of 1882, Sojourner Truth was unable to leave her house. Her daughters Diana and Elizabeth took care of her, and she met happily with visitors. She died early in the morning of November 26, 1883. In 1884, a new edition of her *Narrative* was published. The proceeds were used to purchase a marker for her grave in the Oak Hill Cemetery.

11

Edith Wharton

Edith Wharton grew up surrounded by wealth and what she called "intolerable ugliness." Her parents, George Frederic and Lucretia Rhinelander Jones, were the Joneses with whom everyone tried to keep up. She was born in 1862 in her parents' Manhattan brownstone at 14 West 23rd Street, just off "the old Fifth Avenue with its double line of low brown-stone houses, of a desperate uniformity of style," "cursed with its universal chocolate-coloured coating of the most hideous stone ever quarried." The house was decorated in the fashionable Second Empire style: layers of curtains that shut out all natural light, large pieces of ornate gilded furniture, acres of bric-a-brac, and reproductions of mediocre art created a stifling, airless atmosphere. The family often visited Edith's aunt Elizabeth Jones at Rhinecliff, "an expensive but dour specimen of Hudson River Gothic." The ugliness of the house repelled and terrified her.[1]

When Edith was four years old, the family moved to Europe for six years, living in Rome, Paris, and Florence. Edith was entranced by European architecture and gardens at a time when she was developing an aesthetic sense. "Happy misfortune," she wrote, "which gave me, for the rest of my life, that background of beauty and old-established order!" When the family returned home, she marveled at New Yorkers' provincialism: "How could I understand that people who had seen Rome and Seville, Paris and London, could come back to live contentedly between Washington Square and the Central Park?"[2]

Returning to New York, Edith spent time in the only room she liked: her father's library. Even there, she would "pause on its threshold, averting my eyes from the monstrous oak mantel supported on the heads of the vizored Knights," to reach the "rows of handsome bindings and familiar names."[3] She was fascinated by books, story-telling, and writing. She read voraciously, not only poetry and fiction, but philosophy and logic. She wrote poetry and a novella. Perhaps concerned that she was becoming too bookish to be marriageable, her parents scheduled her debut for 1879, a year earlier than was usual. The family returned to Europe in 1881 for her father's health, and he died in Cannes in 1882. Edith and her mother returned to New York, and in 1885 Edith married Edward ("Teddy") Wharton. She wrote that her "first care was to create a home of my own." She and Teddy moved into a cottage on her mother's Newport estate "and re-arranged it in accordance with our tastes."[4]

In 1893, with a bequest from a distant cousin of Edith's, the Whartons bought two houses at 882 and 884 Park Avenue as well as Land's End in Newport, giving Edith an opportunity to express her architectural and stylistic tastes.[5] The Newport purchase led to a relationship with Ogden Codman, an architect active in the Colonial Revival movement, whom she hired to decorate the house. At that time, interior design was usually delegated to upholsterers who, Edith feared, would cram "every room with curtains, lambrequins [draperies for shelves or mantels], jardinières of artificial plants, wobbly velvet-covered tables littered with silver gewgaws, and festoons of lace on mantelpieces and dressing-tables." Codman, like Wharton, believed that "interior decoration should be simple and architectural."[6]

Codman and Wharton collaborated on a book setting out their shared principles of interior design. *The Decoration of Houses,* published in 1897 and still popular, promotes simplicity and common sense. On the first page, they contrast the undesirable and the desirable: "Rooms may be decorated in two ways: by a superficial application of ornament totally independent of structure, or by means of those architectural features which are part of the organism of every house, inside as well as out."[7] The family houses of Wharton's childhood exemplified the first; the houses she designed, the second. Beginning with Land's End, her houses incorporated structural elements into design, favored light woodwork over dark, and avoided fussy draperies and "gewgaws." Windows connected the house to the landscape, admitting rather than blocking light. When Wharton turned her attention outdoors, she envisioned the garden as a connection between the house and the natural landscape.

In 1903, Richard Watson Gilder commissioned Wharton to write a series of articles about Italian villas and their gardens for *The Century Magazine,* later collected in *Italian Villas and Their Gardens.* Edith and Teddy traveled from Rome through Tuscany, the Veneto, and Lombardy, focusing on less famous sites. The trip expanded her thinking about houses into their gardens. A garden, she wrote, "must be adapted to the architectural lines of the house it adjoined; it must be adapted to the requirements of the inmates of the house, in the sense of providing shady walks, sunny bowling-greens, parterres and orchards, all conveniently accessible; and lastly it must be adapted to the landscape around it." She was critical of gardens that displayed the features she disliked in houses: complicated details, excessive ornament, and artificiality.[8]

The Decoration of Houses and *Italian Villas* set out Wharton's approved stylistic principles. Her novels offer a critique of decorating styles she did *not* approve by satirizing the taste of dislikable characters, whose houses are uncomfortable, artificial, and ostentatious. In *The House of Mirth*, one home of people striving to join New York's elite is described as "a typical rung in the social ladder! ... a complete architectural meal; if he had omitted a style his friends might have thought the money had given out." Another house fulfills "the desire to imply that one has been to Europe and has a standard ... in America every marble house with gilt furniture is thought to be a copy of the *Trianon*." Wharton expresses her opinion of one character simply by describing her drawing room: "A gilt bamboo *jardinière*, in which the primulas and cinerarias were punctually renewed, blocked the access to the bay window...; the sofas and arm-chairs of pale brocade were cleverly grouped about little plush tables densely covered with silver toys, porcelain animals and efflorescent photograph frames; and tall rosy-shaded lamps shot up like tropical flowers among the palms."[9]

The houses of the established elite fare little better. The van der Luydens have the oldest money in *The Age of Innocence*, but their homes are uncomfortable and forbidding. Their country house was said to be an Italian villa, but its garden comprises features that Wharton condemns in *Italian Villas*: "the famous weedless lawns studded with 'specimen' trees (each of a different variety) rolled away to long ranges of grass crested with elaborate cast-iron ornaments." Their town house is unwelcoming: a chill "descended on one in the high-ceilinged white-walled Madison Avenue drawing room, with the pale brocaded armchairs so obviously uncovered for the occasion, and the gauze still veiling the ormolu mantel ornaments."[10]

Another of Wharton's rare garden descriptions focuses the laser beam of her aesthetic judgment on Mrs. Phish, a minor character in *The Mother's Recompense*. The Anglo-American colony on the French Riviera "was assembled on Mrs. Phish's flowery terrace, among the beds of cineraria and cyclamen, and the giant blue frogs which, as Mrs. Phish said, made the garden look 'more natural....' Mrs. Phish beamed, waving a tall disenchanted-looking man in the direction of a palm-tree emerging from a cushion of pansies."[11]

The Mount

In 1901, Wharton finally had an opportunity to create a house from the ground up that would bring her principles to life. The Berkshires were beginning to attract literary figures from New York and Boston seeking summer homes, and the Whartons paid $40,000 for 113 acres in Lenox, Massachusetts. There, they built a house designed by Ogden Codman and the firm of Hoppin & Koen, with a great deal of input from Edith herself. The Mount would incorporate the manifesto set forth in *The Decoration of Houses*, but it would also embody an idea that Edith had expressed in "The Fullness of Life," a short story published in *Scribner's Magazine* in December 1893:

> I have sometimes thought that a woman's nature is like a great house full of rooms: there is the hall, through which everyone passes in going in and out; the drawing room, where one receives formal visits; the sitting room, where the members of the family come and go as they list; but beyond that, far beyond, are other rooms, the handles of whose doors are never turned; no one knows the way to them, no one knows whither they lead; and in the innermost room, the holy of holies, the soul sits alone and waits for a footstep that never comes.

As she had written in *The Decoration of Houses*, "Privacy would seem to be one of the first requisites of civilized life."[12]

Visitors approach The Mount from a long drive, entering a forecourt dug out of the rock on which the house was built. The vestibule provides a transition from the natural world into the house, lined with stucco that imitates the walls of a grotto. This room is completely unlike the interior. We would get no farther without an invitation, leaving us with no idea of the aesthetic of the rest of the house. Invited in, we walk through a glass door and up the stairs, entering the areas of the house open to all. The gallery—with its high, barrel-vaulted ceiling, tall windows with semicircular fanlights, and painted panels outlined with contrasting woodwork—introduces the reigning aesthetic: light, airy, and subtly colorful. But it is also formal and impersonal, offering few clues to the sort of person who lives there. Only the statues and a few pieces of antique furniture add a personal touch. The gallery connects the first-floor rooms, which also open to one another through double doors.[13]

Welcomed into the drawing room, we get a better sense of our hostess's taste, but little sense of *her* beyond her love of art and light. The room is large—36 by 20 feet—with an elaborate plaster ceiling of sculpted ovals and complementary panels. The French doors open onto the terrace, with a view of the gardens. The antique tapestries set into the walls, the Aubusson carpet, and the French marble mantle express Edith's admiration of European art and furnishings. The dining room, too, has a European flavor, with white-painted French dining chairs and elaborate plaster garlands. With a table that seats ten at most, it is designed for intimate dinners, not grand occasions.

11. Edith Wharton

West elevation of The Mount, Edith Wharton's summer home in Lenox, Massachusetts. The drawing, ca. 1901, is by the architectural firm of Hoppin & Koen, which collaborated with Ogden Codman on the design. The image is in the collection of the Avery Architectural and Fine Arts Library, Columbia University in the City of New York. *Courtesy of The Mount, Edith Wharton's Home.*

Admitted into the library and Teddy's "den," we have entered the area "where the members of the family come and go as they list." The library is warm and inviting, with paneling and built-in bookcases of hand-carved oak. French doors admit plenty of light. Edith had a desk in this room but did not write there, though she often read. It was the room where guests gathered in the evening to read aloud and talk. It is a room for use rather than show. Teddy's den is a very masculine space. Smaller than the library, it is both a retreat and a place where he could keep track of the couple's finances and the business of the estate. He may have welcomed male friends there, but it feels more like his "innermost" room, where other footsteps did not venture.

The second floor has a central north-south hall with bedrooms opening off to either side, offering complete privacy to guests housed there. Each bedroom has a bath, and each bathroom has two entrances: one for the resident and the other, opening from the hall, for servants to use when they clean. Teddy's suite—bedroom, dressing room, and bath—connected to Edith's by a door between his dressing room and her bedroom. Edith's suite—bedroom, boudoir, and bath—is at the north end of the hall. Most of the second-floor rooms are plain, but Edith's boudoir is not. Floral paintings are set into the imported Italian paneling, and the room is large enough to accommodate a desk, sofa, and daybed. Only her most intimate friends entered this room. Her adjoining bedroom is simple, with a gray and white marble mantle and practical furniture painted white. This is the room where she worked. In the mornings, she sat up in bed and wrote page after page, tossing each sheet onto the floor for her secretary to retrieve and type. The room was shared rarely, if at all—her "innermost room, the holy of holies," where her "soul sat alone."

The service wing contains a sewing room, a closet for Edith's dresses, her maid's room, and a linen closet on the second floor; a butler's pantry and offices on the first. The kitchen, scullery, laundry room, and servants' dining room are on the ground floor. The attic floor has eight servants' bedrooms and a servants' bath. A stable housed horses and carriages and, later, automobiles.

The gardens also follow the principles in Wharton's writing. An extension of the house, they connect it to the natural world that lies beyond. Wharton had not written her book about Italian gardens until after moving in. She had done a great deal of reading, though, and she enlisted the help of her niece Beatrix Jones Farrand, a landscape architect. The gardens evolved over time into "rooms" connected by gravel walks. The kitchen garden was the first, followed by a rock garden and terraced lawns. A formal enclosed garden built around an oblong pond followed, with gravel walks dividing symmetrical flower beds and grass panels. Wharton used proceeds from *The House of Mirth*, published in 1905, to build a sunken garden around a circular pond.

Construction costs for The Mount totaled just under $85,000, and landscaping eventually cost more than $50,000. Edith had inherited money, and selling Land's End helped finance the new house. She eventually earned more from her writing than from bequests. As the house neared completion, Wharton thanked Scribner's for a royalty payment: "Many thanks for the cheque for $2,191.81, which even to the 81 cents, is welcome to an author in the last throes of house-building."[14]

Wharton published more than forty books in as many years. A shrewd businesswoman, she prodded her publishers to market her work aggressively and bargained for higher royalty rates and advances. In 1905, she earned $65,000 in royalties, fees for serializations, and payments for short stories. She would eventually command higher fees for her short stories and other magazine work than other writers, including F. Scott Fitzgerald. Her most popular books each earned royalties equivalent to a million dollars in today's money, plus fees for serialization and dramatic rights.[15]

The Whartons spent only ten summers at The Mount, but for Edith those were happy and productive times. She wrote in the mornings and spent the afternoons exploring the countryside with guests—a mix of well-known literary figures, academics, and old friends. They walked to

The Mount, with construction nearly complete. *Courtesy of The Mount, Edith Wharton's Home.*

nearby beauty spots or drove into the countryside. Sometimes they went no further than Ashfield, the home of her close friends Charles Eliot Norton, a Harvard professor of literature and translator of Dante, and his daughter Sara. Other neighbors included Richard Gilder, editor of *The Century,* and Frank Crowninshield, editor of *Vanity Fair.*

Edith especially enjoyed chauffeur-driven automobile jaunts—even those that ended in ditches. She later wrote of "inexhaustible delight in penetrating to the remoter parts of Massachusetts and New Hampshire, discovering derelict villages with Georgian churches and balustraded house-fronts, exploring slumbrous mountain valleys, and coming back, weary but laden with a new harvest of beauty, after sticking fast in ruts, having to push the car up hill, to rout out the village blacksmith for repairs, and suffer the jeers of horse-drawn travellers trotting gaily past us."[16] Those explorations inspired her two New England novels, *Summer* and *Ethan Frome.* She spent the evenings reading aloud and discussing books with friends, including Henry James—a frequent visitor—and William Morton Fullerton, who became her lover. Her affair with Fullerton, and Teddy's infidelity, ended their marriage. In 1911, when Edith was sailing to Europe for the winter, Teddy sold The Mount. They were divorced in 1913.

Edith Wharton spent the rest of her life in France. During World War I, she established hostels for refugees and homes for Flemish children, visited the front, and created convalescent homes for tuberculosis patients. She wrote and edited articles and books published in the United States to help in the war effort, and in 1916 the French government awarded her the Legion of Honor. After the war she bought two houses: Pavillon Colombe, a country house outside Paris, and Ste. Claire du Vieux Chateau, overlooking the Mediterranean in Hyères. With the help of the architect Charles Knight and the advice of Ogden Codman, she renovated both houses.

The Pavillon was designed in 1779 by François Joseph Bélanger for Jean André de Vassal de Saint-Hubert as a gift for his mistress, Marie Catherine Ruggieri, an actress known as "Mademoiselle Colombe." Wharton hired the firm of Moreux & Gonse to manage the renovations and Lawrence Johnston to design the landscaping. The biographer Hermione Lee's description of the Pavillon reveals that Wharton was, to a great extent, recreating The Mount with a series of interconnected rooms and features guaranteeing privacy: "a long white house hiding behind the north wall of its courtyard, with a massive carriage-door set into the wall facing the street. Its look says 'private, no entry'; but once inside it has charm, light, and classical elegance.... On the ground floor the rooms (as at The Mount) open sideways into each other through communicating doors, and, on the south side, onto the terrace overlooking the garden." The gardens were much like those of The Mount, though on a smaller scale.[17]

The Chateau had been built by Olivier Voutier, a French naval officer who in 1820 discovered the Venus de Milo while excavating during a voyage in the Aegean. He bought land that had been the site of a convent and built the Castel Sainte-Claire, named after the first mother superior of the order. As Lee notes, this house, too, shared many features with Wharton's other houses: "The moderate-sized ground-floor rooms opened out from each other in the *enfilade* style of the Mount and the Pavillon," and flower paintings from The Mount hung on the walls. The terraced gardens connected the house to the dramatic landscape beyond.[18]

Edith continued to write novels set in America while she was settled abroad, notably *The Custom of the Country* (1913) and *The Age of Innocence,* which won a 1921 Pulitzer Prize. She also wrote an antiwar novel, *A Son at the Front,* reflecting her wartime experience, and two novels about American expatriates: *The Mother's Recompense* (1925) and *The Children* (1928). *The Buccaneers,* her last novel, unfinished at her death in 1937, was published without an ending in 1938 and was completed by Marion Mainwaring in 1993.

Lasting Influence

Today's readers often have difficulty with Wharton's fiction because her characters express opinions, very much shared by their creator, that we no longer tolerate. The anti–Semitism in *The House of Mirth*, which Wharton expects readers to share, makes us uncomfortable. Her snobbery can be off-putting, and her attitudes toward women can be grating. Although at times she seems sympathetic to women's desire for autonomy, at least as often she accepts their subordination. It is certainly impossible to detect feminism in her autobiographical comment praising the "ancient curriculum of house-keeping which, at least in Anglo-Saxon countries, was so soon to be swept aside by the 'monstrous regiment' of the emancipated: young women taught by their elders to despise the kitchen and the linen room, and to substitute the acquiring of University degrees for the more complex art of civilised living. The movement began when I was young, and now that I am old, and have watched it and noted its results, I mourn more than ever the extinction of the household arts."[19] Especially coming from a woman who may not have despised the kitchen and linen room, but who entered them (if at all) only to instruct servants, this does not elicit sympathy.

Unlike the fiction, however, *The Decoration of Houses* remains popular and strikingly modern. Except for some members of the 1 percent who—like their Gilded Age antecedents—slather gold on everything, today's homeowners prefer her cleaner, lighter, more personal aesthetic. Mitchell Owens, writing in *Architectural Digest* in January 2013, compared the book to "the King James Version of the Bible. Thousands of interior design books have come and gone since, but most, I would argue, merely repackage Wharton and Codman's lessons in brighter colors and snappier prose."

To Visit

The Mount (2 Plunkett Street, Lenox, Massachusetts 01240–0974; 413–551–5111; www.edithwharton.org) is open daily May through October and on Saturdays and Sundays, November through February.

New Hampshire

12

Mary Baker Eddy

Mary Baker Eddy spent the first twenty years of her life in a secure, comfortable family home. She, her two sisters, and three brothers grew up surrounded by religious discussions and encouragement to read and learn. In 1844, when she was 23, Mary found herself widowed and pregnant, dependent on her family for a home and basic necessities. It would be thirty years before she owned a house that provided the security she had known as a child. She bought that house with savings from her practice as a healer—a practice based on research for her first book, *Science and Health*, the foundation of Christian Science.

Early Life

The 500-acre farm in Bow, New Hampshire, where Mary Baker was born, had been in the family for generations. The saltbox farmhouse was the gathering place for a large family, friends, and visiting clergy who frequently engaged in theological debates. Her father, Mark, was a conservative Congregationalist and a strict father. Her mother, Abigail, and her grandmother, Mary Ann, balanced Mark's rigor with patience and an interest in books other than religious tracts. Both parents agreed on the importance of education, and all the children attended school longer than was required.

When Grandmother Baker died, in 1835, Mark sold the farm and bought property in the larger town of Sanbornton Bridge. In their new home, the children could attend an academy, extending their education beyond what was offered in Bow. There were social advantages as well. Mary's sister Abigail noted that "the young gentlemen have not been slow in their attentions."[1] Abigail and Martha soon married. Abigail's husband, Alexander Hamilton Tilton, was a member of the town's most prominent family; Martha married Luther Pillsbury, a friend of her brother's. And on December 10, 1843, Mary and George Washington Glover were married.

"The birthplace of Mary Baker Eddy" in Bow, New Hampshire. She remembered the house fondly and visited it late in life. *Prints and Photographs Division, Library of Congress.*

They sailed on Christmas Day to Charleston, South Carolina, and in February moved to Wilmington, North Carolina. George had friends there, and Mary began writing for a local magazine. She had become pregnant soon after the wedding. But this promising start came to an end in June, when George contracted yellow fever. He died on June 27, leaving Mary bereft and penniless. His friends helped her to return to her parents' house, where she gave birth to George Washington Glover II on September 12, 1844.

Mary Glover tried to support herself by writing and by joining her sister Abigail in opening a school, but she remained dependent on her parents. George had been a difficult infant, and he was an active toddler. He resembled the father whom he was named after, whom Mark Baker had never liked. Abigail Baker died in 1849, and in December 1850 Mark remarried and moved to a new house where Mary and George were not welcome. Abigail Tilton told Mary that she could live with her family, but—because she had two frail, timid children—she did not include George in the invitation. Faced with homelessness, Mary sent George to live with a former servant, Mahala Cheney, and her husband, Russell. It was a wrenching choice. But, as she said, "I had no training for self-support, and my home I regarded as very precious."[2]

In 1853, she thought she had solved the problem. She married Daniel Patterson, a dentist and homeopath, and had him named as her son's guardian. She later explained that "my dominant thought in marrying again was to get back my child, but after our marriage his stepfather was not willing he should have a home with me."[3] The Cheneys moved west and told Mary that George had run away and could not be found. In fact, he was living with them and being treated as an indentured servant. George, in turn, was told that his mother had died. Mary did not learn that George was alive until 1861 and would not see him until 1879. When Mrs. Eddy was seventy years old, she wrote indirectly of the pain this caused her: "The true mother never willingly neglects her children in their early and sacred hours, consigning them to the care of nurse or stranger. Who can feel and comprehend the needs of her babe like the ardent mother? What other heart yearns with her solicitude, endures with her patience, waits with her hope, and labors with her love, to promote the welfare and happiness of her children?"[4]

The marriage was not a success. Patterson never managed to earn a living. Her family gave him money to start a practice in North Groton, New Hampshire, where they bought a four-room cottage. By 1856, Patterson was bankrupt, and they were impoverished. Mary was unwell, but she contributed what she could, studying homeopathy and tutoring local children. In 1860, they moved into a small cottage in Rumney, New Hampshire.[5] In 1861, a letter arrived informing her that her son had enlisted in the Union Army—the first time she learned he was alive. He could not write himself, because the Cheneys had never taught him. Mary's health became increasingly precarious, and none of the recommended treatments seemed to help.

Healing and Writing

Patterson contributed to the war effort by traveling to Washington to deliver funds to Union sympathizers in the South. He was captured as a spy and spent months in a North Carolina prison until he escaped. While he was gone, Mary began to seek new kinds of medical help. First she went to Hill, New Hampshire, for a water cure. When that did not work, she went to Portland, Maine, where a healer named Phineas Parkhurst Quimby was reporting success. He described his methods: "there is a principle or inward man that governs the outward man or body, and when these are at variance or out of tune, disease is the effect, while by harmonizing them health in the body is the result.... Now all I claim is this, to put myself into communication with these principles of inward and outward man and act as a mediator between these two principles of soul and body; ... and I find that by bringing his spirit back to harmonize with the body he feels better."[6]

In November 1862, Mary Patterson wrote a letter to the *Portland Evening Courier*: "Three weeks' since, and I quitted my nurse and sick room en route for Portland. The belief of my recovery had died out of the hearts of those who were most anxious for it. With this mental and physical depression I first visited P.P. Quimby, and in less than one week from that time I ascended by a stairway of one hundred and eighty-two steps to the dome of the City Hall, and am improving ad infinitum."[7] She stayed in Portland until April 1865, living in boardinghouses or with friends, and she began to study with Quimby. It was the beginning of her quest to discover a theory and practice of healing that would lead to her own practice, teaching, and the publication of *Science and Health*.

In the winter of 1865–66, when her husband had returned from the South and they had rented a second-floor apartment in Swampscott, Massachusetts, Mary fell on the ice, and the doctor who attended her feared for her life.[8] Mary turned to the Bible and to Quimby's system, and within a few days she was able to walk. As she explained, "My immediate recovery from the effects of an injury caused by an accident, an injury that neither medicine nor surgery could reach, was the falling apple that led me to the discovery how to be well myself, and how to make others so."[9] She would advance that discovery as Mary Glover: Daniel deserted her in 1866, and she returned to using the name of her first husband.

Mary Glover might simply have begun to practice as a healer, as Quimby had, but she wanted to clarify and explain her convictions in writing—a process that would take nearly a decade. She had little money. Patterson had agreed to send her $200 a year, but he usually sent less and soon sent nothing at all. She later earned money by teaching. But for ten years she lived with friends, in boardinghouses, or in rented rooms. The arrangements were often unsatisfactory, or worse. She was occasionally evicted because of work habits that tried the patience of her landlords: "I moved eight times in eight months while writing Science and Health. I would find my trunk and my chair set out on the sidewalk, and sometimes I would find my manuscripts covered with ink by some person in the house through malice. Sometimes people would leave me only the bed slats to sleep on."[10] Sometimes things worked out well. For eighteen months, beginning late in 1868, she received room and board in the home of Alanson and Sally Wentworth in Stoughton in exchange for teaching Sally about healing through prayer.[11] There, she finished teaching materials she called "The Science of Man." She spent the winter of 1872–73 at 78 Chestnut Street, in Lynn, where she got a great deal of writing done.

She stayed in Lynn, renting rooms at 7 Broad Street, when the three-story Victorian house across the street went up for sale. She had saved enough money from teaching for a down payment, and she rented out rooms to help pay the mortgage. At the age of 53, widowed by her first husband and recently divorced from her second, she owned her first home. It was a simple, plain house but spacious enough for her needs. The furnishings were typically Victorian, with dark draperies and carpets, but some of the wallpaper was more cheerful. The parlor was furnished for teaching.[12]

New Beginnings

The house at 8 Broad Street was home from 1875 to 1882, momentous years in Mary Glover's life. Writing in the third-floor attic, she finished both *Science and Health,* the foundational text of Christian Science, and *The Science of Man,* the teaching materials she had been developing. She found writing difficult and demanding because she was grappling with theological questions that required both scriptural research and an examination of her own beliefs. *Science and Health* was published in 1875 in an edition of 1,000 copies. By 1891, she later recalled, 62 printings had been published, and "people were healed simply by reading it."[13]

By the late 1870s Mary Glover had many devoted students who were practicing Christian Science healing and promoting her books. Among them was Asa Gilbert Eddy, the first of her students to describe himself as a Christian Scientist. Eddy was eleven years younger than Mary. They had met through a friend of his whom Mary had treated. He became first a patient and then a student. They were married on January 1, 1877. She was known from that date as Mary Baker Eddy.

Mrs. Eddy and six of her students had founded a Christian Science Association in 1876, and three years later 26 members founded a church in Boston, with Mrs. Eddy as pastor. In 1881 they founded the Massachusetts Metaphysical College, also in Boston. The Church grew rapidly, and with success came hostility. Christian Science was one of many new religions that threatened traditional churches. The Seventh-Day Adventists, Jehovah's Witnesses, Theosophists, and Mormons were also drawing believers away from Catholicism, Congregationalism, and Unitarianism. The *Times* of London reported that in Boston "clergymen of all denominations are seriously considering how to deal with what they regard as the most dangerous innovation that has threatened the Christian Church in this region for many years. Scores of the most valued church members are joining the Christian Science branch of the metaphysical organization, and it has thus far been impossible to check the defection."[14] Jewish leaders, too, worried about the growing numbers of their faith who were being lost to Christian Science.

In 1880, to be closer to the college and Church, the Eddys rented out the Lynn house and moved to Boston. Looking for rooms, they felt the full force of public opinion. Mrs. Eddy wrote to a friend, "Ever since we came to Boston it has been one line of persecution from those inhumans. Our first residence on West Newton we kept but a few weeks, although the lady agreed to rent us the rooms until spring but after we had got all our furniture boxes etc there and set up, she gave us a notice to give up our rooms, and shut off the heat. We moved to Springfield St. I wrote a lease for our rooms they signed it and after we got all moved and before a week had elapsed they gave us a request to vacate.... So it has gone on from one step to another."[15] Finally the Eddys rented a house at 537 Shawmut Avenue that they shared with fellow Christian Scientists George and Clara Choate. Two years later, the Eddys lived in a building at 569 Columbus Avenue that also housed the college.[16]

Gilbert Eddy died of heart failure in spring 1882. Mrs. Eddy carried on as pastor of the Church, teacher, and head of the college. She was still expanding and revising *Science and Health*. Each edition incorporated new ideas and new ways of explaining her beliefs. She also started the *Christian Science Journal,* with thousands of subscribers throughout the country. By 1887 subscriptions and book sales, along with tuition, made it possible for Mrs. Eddy to buy a building at 385 Commonwealth Avenue that became both residence and college.[17] The new quarters, in fashionable Back Bay, were far more elegant than any of Mrs. Eddy's previous homes, and she enjoyed giving visitors—mostly former students—tours of the building.

Rapid growth came at a cost. The first problem was internal dissension and rivalries. Some of the students who set up their own practices deviated in important ways from the Church's teaching, often causing embarrassment. Every time a disagreement among Christian Scientists came to light, the press leaped on it. Much of the hostility was directed at Mrs. Eddy personally. In 1889, she took measures to distinguish the Church from her person. She disbanded the college and the Christian Science Association, and she bought property on Boston's Massachusetts Avenue where a new church would be built, to be run by a trust. The Mother Church, which was to serve Christian Scientists throughout the world, is a large Romanesque building of New Hampshire granite, with a 126-foot steeple. The octagonal auditorium seats nine hundred people. Miraculously, it was completed in only eight months. The new Church would be administered by a variety of boards, with no one person in charge. As one historian explained, Mrs. Eddy "presided over the transformation of her church from a charismatic into a bureaucratic institution."[18]

Mrs. Eddy also removed herself from Boston, first renting a furnished house at 62 North State Street in Concord, New Hampshire.[19] The elegant Greek Revival building was too small for her staff, and it was on a noisy downtown street. Two years later, she bought a farmhouse on a hill and began to remodel it as her home and headquarters. Mrs. Eddy supervised every detail of the renovation of the house she named Pleasant View. The biographer Gillian Gill wrote that the changes "were designed to make the most of the scenery, with a veranda built on at the back ... a porte-cochère built onto the front so she could easily embark in her carriage every day, and a side tower built to house her own apartment from which she had a clear view in several directions. Living in a setting of natural beauty was an important thing for Mary Baker Eddy.... Having ample space around her and almost no uncontrollable ambient noise had also become vital requirements."[20] Once the remodeling was completed, the farmhouse had become a large three-story Victorian with turrets and bay windows. The entire back of the house had verandas on the first and second floors. The house was furnished with Mrs. Eddy's own furniture and gifts she had received. The decor was typically Victorian, with heavy upholstery and draperies and the clutter of knickknacks, antimacassars, and doilies.

In addition to the house, the site provided lodgings for permanent and visiting staff. Although the Church was headquartered in Boston, Mrs. Eddy remained active. People from the Boston office visited frequently, and a rotating cadre of people helped with correspondence, domestic chores, and farm work. (Pleasant View was a working farm with cows,

Pleasant View, Mary Baker Eddy's house, on the south side of Pleasant Street in Concord, New Hampshire. Eddy lived there from 1892 until 1908. In 1917 the house was demolished, and in the 1920s the Pleasant View Home, a retirement facility for Christian Scientists, was built on the site. *Detroit Publishing Company, Prints and Photographs Division, Library of Congress.*

horses, pigs, and gardens.) The household staff kept the house immaculate and ensured that everything remained in its proper place.

At Pleasant View, Mrs. Eddy finally found the home she had been seeking since her childhood. "'The strongest tie I have ever felt,'" one of her students reported her saying, "next to my love of God, has been my love for home."[21] Pleasant View—with its spacious rooms and gardens, pleasant and efficient staff, and time for both work and relaxation—was nearly Edenic, but there was more than one serpent.

Under Attack

The first problems arose from what should have been a blessing: her son George and his family reestablished contact. The only connection George seemed interested in establishing, though, was financial. He was always short of funds, and his mother was prosperous. She gave him money for his children's education and for other purposes, but she worried about his making larger claims on her estate.

Then an old disagreement with a church member became a major scandal. In 1889 Mrs. Eddy advised Josephine Woodbury, a prominent Christian Science practitioner, to end an extramarital relationship. In 1890, Woodbury gave birth to a child whose father was not her husband. She announced that the baby was the product of an immaculate conception and that he represented the second coming of Christ. Mrs. Eddy expelled her from the Church, and in 1899 Woodbury sued for libel. Mrs. Eddy won the suit, but the press coverage was damaging.

A few years later Mark Twain attacked Mrs. Eddy personally in *Cosmopolitan* and the *North American Review*. He said that he had nothing against Christian Science: "Making fun of that shameless old swindler, Mother Eddy, is the only thing I take any interest in," he wrote, and referred to a "cult of personality."[22] Mrs. Eddy—already uneasy about the conflation of herself and the Church—asked to be called "Leader" instead of "Mother" and had her "Mother's Room" in the Mother Church closed.

The most harmful attacks came from two giants of the newspaper world: Sam McClure, founder of *McClure's Magazine,* and Joseph Pulitzer, publisher of the *New York World*. Hoping to find evidence of financial wrongdoing—or anything scandalous—they sent out teams of investigators. They spied on Pleasant View, and Mrs. Eddy responded by granting an interview. Although she was perfectly healthy, they reported that she was terminally ill, or possibly already dead, or perhaps being held prisoner.[23]

Pulitzer went a step further, recruiting Mrs. Eddy's son, George, and a nephew, George Waldron Baker, to sue Church officials in what was referred to as the Next Friends Suit, filed in 1907. They alleged that the officials had improperly appropriated Mrs. Eddy's personal assets, and asked that the court appoint a receiver to handle her property. The two Georges saw themselves as Mrs. Eddy's heirs and wanted to maximize their potential inheritance. But to win, they would have to prove Mrs. Eddy incompetent.

In anticipation of the trial, Mrs. Eddy demonstrated that she was not only competent but extremely adept at public relations. She granted interviews to friendly journalists, submitted to medical examinations, and explained her finances to the judge. When the judge and the attorneys met with Mrs. Eddy at Pleasant View, it became clear that the plaintiffs were fighting for a lost cause. According to a witness, they "were greeted by a slim, frail, slightly deaf old lady, charming, polite, authoritative, who answered their questions of fact, insisted despite their demurrals upon giving a brief and lucid history of Christian Science and its doctrine, and begged them to take the time to listen to her marvelous new gramophone.... [Judge] Aldrich was reminded of his mother." The plaintiffs' attorney was overheard saying that Mrs. Eddy "had a mind like a steel trap."[24]

Although she won the suit, Mrs. Eddy became painfully aware of how vulnerable she was at Pleasant View. She was physically afraid of her son, and she had been besieged by reporters and sightseers. The house was no longer a refuge or a source of pleasure. She decided to return to Boston, and church officials found a house that they hoped she would approve. Their job was to create a home where a woman in her eighties, to whom home was extremely important, could once again find the comfort and security she had found at Pleasant View.

Last Home

The house is in Chestnut Hill, a leafy suburb of large mansions and estates six miles west of Boston.[25] Set in 12 acres, the three-story stone house is large (25 rooms), elegant, with extensive gardens, beautiful views, a large carriage house, and paths for carriage rides. Church officials remodeled the house to make it suitable as both a home and a workplace for Mrs. Eddy. She had agreed to the move, but with the condition that her own apartment was to replicate her quarters at Pleasant View.

When Mrs. Eddy arrived on January 26, 1908 (traveling in secret on a special train), she was not at all pleased. The electric lighting was too bright, and the house was overheated. But the worst problem was her own apartment, which was simply *not* a replica of her Pleasant View rooms.

It was, she said, "a *great barn* of a *place*.... The rooms are so large that it is really a great deal of exertion for me to walk the distance." The window was placed so high that, seated in her chair, she could not see out. She moved up to the third floor so that the problems could be resolved. According to her biographer Gillian Gill, "In three weeks' time the rooms of her second-floor apartment were converted to Pleasant View dimensions, the window frames were lowered, a small elevator was installed, the slope of the driveway was changed to afford more privacy when Mrs. Eddy came out, and a large tree was cut down to allow her to look out on nearby homes.... Mrs. Eddy had her old gaslight fixture installed at the head of her bed."[26] Pleasant View remained Mrs. Eddy's favorite house, but Chestnut Hill did become a genuine home. Each staff member had a bedroom and bath. Every evening they dined together and often spent the evenings in the parlor or on the roof, where a telescope allowed them to view the heavens. She and her staff once again enjoyed privacy and safety.

Mrs. Eddy continued to deal decisively with internal disputes and to revise *Science and Health*. She reached a settlement with her son in which he agreed not to contest her will. Most important, benefiting from her experience at the hands of the press, she launched a daily newspaper, the *Christian Science Monitor*, which now publishes both print and online editions.

In the summer of 1910, Mrs. Eddy became noticeably weaker. The daily carriage rides became a strain, but she insisted on them. Someone sat with her throughout the day and night. On December 1, she asked for a piece of paper and wrote, "God is my life." The next day she remained able to talk with her companions but could not leave her bed. On the night of December 3, she died in her sleep.

On Sunday, December 4, at the Mother Church, Clifford P. Smith announced Mrs. Eddy's death and read a passage from an 1891 letter that she had written to the students at the Metaphysical College: "You can well afford to give me up, since you have in my last revised edition of Science and Health your teacher and guide."[27] It is an extraordinary statement of identity between author and work, of writing as a source of immortality.

To Visit

The Longyear Museum has restored Mrs. Eddy's homes in North Groton, Rumney, and Concord (State St.), New Hampshire; and Chestnut Hill, Amesbury, Lynn, Stoughton, and Swampscott, Massachusetts. For information on visiting hours, as well as virtual tours of the houses, see www.longyear.org/visit/historic-houses/.

13

Sarah Josepha Hale

Sarah Josepha Hale, for fifty years the editor of *Godey's Lady's Book*, is remembered for all the wrong reasons. She was, indeed, the author of "Mary Had a Little Lamb," and she was the most persistent voice in establishing Thanksgiving as a national holiday. Those were the least of her accomplishments. Similarly, *Godey's Lady's Book* is remembered, and collected, for its tinted fashion plates, but they were the magazine's least remarkable feature. In its pages, Hale advocated tirelessly for elementary education for all children and higher education for women, and for women's economic rights. Her magazine and her many advice books shaped American social and domestic life for decades.

Roots

Sarah Josepha, born to Captain Gordon and Martha Whittlesey Buell on October 24, 1788, was a child of the New Hampshire frontier. Captain Buell, as a veteran injured in the Revolutionary War, was awarded 400 acres in New Hampshire. The Buells moved there from Connecticut, farmed, and built the Rising Sun Tavern in Newport. Two of their children died young, but Sarah grew up with a brother, Horatio Gates, a year older than she.

Martha Whittlesey's parents valued education, sending their sons to Williams College and educating their daughters at home. She taught Sarah and Horatio, and Sarah later wrote that "I owe my early predilection for literary pursuits to the teaching and example of my mother." In addition to the Bible and *Pilgrim's Progress,* the children read the works of John Milton, William Shakespeare, Alexander Pope, and William Cowper. *The Mysteries of Udolpho,* a gothic novel by Ann Radcliffe, made a special impression on Sarah because it was a novel and it was written by a woman. Horatio was sent to Dartmouth College, and during the summer vacations he taught Sarah Latin and mathematics. She explained that "in childhood our studies had been pursued together, and he seemed very unwilling that I should be deprived of all his collegiate advantages."[1]

Sarah began teaching school when she was eighteen and continued until 1813, when she married a local lawyer, David Hale. They lived in a house on Main Street known as "Lawyer Hale's Mansion."[2] Her first biographer, Ruth Finley, believed that the house described in Hale's novel *Northwood* was based on their home: a Federal-style house with six windows on the second floor and, on the first, five windows and a door with a fanlight. In their parlor, Sarah and David read every evening from eight to ten. Together they studied French, botany, and geology. Sarah began to write, and David encouraged her to use plainer, less pompous language than the English writers she admired.

Their first child, David Emerson, was born in 1815. Horatio followed in 1817, Frances Ann in 1819, and Sarah Josepha in 1820. In 1822, Sarah was pregnant when David died of pneumonia. Their fifth child, William George, was born two weeks after his death. David Hale had been a successful lawyer, but he had been in practice too short a time to save much money. As Sarah remembered, "We had lived in comfort, but I was left poor." She needed to find a way to remain in her home, and to support and educate her children. After an unsuccessful attempt to start a millinery business, she began writing for newspapers and magazines. She was

"Lawyer Hale's Mansion," Sarah Josepha Hale's marital home, on North Main Street. The photograph was taken between 1888 and 1893, when the house was moved to Myrtle Street and made into a duplex. *Courtesy of the Newport Historical Society Museum.*

prolific: in 1826 alone, she had 17 poems, two short stories, and one review published in the *Boston Spectator and Ladies' Album*, winning a prize of 20 dollars and a gold medal for the best poem. She also wrote for the *New York Mirror, American Monthly,* and the *United States Review and Literary Gazette*. She earned a small amount from a poetry collection, but real success came with the 1827 publication of her first novel, "written literally with my baby in my arms." *Northwood, a Tale of New England,* in two volumes, was an instant success and was republished in England in three volumes as *Sidney Romelee: A Tale of New England*.[3]

Boston

Hale's literary activity brought her to the attention of the Rev. John Lauris Blake, who was looking for an editor for a new magazine to be published by the firm of Putnam and Hunt. Hale accepted his invitation, moving to Boston in 1828, although it meant separating from her children. Only William, the youngest, would live with her. The others went to stay with various relatives and, as they grew older, were sent to boarding school and college.

The first issue of the *Ladies' Magazine,* "conducted by Mrs. Sarah J. Hale," appeared in 1828. Hale's introduction set out the theme that would dominate her work for the next half-century: "Perhaps no experiment will have an influence more important on the character and happiness of our society, than the granting to females the advantages of a systematic and thorough education." She presented it as a patriotic challenge:

> The honor of this triumph, in favor of intellect over long established prejudices, belongs to the men of America. They appear willing to risk the hazard of proving, experimentally, whether that degree of literature, which only can qualify woman to become a rational companion, an instructive as well as agreeable friend, be compatible with the cheerful discharge of her domestic duties, and that delicacy of feeling, and love of retirement, which nature so obviously imposes on the sex ... not that they may usurp the station, or encroach on the prerogative of the man; but that each individual may lend her aid to perfect the moral and intellectual character of those within her sphere.

Her sales pitch was directed at men—husbands, fathers, and brothers—because they were the ones who would pay for the subscriptions. She pointed out that any husband who was away from home all day, hard at work, would surely wish to give his wife "the means of agreeably beguiling the interval of his absence." If he was worried about the quality of his dinner, "He may rest assured, that nothing found on the pages of this publication, shall cause her to be less assiduous in preparing for his reception, or less sincere in welcoming his return."[4]

Though many magazines focused on women as an audience, the *Ladies' Magazine* was innovative in encouraging them as contributors. Equally important, Hale insisted on original, *American* writing. Because American copyright law did not protect English works, most American magazines simply reprinted poems, essays, and stories from English periodicals, paying neither authors nor the original publishers. The *Ladies' Magazine* did pay its authors, and paying a fair wage was a principle that Hale promoted in practice as well as theory. The emphasis on American writing appealed to patriotic sentiments, too.

Although she was busy writing and editing, Hale found time to promote causes particularly relevant to Bostonians. The first was the welfare of seamen and their families. When men went to sea, many were not paid until the end of a voyage, sometimes leaving their families without income for months or years. Seamen were also exploited by the outfitters who supplied overpriced clothing and equipment. Hale and her colleagues solved both problems by training sailors' wives to sew and produce clothing, for which they were paid a fair wage. The clothing was then sold to the seamen in nonprofit shops at a fair price. The Seamen's Aid Society, of which she was president from 1833 to 1840, also set up Mariner's House, a day nursery for the children of the working women, and a free library. The Boston model was copied in port after port, and the Boston Mariner's House still provides housing and services to seamen.

Another Boston project was the Bunker Hill Monument. Work on a monument to commemorate the battle had begun in 1823, but the project stalled time and again for lack of funds. An editorial in the March 1830 issue of the magazine raised $3,000, but that wasn't nearly enough. In 1840, Hale and her colleagues organized fairs at which women sold handmade goods. The Boston fair netted $30,000 and inspired a few large donations in addition. The monument was completed in 1843, and women's fairs became an institution. They were used with great success during the Civil War to support the Sanitary Commission.

In 1837, Hale compiled a collection of poetry by women, *The Ladies' Wreath: A Selection from the Female Poetic Writers of England and America*. She approached the firm of Carey & Hart, who had published her *Traits of American Life*, and her letter to them shows how quickly she had grasped the economics of authorship, publishing, and marketing:

> You wish to know my terms for The Ladies Wreath. I shall ask ten percent premium on the first edition and I wish that edition to be not less than 2000. I do not choose to sell the copyright or I should value it higher than you probably would be willing to give.... I am confident the work will be popular and continue to sell for years....
>
> There is no work extant on this plan....

I always stipulate for six sets of every work of mine published, that is one for myself and one for each of my five children.

Have you forwarded any of my books to New York? The editors of the New York Mirror and the American Magazine would notice the work.[5]

Carey & Hart apparently refused to meet her terms, and the book was published by other firms in Boston and New York.

Philadelphia and Godey's Lady's Book

The *Ladies Magazine* had a serious rival in Louis Godey's *Lady's Book*, launched in Philadelphia in 1830. In 1836, he bought Hale's magazine and made her editor of the merged publication. Like other magazine editors, Godey had simply reprinted English work, but Hale's arrival changed that. In September 1836, Godey announced: "The publisher of this work, with a view to securing *original contributions* for its columns, will give for such articles as he may approve and publish, the highest rate of remuneration offered by any periodical in the country." In the December issue, he made Hale's appointment public: "The present number of the Lady's Book closes our career as sole editor.... We are confident our readers will not regret this change, when they learn that Mrs. Sarah Josepha Hale, late editor of the American Ladies' Magazine (which work is now amalgamated with the Lady's Book), will superintend the Literary Department of the Book. Mrs. Hale is too well known to the public to need eulogy from us. For nine years she has conducted the magazine, which she originated, how! its readers well know."[6]

Hale published work by well-known men and women. She counted Edgar Allan Poe, Harriet Beecher Stowe, Horace Greeley, Lydia Maria Child, Henry Wadsworth Longfellow, Catharine Maria Sedgwick, Ralph Waldo Emerson, Catherine Beecher, John Greenleaf Whittier, and Lydia Sigourney among her contributors. All were paid well. She commissioned reviews of books by women that were often ignored in periodicals edited by men.

Hale was unable to change one feature of *Godey's*: the fashion plates. She was not merely uninterested in fashion; she disliked it. She believed that women should dress neatly and even stylishly, but corsets and bustles, ruffles and lace, the extravagance and waste involved in the industry, appalled her. She was much more concerned with women's health and encouraged her readers to exercise, enjoy the outdoors, ride, and swim. She promoted an "American" style, with sensible clothing. Her readers disagreed, and European fashions prevailed among those who could afford high style. (She was similarly ineffective in discouraging men from growing facial hair.) The illustrations were one of the magazine's most popular features. Because they were individually tinted by hand, the illustrations might differ from one copy to the next. If a colorist ran out of red, she might simply use green instead. When readers complained, Godey disingenuously made a virtue of a necessity: "We now colour plates to different patterns, so that two persons in a place may compare their fashions, and adapt those colours that they may suppose may be most suitable to their figures and complexions."[7]

Godey's Lady's Book provided advice about designing and furnishing homes, and reading the magazine over the fifty years of its existence provides a guide to what Americans were building—or wished to build. From "Godey's Model Cottages" of 1846, with their gothic rooflines, porches, and gingerbread trim, to Italianate towers, to mansard roofs, from Georgian architecture to Victorian, every trend can be traced in the magazine's pages. Recipes, too, reflected the changing tastes of the times. Each issue included the music and lyrics of a song, and those too provide clues to popular taste.

Hale promoted technology that would improve women's lives—praising the 1854 invention of the washing machine and introducing readers to the wonders of the double boiler and the rotary egg beater. She began a feature called "Everyday Actualities," noting such advances as the shift from whale oil to gas for lighting. She featured accounts of travel by steamship and rail, including a trip to Niagara Falls. She added a column by someone who called herself "Hickory Broom" that exposed popular swindles.

Hale's campaigns for social reform included efforts to improve child welfare, end corporal punishment, improve sanitation and public health, and organize charity. Above all, she promoted women's causes. She wanted equality in education, property rights, legal rights, and professional opportunity. Every institution—from kindergartens and infant schools to professional schools—should be available to girls and boys, women and men. When Elizabeth Blackwell sought a medical education, the *Lady's Book* supported her, and the editor expressed her pleasure at the establishment of the Female Medical College of Philadelphia. Male doctors, she insisted, should not infringe on the practice of female midwives. Having given birth to five children, Hale agreed with Queen Victoria that anesthesia was a wonderful invention.

Hale regularly published notes about schools for girls and young women, and she was delighted when Matthew Vassar announced a plan to create the first college for women to rival elite men's colleges in quality. She was not pleased that Vassar's board members planned to hire only male faculty members, and in editorials in February, May, and June 1864, the *Lady's Book* urged them to hire women. When the college opened in September 1865, the majority of the faculty were women.

Despite her support of opportunities for women, Hale's credentials as a feminist are often questioned. In all her writing, she insisted on "separate spheres" for men and women. Women's role was domestic. Middle-class women should stay at home; women who needed employment should not work alongside men. The fact that she violated these rules daily did not trouble her. *Godey's Lady's Book* was the bible of the domestic sphere, with its recipes, clothing patterns, and stories emphasizing romance.

Another strike against her as a feminist came from her staunch opposition to women's suffrage. She argued that women should not vote because involvement in politics and government would undermine their moral superiority and authority. She also suggested that women were not yet well enough educated to vote intelligently and that once her educational goals were achieved, the right to vote would follow. Neither of those arguments stood up well. Hale never changed her views on suffrage, and when she published *Woman's Record,* which purported to provide "sketches of all distinguished women to A.D. 1869," Elizabeth Cady Stanton and Susan B. Anthony were conspicuously absent.[8]

The Civil War

When *Uncle Tom's Cabin* was published in 1852, Hale republished *Northwood* with a new introduction and subtitle: *Life North and South.* She regarded Stowe's novel as inflammatory, and she did not support abolition. In her preface, she wrote, "The great error of those who would sever the Union, rather than see a slave within its borders, is that they forget the *master* is their brother as well as the *servant.*"[9] She maintained that protecting the Union was more important than emancipation, and that slavery was a false issue. She backed the movement for colonization: enslaved people should be trained for independence; slaveholders should be compensated for the loss of their "property"; and the formerly enslaved should be sent to Africa. She set out these views in an 1853 novel, *Liberia.* But if you had been reading *Godey's Lady's Book* in the following decade, you would not know her views.

In fact, even after the attack on Fort Sumter, reading the magazine would not tell you anything about the war. By mid-century, *Godey's Lady's Book* had 150,000 subscribers, about one-third of them in the South. Neither publisher nor editor wished to offend them. They may also have believed that their female readers were not interested in politics. Whatever the case, the magazine simply remained silent. During the war, Southern subscribers did not receive the magazine, because the U.S. Postal Service did not deliver mail to the Confederate States. Their opinions were no longer a reason to avoid the issue. Nevertheless, the magazine continued to ignore the war and failed to support the Union cause. Hale had enthusiastically backed Elizabeth Blackwell's quest for a medical education, but when Dr. Blackwell sent out a call for nurses to serve in military hospitals, the magazine did nothing to publicize it. They wrote nothing about the efforts of Northern women to support the war by rolling bandages, knitting stockings, and sewing uniforms and blankets. Although Hale had been instrumental in creating women's fairs to raise money, the magazine published nothing about the fairs to support the Sanitary Commission.

Hale took notice of the war only in her ongoing campaign for a national Thanksgiving Day. In 1859, she had written an editorial: "If every state would join us in Union Thanksgiving on the 24th of this month, would it not be a renewed pledge of love and loyalty to the Constitution of the United States which guarantees peace, prosperity, progress and perpetuity to our great Republic?" In 1861, she editorialized for a Thanksgiving Day on which "we lay aside our enmities and strifes" for that day at least.[10] She wrote letters to anyone who might read them, and Secretary of State William H. Seward forwarded one of her letters to the president only a few days before October 3, 1863, when Lincoln issued the Thanksgiving Day Proclamation. There was no daylong truce, the war would continue for more than a year, and thousands more lives would be lost.

Last Home

From the time she left "Lawyer Hale's Mansion" in Newport until the 1850s, Hale lived in boardinghouses in Boston and Philadelphia. She had become a very wealthy woman, with a generous salary from the magazine and royalties from her many books, but she worked too hard to maintain a home. She later lived with her daughters, first at a four-story brick town house at 922 Spruce Street, where Sarah ran a school, and later with Frances Ann, who had married Dr. Lewis Boudinot Hunter, a naval surgeon, in 1844. She lived with the Hunters and their children at 1413 Locust Street. As she grew older, she worked at home, sending manuscripts to the office by messenger.[11]

She had a large upstairs room with an alcove for her bed, a rocking chair near her Franklin stove, a sofa, and a birdcage with four pairs of canaries. The center of the room was taken up with a large table with drawers at each end, with neat piles of books and papers, a tray with an inkpot and her gold pen, and a student lamp with green glass shades. She worked hard six days a week, till sundown. After supper, she told her grandchildren stories and played the piano while the children sang.

In 1877, *Godey's Lady's Book* was sold to Munsey's, a New York publisher, and Hale wrote her last editorial: "Having reached my ninetieth year, I must bid farewell to my countrywomen, with the hope that this work of half a century may be blessed to the furtherance of their happiness and usefulness in their Divinely appointed sphere. New avenues for higher culture and for good works are opening before them, which fifty years ago were unknown. That they may improve these opportunities, and be faithful to their high vocation, is my heartfelt prayer."[12] Louis Godey died a year later, and on April 30, 1879, Sarah Josepha Hale died at home.

14

Grace Metalious

The residents of Manchester, New Hampshire, where Grace De Repentigny was born in 1924, segregated themselves into ethnic neighborhoods. Grace's mother, Laurette, with pretensions of cultural and social superiority, chose to live outside the French-Canadian enclaves. Their apartment at 104 Ash Street was close to the north-central "Protestant" section of town. On another side, it wasn't far from a Greek American neighborhood, and one of Grace's childhood playmates was George Metalious—a friend of whom her mother did not approve. Laurette worked as a dental assistant; her husband, Al, was a printer; both jobs were a step up from those Grace's grandmothers had held in the local textile plant. The grandfathers had left their families long ago. Al soon left as well, to join the Merchant Marine, and the couple divorced in 1936.

Laurette wanted Grace and her younger sister, Doris (known as Bunny), to share her aspirations. She could not afford to send them to Catholic schools, but she made sure they attended the public schools and read a great deal. Although they had little money, the girls always dressed well. They were not expected to do household chores. Laurette read the *New York Times Book Review,* and the girls made good use of the public library. Grace outgrew the children's section and managed to borrow books from the adult section by saying they were for her mother. She read everything, from Nancy Drew and murder stories to historical novels, Charles Dickens to F. Scott Fitzgerald. She also wrote from early childhood. Even then, as she would later say, "somewhere in my head there is always a story."[1] In seventh grade she completed her first novel, "Murder in the Summer Barn Theater," featuring a girl sleuth.

Grace was a mediocre student, but in high school she joined a few of her classmates in a little theater group. They read Shakespeare and O'Neill, wrote, and performed plays. Grace was never short of boyfriends, and in her senior year she started dating George Metalious. No longer a childhood pal, the tall, dark, handsome young man had graduated from high school in 1941 and had gone on to the University of New Hampshire the following September. He came home on weekends, and by Christmas they were lovers. When both their mothers opposed their marriage, they threatened to live together anyway. The ploy worked. They were married in February 1943, and George left college to work in a defense plant. Their daughter Marsha was born seven months and three weeks after the wedding. It was a complicated, difficult delivery, and the doctor warned Grace against having more children.

Grace had never learned to keep house. She did not clean, and she picked up dinner cooked by her grandmother and passed it off as her own. When George was drafted in July 1943, she moved to an apartment on Third Street with her mother, grandmother, and sister. She supported all of them by working as a clerk while her grandmother took care of the baby. In the evenings, she dated pilots at a nearby Air Force base. George had been posted to Texas and Missouri, and then was sent to England. He fought in the Battle of the Bulge, December 1944 through January 1945— the largest and deadliest battle of the war. When he returned to Manchester on New Year's Eve, he threw his in-laws out of the apartment. He went to work in a textile mill, and the young couple and their infant moved in with his family.

Finally, in 1947, George was given an apartment in a housing project for veterans, and they were living there when their son, Christopher George, was born in February. A year later, George returned to the University of New Hampshire, and they moved into student housing—converted wooden barracks from Fort Devens, with the only heat provided by kitchen stoves. A daughter, Cynthia Jean, was born in July 1950, and Grace nearly died giving birth. She was again told not to risk another pregnancy, and the next spring she had a tubal ligation. The decision was traumatic: "You don't feel like a woman at all. You are sterile. Barren.... You begin to look for a substitute. Somehow you are going to create something. And then one day you look at your typewriter."[2]

Small-Town Life

When George graduated from the University of New Hampshire, he began a series of teaching jobs in small New Hampshire towns. In 1954, he was teaching at the State School in Laconia, and that fall the family moved into a house that the owner had named "It'll Do." On a dirt road, it was more falling-down shack than house. The asbestos siding fell off when it rained, windows didn't work properly, and there was no insulation. When the well went dry—as it once did for nine weeks—Grace said that "there was a certain ripe smell about all of us." The owner's brother continued to live in one of the tiny rooms. But the rent was only $35 a month. A visitor described it as "a little shanty house, with dirty dishes everywhere." The only clean place was the corner where Grace kept her typewriter.³ She had written more than three hundred stories, but she had never tried to publish any.

Grace did not fit the stereotype of a small-town teacher's wife. She had already adopted what became her signature outfit: blue jeans, flannel shirt, sneakers, and ponytail. Her housekeeping had not improved, and her children looked neglected. George did the cooking and housework. Her writing became the subject of gossip. What was she writing *about*? Is she writing about *us*? But she made one friend who encouraged her writing and told her stories about the nearby town of Gilmanton.

Laurie Wilkens came from a wealthy New York family, but she and her husband Bill had bought a two-hundred-year-old farmhouse, and she was writing for the Laconia *Evening Citizen*. When she heard that a writer had moved to town, she arranged to meet her. Soon they were getting together, usually at Laurie's house, to talk about books and writing. Grace read her work in progress aloud, and Laurie made suggestions. Grace was working on two manuscripts. "A Quiet Place" told the story of a young married couple, with the husband attending college on the G.I. Bill. She wrote to a New York literary agent, Jacques Chambrun, chosen from a list she found at the library because of his French name. He agreed to represent her and sent the manuscript out only to have it rejected by a half-dozen publishers.

In the meantime, Grace was working on "The Tree and the Blossom," a novel of small-town life. One of the central stories was based on a crime that Laurie had told her about: the 1947 "sheep pen murder," in which a young woman had killed her abusive father and buried him under the sheep pen. Grace later described her work on the novel: "I thought twenty-four hours a day for a year. I wrote ten hours a day for two and a half months." She would later say, "I think I began *Peyton Place* the day I was born." When asked why she wrote it, she said, "I thought about it a good long time ... and frankly I needed the money."⁴ In spring 1955, she sent more than 600 manuscript pages off to Chambrun. Houghton Mifflin, Lippincott, and Little, Brown rejected it, but Leona Nevler, who had read it as a freelancer for Lippincott, recommended it to Kathryn G. Messner, president and editor-in-chief of Julian Messner, who asked Chambrun to send it.

On August 17, 1955, Grace took the children swimming: the well had gone dry and the outing would take the place of a bath. When they got home, there was a telegram from Chambrun asking her to call. He told her that he had sold the manuscript to Messner. She was so excited that she didn't ask how much they would pay. Kitty Messner told her, "Sweetie, I've read your book. I love it." Two days later, Grace went to New York to be wined and dined and to sign her contract. She received an advance of $1,500.[5] Laurie Wilkens wrote a story about Grace's success for the Laconia *Evening Citizen*.

Becoming an Author

It took a while for the manuscript to become a book. The publisher hired Leona Nevler, who had recommended the manuscript, to edit it, and she had a heavy hand. Grace was so hurt and furious at Nevler's changes that Kitty Messner took over the job. She was more tactful and had a lighter editorial touch, but the process took a full year. Kitty had high hopes for the book, and her company invested $5,000 in publicity—an unheard-of sum for a first novel.

The publicity campaign would portray Grace as an ordinary housewife who, as an emancipated modern woman, had blown the lid off small-town life. In her signature denim and flannel, she became "Pandora in blue jeans." The publicists were undaunted by their first visit to Grace at "It'll Do." According to the biographer Emily Toth, "To enter the house, they had to step over a pile of garbage at the door. Inside it seemed that nothing put down was ever put away. Dirty dishes lay everywhere. Flies swarmed around an open jar of marshmallows, and when the children said they were hungry, Grace told them, 'Make yourself a peanut butter and marshmallow sandwich'—and handed them a goo-covered knife. On another occasion, she picked up what she thought was a Brillo pad—and found a dead mouse."[6] Nevertheless, the publicity photo they used repeatedly showed her in her blue jeans and flannel shirt at a typewriter in the kitchen—not her kitchen, of course, but Laurie Wilkens's. Other publicity photos showed the family eating breakfast together or doing jigsaw puzzles. Perhaps the thinking was that the book couldn't be too scandalous for the American public if it came from such a wholesome background. And one of the publicists suggested changing the title to *Peyton Place*.

In July 1956, advance copies arrived. Grace said "it was the most beautiful sight in the world to see my name on the spine of a hard cover." The publication date was September 24, but word quickly spread in Gilmanton. In August, George's $3,000 annual teaching contract was not renewed, and Grace's publicists saw that as a gift. The Boston *Traveler* headline said it all: "Teacher Fired for Wife's Book / Gossipy, Spicy Story Costs Him His Job." In an interview by Hal Boyle, a syndicated columnist, Grace said, "To a tourist these towns look as peaceful as a postcard picture. But if you go beneath that picture, it's like turning over a rock with your foot—all kinds of strange things crawl out. Everybody who lives in town knows what's going on—there are no secrets—but they don't want outsiders to know."[7]

A novel is a work of fiction, and Gilmanton was not Peyton Place. The things that crawl out from under the Peyton Place rock—teenage sex and pregnancy, divorce, adultery, rape, incest, abortion, and murder—appear to characters who came from Grace's imagination. But they were not unknown to the residents of Gilmanton, who did not want outsiders to see their town in the book's pages. Grace had betrayed the silence. She was shunned, the children were harassed, and the book broke all sales records.

Bestseller and a New House

Peyton Place was on the bestseller list for 26 weeks and sold more than 100,000 copies in its first month. It was reviewed nearly everywhere. It was also banned in several cities and libraries, with each ban increasing sales. In October Chambrun sold the movie and television rights for $250,000. British and paperback rights were sold as well. Within two years, *Peyton Place* had sold more copies than *Gone with the Wind,* and by 1960 it had sold more than 8.5 million copies. Everyone read it, though not everyone admitted doing so. Wives hid the book from husbands; husbands hid the book from wives; teenagers found the hidden copies and shared the page numbers of the most salacious passages. The filmmaker John Waters "found the book at his grandfather's when he was ten. 'I never got over it.... She put me on the wrong road early on, and I am better for it.'"[8] Grace's lawyer, concerned about her ability to deal with sudden wealth, set up a financial plan that would

"Pandora in Blue Jeans." The nickname, used by her publicists to portray Grace Metalious as a typical American housewife, has persisted in this bobblehead doll. *New Hampshire Historical Society.*

pay her annual living expenses and set up trust funds for the children. She never signed the papers. She did pay off her debts and bought a used Cadillac.

Grace also bought a house. She had long admired a small white Cape, built in 1756, known as the Mudgett homestead, set in 14 acres on Meadow Pond Road. The first floor had a living room with a beamed ceiling and fireplace, a center hallway, two bedrooms, and a bathroom. The second floor had two bedrooms. The best-known member of the original family was Herman Webster Mudgett, who had taught school in Gilmanton. He was better known as H.H. Holmes, a serial killer said to have murdered 36 people in Chicago to collect their life insurance. He was hanged in 1896.[9] The house was vacant but furnished, and in August the family moved in with their books, clothes, and personal items. Grace bought a large new refrigerator and filled it with food. It was going to be the family's first real home. ("It'll Do" burned down a few years later.)

The family was falling apart, though. George had taken a job in Stow, Massachusetts. He and Grace had both been unfaithful, and the town's hostility was taking a toll. In September, Grace did a radio interview with Thomas James Martin, known as TJ the DJ. Before the end of the year, they were living together. TJ took charge of renovating the house. He had Grace buy more land, to ensure privacy, and he made the property less rural, planting a huge lawn and adding a gravel driveway and a two-car garage with a loft, a flagstone patio, and a stone wall. To ensure the water supply, he had an artesian well dug. He also added four fireplaces, a wall of windows, a dining room with pine paneling, a playroom, laundry room, and a new kitchen with barbecue, and a bar. On the second floor, he added a master bedroom with a fireplace and an adjoining writing studio. The renovations cost $100,000.

In February 1958, Grace and George were divorced, and three days later she married TJ. They spent the next two years partying, traveling, and spending more money than even Grace could afford. They were often seen in his-and-hers outfits. Grace began to drink heavily—fashionable cocktails in New York, but Canadian Club and 7-Up at home. She gained a great deal of weight and began to have occasional blackouts. She was also under pressure to write. Had she been wiser about money, *Peyton Place* might have supported her forever. But her agent, Jacques Chambrun, had been cheating her, and she had spent too freely. In 1959 she devoted a month to writing *Return to Peyton Place*. The reviews were terrible, but it sold well (4.5 million in paperback), and the movie rights were bought. Another book, *The Tight White Collar*, was published in 1960 and sold moderately well.

Grace's marriage to TJ ended in October 1960. She said that TJ expected her to "conform to his image of a suburban housewife while still embodying the glamour of theatrical and literary life."[10] She joined George, who was living with the children on Martha's Vineyard. It is not clear whether they remarried, but they stayed together on the Vineyard until November, when they returned to Gilmanton. Despite George's efforts to help her, Grace was still drinking. They separated again in October 1963. Her last book, *No Adam in Eden*, based on her family, was published that year. The jacket copy, transparently false, said that the author "still lives, simply and happily, in rural New Hampshire with her husband and her children."

Death and Afterlife

In October 1963, a British journalist named John Rees arrived in Gilmanton to interview Grace. He found "chaos. In a large paneled room there were hundreds of books, magazines, and newspapers, the remains of several meals, unwashed glasses and an unbelievable confusion of classical and popular records."[11] They soon became lovers, and by December they were living together in Gilmanton. Grace's financial affairs were as chaotic as her house. She had bought a motel on Lake Winnipesaukee that was in bankruptcy; she owed more than $200,000 in back taxes and interest; and the revenue from *No Adam in Eden* was less than her debts. Her house had been burglarized. Rees tried to sort out her finances, but it was nearly impossible.

On February 23, 1964, Grace and John Reese were staying at the Parker House in Boston when she began hemorrhaging. She was taken to Beth Israel Hospital, where doctors diagnosed cirrhosis of the liver. On February 24 she wrote a will leaving everything to Rees, and on February 25, she died. She was 39 years old. Rees promptly renounced any claim to her estate and promised her children 50 percent of anything he earned from writing about her. In fact, there was nothing to renounce. The estate had $211,153 in liabilities and only $37,690 in assets. When the house and motel were auctioned off, the proceeds went to the Internal Revenue Service.

Peyton Place outlived its creator. In September 1964, the television version aired, starring Mia Farrow, Ryan O'Neal, and Dorothy Malone. It ran for five years and became an international hit. In the United States it had 60 million viewers. The book itself has never been out of print and has achieved respectability as a cultural phenomenon. The most recent edition was issued by Northeastern University Press. It has become the subject of analysis by women's studies scholars. Ardis Cameron, a distinguished scholar of history and gender studies, gave the book its own biography: *Unbuttoning America: A Biography of Peyton Place*. Peyton Place became a synonym for one version of small-town America, even finding its way into congressional debate. As Cameron notes, during the 1998 hearing over the Bill Clinton–Monica Lewinski scandal, Representative Lindsey Graham asked, "Is this Watergate or *Peyton Place?*" The book, she notes, had been "reduced to common shorthand for idle philandering, its edginess dulled by the mystic chords of memory."[12]

Rhode Island

15

Elleanor Eldridge and Frances Green

Elleanor Eldridge spent her childhood cleaning other people's houses and died the wealthiest Black woman and property owner in Rhode Island. When dishonest businessmen and politicians seized her real estate holdings, she needed money for legal costs. Frances Whipple, a white writer, became interested in her cause and offered to help Eldridge tell her story as a way of raising money. Their collaboration enabled Eldridge to pay her debts, and it helped Whipple advance her career as an author.

Complex Marriages

In the middle of the eighteenth century, a Narragansett woman named Mary Fuller was hoping to marry. Few Narragansett men had survived the diseases and wars brought by whites. She solved her problem in a way that was becoming common among the women of her community: she bought a slave named Thomas Prophet, freed him, and married him. Their daughter Hannah also married a man who had arrived with his parents and siblings on a slave ship. The father of this family became known as Dick Eldridge, and he and his wife had four children: a daughter, Phillis, and three sons, Dick, George, and Robin. When the American Revolution started, all three brothers enlisted, trading their service for a promise of freedom. At the end of the war, Robin—now a free man—married Hannah Prophet. They settled in Warwick and had nine children. Elleanor, the youngest, was born in 1784 or 1785.

A Servant in Other People's Houses

Hannah Eldridge worked as a laundress in the Warwick home of Joseph Baker, and Elleanor often accompanied her to work. After Hannah died, Elleanor—then ten years old—took over the job. For twenty-five cents a week, she boiled water, scrubbed soiled linens, wrung them out, hung them to dry, and ironed. She stayed with the Bakers for nearly six years, with periodic raises in pay. As she grew up, she took on other jobs—gathering eggs, tending to cows and pigs, spinning, and weaving. She became adept at double weaving—a complex process requiring both mechanical skill and mathematical calculation. In addition to utilitarian items, she wove ornamental carpets and damask.

From 1803 to 1812, Elleanor worked in the home of Captain Benjamin Greene, a farmer who had served in the Revolution. For the first year, she worked at spinning, but she then took charge of the dairy, creating prize-winning cheeses. She remained with the Greene family for eight years. During that time, her brother George was elected governor of the Black community. Since 1756, people of color in Rhode Island had held annual Negro Election festivals in June, at which the male voters chose a governor and judges. While they had no official standing, election to these offices indicated respect in the community. The festivals were great celebrations, with music, dancing, and costumes. As the governor's sister, Elleanor was highly visible at the ceremonies and dressed elegantly. She had become an attractive young woman, "quite a belle."[1]

Elleanor attracted the attention of a young man, a cousin, identified only as Christopher G. Their relationship survives in letters written when he was at sea. He traveled around the world, was impressed by the British Navy, and returned to Rhode Island occasionally. Their long-distance courtship continued for six years, until he died in a shipwreck.

In 1806 Robin Eldridge died, and that fall Elleanor, named executor in his will, left Warwick to settle his estate. She needed the signature of her sister Fettina, who was living in Adams, Massachusetts, nearly two hundred miles away. She traveled on foot. Adams was also home to an aunt, Hannah's only sister, and several cousins. Elleanor stayed until spring, working as a weaver and enjoying the company of her family and the admiration of the community's young men. When she returned to Captain Greene's household, she had Fettina's power of attorney in hand.

Captain Greene died in 1812, and Elleanor decided it was time to stop being a servant in other people's homes. Together with her sister Lettise, she embarked on a career as an independent businesswoman.

A Woman of Property

Elleanor moved in with Lettise, and together they began to do whatever jobs came to hand: laundering, nursing, weaving, spinning, and making soap, which they sold in Providence. Elleanor managed to save enough money to buy a house in Warwick. She lived there, but she also rented part of it out for $40 a year. In 1815 she moved to Providence to start another business: papering, painting, and whitewashing. Because that was a seasonal operation, she worked in other people's homes in the winter. Her employers included prominent families. As her memoir notes, "*Elleanor has always lived with good people.*"[2] She moved back to Warwick temporarily, living in her house with her brother Jetter as a tenant. Her brother George had his own house next door.

She continued to live frugally and save, and by 1826 she had accumulated enough money to buy a lot with a house on Spring Street in Providence, between Broad and Westminster streets, near where Classical High School is now located. She had also acquired a reputation for business acumen and honesty that made people willing to extend credit. She paid $1,700 for the house, $1,600 of which was borrowed. She added two wings: one to live in and one for tenants, collecting $150 a year in rent. Eldridge was borrowing sums that were very large for a working person; for a woman of color, they were nearly unheard of. Banks at that time did not make loans to individuals, so she borrowed from people she knew, most likely her former employers.

In the 1820s Providence had two neighborhoods that were predominantly Black: Hard Scrabble and Snow Town, where the state capitol is now located. Both were the victims of violent, destructive attacks by white mobs, Hard Scrabble in 1824 and Snow Town in 1831.[3] Eldridge's home was in a predominantly white neighborhood and was never attacked by rioters, but later events suggest that her ownership provoked hostility.

Litigation

As executor of her father's will, Eldridge had learned something about estate law, and in 1830 she acted as executor of the estate of a woman named Lucy Gardner. As the historian Jacqueline Jones notes, "as required by law, a 'notice' ran in a local paper, informing creditors of Gardner's death and requesting them to submit their claims to 'the subscriber'—Eldridge—'for settlement.' Elleanor was educating herself about property law."[4] She was also learning about the risks of borrowing. In 1831, Eldridge defaulted on a loan of $94 and was taken to court, where she was told to repay the loan and pay costs. And after returning from another trip to Adams, she found that her house had been repossessed because she had failed to repay an outstanding loan.

Her legal troubles were not limited to civil cases. In 1832, her brother

George was arrested for assaulting Samuel Gorton, a descendant of one of Warwick's founding white families. He was jailed in East Greenwich. To raise the $500 bond, she obtained a mortgage from George Carder, who had loaned her money earlier. She hired Joseph L. Tillinghast, a prominent lawyer and member of the state House of Representatives, to defend her brother. George Eldridge was acquitted.

By 1835, Elleanor's legal and financial troubles had grown extraordinarily complex. When she had borrowed $250 from George Carder, he had agreed that she could pay only the interest on the loan (at 10 percent) indefinitely. After George Carder died, his brother John sued her in January 1835 for the outstanding balance, which she could not pay. On September 12, Sheriff William Brayton Mann auctioned off her house, and it was purchased by a neighbor named Benjamin Balch for $1,700. He demolished the wings she had added and evicted her tenants. Neither Balch nor the sheriff knew how many friends Eldridge had in high places. As Jones notes, "If creditors had thought her an easy mark—someone unable to afford legal counsel, someone from whom they could strip all earthly belongings on the pretext of recalling a loan—they were mistaken. And throughout this period she called upon her employers for support that went well beyond the financial and in fact made a dramatic statement about her respectability and her creditworthiness."[5]

Joseph Tillinghast, who was planning to run for the U.S. House of Representatives, agreed to represent Eldridge in suing Balch. She consulted Rhode Island Attorney General Albert C. Greene, who advised her that, if the sheriff had failed to advertise the auction properly, it might have been illegal. Balch won the case in January 1837, but Eldridge continued to pursue the matter. Finally, with the help of an unknown "gentleman," Eldridge and Balch came to an understanding that would allow her to recover her property but left her deeply in debt. At this point Frances Whipple appeared with the suggestion that she help Eldridge tell her story as a way of raising money.

The Entrepreneur as Author

Like Eldridge, Frances Whipple traced her Rhode Island roots back to colonial days. Born in Smithfield in 1805, she was descended from two of the colony's founding families. Her parents were nevertheless of modest means, and she decided as a young woman that she would earn her living as an author and editor. Eldridge had worked for her at some point, and the court cases outraged her. She had become committed to women's rights, respect for Native people, and abolition. Here was a story that could advance her causes, as well as her writing, and could materially aid someone in need.

Eldridge is the author of *Memoirs* because it is her story; Whipple is the author because she wrote it. If published today, the title page would probably read "The Memoirs of Elleanor Eldridge, *as told to* Frances Whipple." It is written in the third person. The book is not an objective telling of Eldridge's life, but it is often difficult to determine whose agenda is being advanced by the omissions, inaccuracies, and embroideries. What is certain is that the voice we hear—at once angry and romantic, political and sentimental—belongs to Whipple.

The book begins with a fanciful version of the enslavement of Eldridge's grandfather, Dick. We are told that he was a chieftain and merchant in the Congo who had been selling tobacco to the owners of a ship. They invited him and his family to come on board for refreshments and a tour of the vessel, and the family suddenly found themselves in chains. This is not how people in the Congo became enslaved in the 1740s. The slave trade was a brutal system of kidnaping and the selling of Africans by Africans. But whose fantasy was this? It might have been a story that the Eldridges grew up with, or it might have been Whipple's way of providing the family with a noble African ancestry.

The two authors shared certain goals. Both wanted the book to make money, and the volume includes testimonials as to the importance of the cause from several of the 19 sponsors who had paid for the printing. Both wanted to present Eldridge in the best possible light, omitting or downplaying her failures to make timely payments on loans and emphasizing that she was a person of good character, charitable toward others, and the provider of housing for deserving Black tenants. Yet I hear Whipple's voice in the description of "poor, simple-hearted, honest Ellen."[6] The frontispiece of the book promotes that view by showing Eldridge carrying a broom. It is not congruent with Eldridge's canny management of her case or her ability to take advantage of her connections to powerful white people. Whipple also claims that Eldridge was illiterate, which is not credible, given her ease in dealing with legal matters.

Both wanted to portray the Carders, the sheriff, and Benjamin Balch as conniving, cruel, and acting in bad faith. Balch evicted Eldridge's tenants: "All her families had been compelled to leave, at a single week's notice; and many of them, being unable to procure tenements, were compelled to find shelter in barns and out-houses, or even in the woods. But *they were colored people*—So thought he, who so unceremoniously ejected them from their comfortable homes." And he tore down the wings Elleanor had added: "There seems to be a spirit of wilful malignity, in this

15. Elleanor Eldridge and Frances Green

wanton destruction of property, which it is difficult to conceive of as existing in the bosom of civilized man."[7]

Eldridge's motivation was personal, and it is not clear to what extent she shared Whipple's political agenda. Whipple and Eldridge—and today's readers—would agree that Eldridge's race and gender weighed against her, but Eldridge might not have been as eager as Whipple to go into more general discussions of bias. Before naming Eldridge's ancestors, Whipple introduces the topic of race: "Elleanor Eldridge, on the one hand, is the inheritress of African blood, with all its hardship of woe and shame; and the subject of wrong and banishment, by her Indian maternity on the other. Fully, and sadly, have these titles been redeemed. It seems, indeed, as if the wrongs and persecutions of both races had fallen upon Elleanor." And she concludes, "the subject of this wrong, or rather of this accumulation of wrongs, was a woman, and therefore weak—a *colored woman*—and therefore contemptible. No *man* ever would have been treated so; and if a *white woman* had been the subject of such wrongs, the whole town—nay, the whole country, would have been indignant."[8]

Elleanor Eldridge, as portrayed in the frontispiece to *Memoirs of Elleanor Eldridge* (Providence: B.T. Albro, 1838). By the time the book was published, she was an entrepreneur and real estate owner, not a domestic servant. The image was probably chosen to present her as the naive victim of scheming businessmen.

Whipple's most obvious intervention in Eldridge's story was the addition of two long poems that she wrote about slavery and freedom. "The Supplication of Elleanor" speaks of the heritage of African and Indigenous ancestry and of military service as the road to freedom. "The Emancipated" continues the theme of slavery and freedom. The inclusion of the poems reminds us that, for Whipple, *The Memoirs of Elleanor Eldridge* was as much literary as charitable, an important step in developing her career as a writer.

Both authors played a role in marketing Eldridge's story. Whipple recruited 19 women to sponsor the book and others to write testimonials to Eldridge's character that were included in the volume. She arranged the printing and negotiated with William Lloyd Garrison to publicize the book. One of the poems in the book, "Hard Fate of Poor Ellen," by "A Lady of Providence" with the initials S.P., was also published in *The Liberator,* as were advertisements for the book. Eldridge set out on a book tour, promoting the *Memoirs* with talks in Bristol, Warren, and Newport; in Boston, Fall River, New Bedford, and Nantucket; and as far afield as New York City and Philadelphia. The book, which sold for fifty cents, had eight printings by 1847. The first edition sold nearly two thousand copies, so total sales must have been quite respectable.

Whipple wrote a sequel, *Elleanor's Second Book,* published in 1839, again to raise money but also clearly to advance her own writing career. In the book, a group of young women call on Elleanor Eldridge in her home; she provides a summary of her life so far; and the young women take turns telling unrelated sentimental stories. The book allows Whipple to bring us up to date on Eldridge: she is living in her house in Providence, she has been on a book tour, her *Memoirs* have sold about 1,900 copies. A year later, Whipple wrote an antislavery tract meant for children, *The Envoy: From Free Hearts to the Free,* and a novel, *The Mechanic.* In 1842, she was the editor of the *Wampanoag and Operatives Journal,* concerned with the rights of women factory workers.

In 1842, she married Charles C. Green, and her subsequent writings were under the name Frances Harriet Whipple Green. The marriage lasted five years. Although she wrote another antislavery book, *Shahmah in Pursuit of Freedom* (1858), most of her later writings were spiritualist tracts. In some of these, the returning spirits spoke against slavery and in favor of women's rights. She lived in New York and California and, in 1861 married William C. McDougall. She died in Oakland, California, in 1878.

Eldridge continued to live on Spring Street, with a series of tenants, and in 1847 bought a lot next door to her house. When she died in 1862, her real estate holdings were valued at $4,800, making her the wealthiest Black woman, and the second-wealthiest Black person, in Providence. Her house no longer stands; even Spring Street is gone.

16

Charlotte Perkins Gilman

Readers in the 1960s discovered Charlotte Perkins Gilman as the author of "The Yellow Wallpaper," a fictionalized account of her postpartum depression and the "rest cure" to which she was subjected. Some went on to read her novel *Herland*, set in a utopia without men. Both have become part of the feminist canon. But during her lifetime, she was best known for controversial books and lectures on political economy. In a review of Gilman's autobiography, Dorothy Canfield Fisher summarized her accomplishments: "the vigorous radicalism which in her younger days seemed shocking ... by the time she was an old woman seemed only what any intelligent person believes as a matter of course."[1]

An Unhappy Marriage

Charlotte Anne Perkins was born on July 3, 1860, to Frederick and Mary Westcott Perkins. Frederick was the grandson of Mary Beecher Perkins, the private, domestic sister of the activists Harriet Beecher Stowe, Catharine Beecher, and Isabella Beecher Hooker. Mary Westcott, Frederick's second cousin, was also his second choice. He had been engaged to Frankie Johnson, but his mother forced him to break the engagement. Frankie then married James Beecher, Frederick's uncle. (Frederick and Frankie eventually married, after both their spouses had died.)

Frederick and Mary had two children who survived infancy: Thomas Adie, born in 1859, and Charlotte, born a year later. Soon after Charlotte's birth, Frederick deserted the family. Mary and the children moved to her grandfather's house, where they lived for nine months. Frederick visited occasionally but failed to pay for their support as he had promised. From 1863 to 1873, the family lived with relatives or in rented homes in Rhode Island, Connecticut, New York, and Massachusetts. At one point, they lived in a cooperative house in Providence that would contribute to Charlotte's later writings about the need to change our conception of home.[2]

Charlotte visited Great-Aunt Harriet Beecher Stowe at Oakholm, in Hartford's Nook Farm, and the family stayed connected with their Beecher relatives until 1873, when Mary filed for divorce. Except for Frederick's aunts Charlotte and Anna Perkins, the Beecher family took Frederick's side, even though he was hostile to them. In 1877, he would publish a book of short stories ridiculing his grandfather, uncles, parents, wife, and children. The last story was "What's the use of a baby?": "an 'awful example' for the warning of maids and bachelors, as terrific consequences universally follow great follies. It is the delirium tremens of matrimony." Not surprisingly, Gilman would later write, "The word Father, in the sense of love, care, one to go to in trouble, means nothing to me."[3] The Beecher heritage of intellectual accomplishment and public service, though, remained a source of pride and inspiration throughout her life.

Although their frequent moves and lack of funds meant that Charlotte had little formal schooling, her mother made sure that she attended classes when possible and gave the children access to books and magazines for children as well as volumes of natural history and novels by Charles Dickens, George Eliot, and Louisa May Alcott. Charlotte had a lively imagination and wrote stories about princes, princesses, kings, and fairies. As adolescence approached, her mother became alarmed by her fantasizing,

A house where Charlotte Perkins Gilman once lived. The arrow pointing to the third floor is explained by the inscription on the verso: "House N.W. cor. Manning & Ives sts Providence, 1871–1874 I had the third floor front room." *Charlotte Perkins Gilman Papers, Schlesinger Library, Harvard Radcliffe Institute.*

and when Charlotte was 13 she was told to end her imaginings. She turned her creative thinking toward goals that were based in the real world: ambitious ways to make it a better place.

Adolescence and a Career

Charlotte continued to read, including books about Darwinian thought and other scientific material. She attended parties and the theater, visited relatives in Boston, played board games, and socialized informally with people of her own age. As a teenager, Charlotte found her mother's attempts to control her thinking and her social life intolerable. She longed for a home that would offer her privacy and began to think seriously about how she could become independent. One line of effort focused on developing good habits and self-control, including a program of physical self-improvement. She went without corsets, wore comfortable shoes, got lots of fresh air, and took cold baths. A gymnasium for women had recently opened in Providence, and she exercised there twice a week, in addition to running a mile every day.

She also began to think about establishing financial independence as an artist. She sold her watercolors and gave art lessons. In 1879, her father agreed to pay her fees at the recently established Rhode Island School of Design, and the school certified her credentials as an art teacher. In 1880, she began painting advertising cards for "Soapine," a laundry detergent. She earned a respectable amount of money for this part-time venture until 1884.[4]

Charlotte also entered into the first of several intense friendships with young women. She met Martha Luther at an 1879 performance of *H.M.S. Pinafore*. They soon exchanged secrets and the pledges of love that were common among young women at the time. In her old age, she said that she had known perfect happiness with Martha—"love, but not sex."[5] They had both renounced marriage, but in October 1881 Martha married Charles Lane, and a year later Charlotte had her first marriage proposal, from Walter Stetson, an artist whom she had known only three weeks. She refused him, in part because he would have expected her to become a traditional housewife—a role that was repugnant to her. By the time she was twenty, she was convinced that work was essential to being human. If marriage interfered with work—with one's real purpose in life—it was to be avoided.

Walter offered her a pledge: "I hereby make my solemn oath that I shall never in future years expect of my wife any culinary or housekeeping proficiency. She shall never be required, whatever the emergency, to DUST! Signed by Charles Walter Stetson on October 22, 1882." That was not enough. Charlotte did not agree to marry him until May 1883, and the wedding took place a year later. In a letter to a close friend a few months before the wedding, she described marriage as "a concession, a digression ... a means, not an end.... It fills my mind much; but plans for teaching and writing and studying for *living* and helping are more prominent and active."[6]

Marriage and Motherhood

Charlotte and Walter moved into a second-floor apartment at 1 Wayland Street in Providence. She remembered that "the house stood on a high bank, looking southward over the chimneys of a few small buildings below to the broad basin of the Seekonk, ringed at night with golden lights. White ducks drifted like magnolia petals along the still margins. Opposite us was a grove of tall pines—a pleasant place to walk and sit." Mercifully, "the housework for two in this tiny place was nothing to me." She learned to cook by experimentation: "I won't have a cook-book in the house."[7]

Charlotte became pregnant almost immediately and fell into a severe depression, which she assumed would lift when her child was born. On March 23, 1885, she gave birth to a daughter, Katharine, and hired a nurse to help for a month, but she "was already plunged into an extreme of nervous exhaustion which no one observed or understood." When the nurse left, "and I was left alone with the child I broke so fast that we sent for my mother ... to take care of the darling, I being incapable of doing that—or anything else, a mental wreck." Despite a move to a nicer house and the additional help of a servant, "I lay all day on the lounge and cried."[8]

Her depression did not lift, and it took a toll on Walter, who wrote in his diary: "I felt that I was sorry that I had married, for the first time distinctly I would not marry if I had the chance again, knowing what I do now."[9] That winter, Charlotte visited her friend Grace Channing in Pasadena, leaving Katharine at home. She wrote, painted, and enjoyed herself. As soon as she returned home, though, she became irritable and lethargic. The only thing that helped was activity—exercise at the gymnasium, painting greeting cards, writing a column on suffrage for *The Women's Journal*, writing poems, drawing, and spending time with friends. At home, facing domestic responsibilities, she became listless and depressed. In April 1887, she sought the help of Dr. Silas Weir Mitchell, a world-renowned specialist in women's neurological disorders. In addition to his general reputation, he had the virtue of having treated two women in the Beecher family.

Mitchell diagnosed Charlotte as suffering from neurasthenia, or nervous exhaustion—a catchall name for women's psychological problems other than hysteria. The treatment was a "rest cure": total bed rest away from home, isolation from family and friends, massage, and electrical stimulation. Patients were not permitted even to feed themselves. Reading, writing, sewing, and conversation were forbidden. Charlotte stayed for a month and left with the following instructions: "Live as domestic a life as possible. Have your child with you all the time. Lie down an hour after each meal. Have but two hours' intellectual life a day. And never touch pen, brush or pencil as long as you live." She "followed those directions rigidly for months, and came perilously near to losing my mind."[10]

Mitchell's advice ran counter to Charlotte's own experience. She knew that she was happy only when she avoided domestic chores; had an intellectual life; and held a pen, brush, or pencil in her hand. Work was essential. That November, she wrote to Grace Channing: "I decided to cast off Dr. Mitchell bodily, and do exactly what I pleased."[11] She also cast off Walter Stetson: the couple agreed to separate in 1888. Charlotte went back to Pasadena, this time taking three-year-old Katharine. She rented a four-room cottage on the corner of Orange Grove Avenue and Arroyo Drive for ten dollars a month. Two years later, she completed "The Yellow Wallpaper." She sent the manuscript to the *Atlantic Monthly*, and the editor's rejection was not encouraging. After reading it, he said, "I could not forgive myself if I made others as miserable as I have made myself!"[12] The editor of the *New England Magazine* disagreed and included it in the issue for January 1892 (with "Wallpaper" hyphenated).

Work

"The Yellow Wallpaper" added a publication in a major regional magazine to Gilman's credits. It allowed her to exorcise the experience of the rest cure and its aftermath, to repudiate Mitchell publicly, and to prevent other women from subjecting themselves to the treatment. She also hoped to convince Weir Mitchell "of the error of his ways." Mitchell never acknowledged the copy she sent him, but he told friends "that he had altered his treatment of neurasthenia since reading the story." In 1913, she summarized her motivation: "to save people from being driven crazy." The cure for depression, she wrote, is "work, the normal life of every human being; work, which is joy and growth and service, without which one is a pauper and a parasite."[13]

Gilman lived in Pasadena for two years, giving art lessons, tutoring, lecturing, and writing. She was extraordinarily productive—as she would be throughout her active writing life. In one year, she wrote 33 articles and as many poems. She joined a theater group, and she and Grace wrote plays together. Several of her articles were published, and the novelist and literary critic William Dean Howells sent her a fan letter.

In 1891, Charlotte and Katharine moved to Oakland, and her mother, who was ill, joined them. In the Bay Area she expected to find a more reform-minded audience for her lectures, as well as more politically congenial companions. She was soon lecturing and writing on socialism, utopian thought, women's rights, the labor movement, and communalism. Her radicalism and growing fame made her a target for the conservative mainstream press. Her personal life as well as her politics came into the spotlight. When Walter filed for divorce in 1892, the San Francisco papers reported it disapprovingly, including a full page in the *Examiner* asking "Should Literary Women Marry?"

Gilman had become attached to Adeline Knapp, a woman whom she called Dora in her autobiography. Knapp lived with Gilman and her family in a boardinghouse at 1258 Webster Street. Eventually Gilman took over management of the house and coped with nine boarders. She remembered that "I did all the housework and nursed mother till I broke down; then I hired a cook and did the nursing till I broke down; then I hired a nurse and did the cooking till I broke down." Her mother died on March 7, 1893, and the relationship with Dora ended in the same year. That spring she published her first volume of poetry, *In This Our World*, which in her words "brought small returns in cash but much in reputation."[14] It was widely reviewed and had a second printing in the United States and one in England.

Although Walter had filed for divorce in 1892, Rhode Island had denied his petition. Charlotte then filed in California, and the decree was granted in April 1894. Walter and Grace Channing married later that spring. With their marriage, any guilt Gilman felt over the divorce ended. She made a decision—scandalous at the time—to send Katharine to live with Walter and Grace. Walter was, after all, the girl's father, and Gilman thought that Grace, a close friend to whom Katharine was already attached, would be a better mother than she. Charlotte visited and wrote frequently, but they did not live together again until Katharine was an adult.

Rootless

At 35, Gilman considered herself a failure. She was in debt. Her mother was dead, her daughter was being cared for by Walter and Grace, and her friendship with "Dora" had ended. Yet that set her free to live wherever she wished and to pursue the work she loved: to diagnose society's ills, discover how best to treat them, and encourage people to act. In San Francisco, Gilman had helped to arrange several Woman's Congresses. There she met Jane Addams, the founder of Hull House, who invited her to visit. She borrowed enough money for a train ticket to Chicago.

Hull House was a settlement house for immigrants and a meeting place for social reformers of every sort. Gilman found "companionship, fellow feeling, friendly society."[15] Invitations to lecture began to arrive from cities in the Midwest, the South, and the East Coast. She called this chapter of her autobiography "At Large." She had no base, no home. She stayed with friends and followers as she traveled, earning an average of ten dollars per lecture. Her lectures had titles like "Collective Ethics," "America's Place Today," "A New Way to Heaven," and "Woman Suffrage and Man's Sufferings." In 1896, she addressed the House Judiciary Committee on suffrage, though she had come down with a mild case of mumps.

Gilman turned much of her lecture material into articles and books, so we can get a sense of why her audiences were enthusiastic. She brought theory down to earth and personalized abstractions, often with humor. In dissecting the glorification of motherhood, she noted, "Our voices thrill and tremble with pathos and veneration as we speak of 'the mothers of great men'—Mother of Abraham Lincoln! Mother of George Washington! and so on. Did Wilkes Booth have no mother? Was Benedict Arnold an orphan?"[16] She had a commanding presence and had learned to speak extemporaneously—although her lectures became polished through repetition. She reached her controversial conclusions by citing historical background, choosing examples carefully, and arguing clearly.

Her stage presence was commanding. A reporter for the *Woman's Journal* described her as "tall, lithe and graceful, with fine dark eyes, and spirit and originality flashing from her at every turn like light from a diamond." To illustrate the ill effects of corsets, she displayed a chart "depicting the effects of habitual corset-wearing on a horse." Her composure on stage was remarkable: she once continued to speak after swallowing a fly. Spontaneous applause broke out throughout her presentations.[17] If she had considered herself a failure at 35, she was surely a success at 37.

Productive Years

In March 1897, Gilman sought legal advice from George Houghton Gilman, the son of William and Katherine Beecher Perkins Gilman, at his New York office. He was her first cousin, and they had played together and corresponded as children. Houghton was well educated, a linguist and music lover, but politically conservative. For the next month, they saw the sights and went to the theater. When Charlotte left the city, they began writing to each other daily—long, confiding letters unlike any that Charlotte had ever written to a man. They rarely saw each other, because Charlotte was traveling constantly. In 1899 alone she lectured in Michigan, Illinois, Missouri, California, Utah, Colorado, Georgia, Tennessee, Alabama, North Carolina, and New York, and spent five months in England.

She was also writing thousands of words a day. Her main project was *Women and Economics: A Study of the Economic Relation Between Men and Women as a Factor in Social Evolution,* which would establish her reputation as a political economist and feminist. She argued that women's economic independence would solve many of society's economic and social problems, as well as improving women's mental and physical health. The book, published in 1898 by the Boston firm of Small, Maynard and in England by Putnam's, was an immediate success. It went through nine printings and was translated into Danish, Italian, Dutch, German, Hungarian, Polish, Russian, and Japanese. As she did in her lectures, she connected theory to personal experience. One reviewer wrote that "no woman, whatever her position or the conditions surrounding her, can read the book and not feel that the whole argument applies to herself and her concerns almost like a personal appeal."[18]

As her relationship with Houghton deepened, she reexamined her ideas about marriage. His family disapproved: she was seven years older than he, divorced, and his first cousin. Yet soon she was consulting doctors about the possibility of pregnancy at her age and the problems associated with the marriage of first cousins. They decided to marry but not have children. On June 12, 1900, as Charlotte wrote, "we were married—and lived happy ever after. If this were a novel, now, here's the happy ending."[19]

Charlotte, Houghton, and Katharine lived in apartments in New York City from 1900 to 1922. During that time, Katharine—now an artist—married and moved to Pasadena. Walter Stetson died, as did Charlotte's father. Gilman lectured in Germany, Italy, England, Austria, Hungary, and the Netherlands until World War I put an end to her international travels. And she continued to write thousands of words every year. She followed *Women and Economics* with sequels developing her argument further: *Concerning Children* (1900), *The Home: Its Work and Influence* (1903), *Human Work* (1904), and *The Man-Made World; or, Our Androcentric Culture* (1911). She also created a 32-page monthly journal, *Forerunner,* which published fiction, nonfiction, and poetry—all written by Gilman. She often serialized material in *Forerunner* and then published it in book form. That is how *Herland* appeared—first in monthly installments, and then as a book in 1915. *With Her in Ourland,* a sequel, also appeared first in the journal. She continued this marathon effort for seven years until, as she explained, "I had said all I had to say."[20] Her other venture into fiction was *Unpunished*, a mystery novel published after her death that featured husband-and-wife detectives.

House and Home

In *The Home*, Gilman had made an economic case against the traditional nuclear-family home: It was inefficient. It deprived women of the opportunity to do real work in the real world. It did not offer the privacy or security that it promised. Outsourcing chores like cooking, laundry, sewing, and childrearing to qualified specialists would free women to do productive work outside the home—and get these jobs done better. Men, she argued, had learned to specialize in their work, but women remained Jills-of-all-trades in the home. Her arguments are both entertaining and compelling. Yet in 1903, when the book was published, Gilman had rarely lived in a nuclear-family home. In fact, she had never lived anywhere for very long.

That changed in 1922. Houghton inherited half of a family home in Norwich, Connecticut. The other half was left to his brother Francis. They decided that Houghton, Charlotte, Francis, and his wife Emily would share the house and the expenses. Emily would run the household, with Charlotte still writing and lecturing. "Lowthorpe," at 380 Washington Street, had been built in 1660, with subsequent additions of ells and gables. Previous occupants included Benedict Arnold. It sits on an acre of land, with a park called Lowthorpe Meadows on two sides. The original section was a center-hall colonial with a gambrel roof and two chimneys. Its clapboards are painted dark red, and since rebuilding after an 1818 fire, four chimneys served its nine fireplaces. Because of the additions, some parts of the house required going upstairs and down again to get from one part of the first floor to another. The ceilings are low, with exposed beams. The house was expensive to maintain, and more picturesque than convenient.[21]

Gilman found Norwich congenial, full of well-educated people who read books. She and Houghton started a garden, and she enjoyed the physical labor. The vegetables they grew became useful as their incomes dwindled. Relations with Francis and Emily deteriorated, though. Houghton avoided conflict, and Charlotte and Emily stopped speaking. Their dining arrangements were antithetical to Charlotte's ideas of communal meals: they ate separately, with different menus, to avoid arguing at the table. They once came close to physical violence over what to have for dessert. Underlying the petty squabbles were financial resentments: Charlotte and Houghton were the only ones earning money. Gilman ended by holding the couple in contempt, writing to her friend Grace that "Francis is sub-normal.... Poor Emily a cripple & F. almost a dwarf and moron."[22]

"The Gilmans clowning on the front steps, possibly of their home in Connecticut," ca. 1920–25. *Charlotte Perkins Gilman Papers, Schlesinger Library, Harvard Radcliffe Institute.*

The End

On May 4, 1934, Houghton collapsed in the street after suffering a cerebral hemorrhage. Gilman sold her share in the house to Francis and moved to Pasadena with Grace Channing Stetson, living one door away from Katharine and her husband. Gilman had been diagnosed with breast cancer but told no one. She continued to lecture from time to time, and signed a contract with Appleton-Century for her autobiography, to be titled *The Living of Charlotte Perkins Gilman*. When she started radiation treatments, she discovered that the cancer had metastasized to her lungs. She could no longer keep her illness secret and moved in with her daughter. Early in August 1935, she finished her autobiography. On August 17, she took her life, leaving a letter that ended, "I have preferred chloroform to cancer." At the close of her life, she could write: "Much, very much of what I have worked for has been attained. Far more is waiting to be done."[23]

17

Cynthia Taggart

William Taggart had been president of the Newport Town Council, a county court judge, and a judge of the Supreme Court when in 1770 he and his oldest son, also William, went to sea, leaving his wife Mary and 11 children at home. When they returned, William Senior bought a farm in Middletown, about six miles from Newport. He built a "commodious mansion house" where—according to the younger William—"the greatest harmony prevailed."[1]

When British troops invaded Rhode Island in December 1776, a Hessian officer took part of the house as quarters for himself and his officers. They did not ask the family to move, but Mary did not want her family—especially her daughters—living in the same house as British soldiers. The Taggarts, except for William and his second and third sons, moved to Little Compton with William Jr. as their protector. William became a major in the Continental forces, transporting troops by boat to defend Newport. He also delivered information from Patriot spies to commanding officers. The next summer, Major William sent for his son, and his trip back to Newport became a reconnaissance mission. William and the officers who accompanied him reported that the British had no more than two thousand men, with a small naval force. William returned to Newport several times, gathering further intelligence. Whether the intelligence was flawed, or the attack was ill conceived, it did not go well. William reported:

> A party of about thirty, of which I was one, was detached in three boats: and having landed, well down to the mouth of the river, we immediately proceeded to my father's house. He, with his two sons, who, until this period, had remained on the Island, and had communicated much important information to the American commander, now joined us. Our orders were, to proceed to Black Point, so called, which was the place designated for the landing of our army.... On our way we captured two mounted light-horsemen, who were patrolling the shore; and, after our arrival at the appointed station, we waited until near day break, for the signal. But it was not given; and to our great mortification and disappointment, we were under the necessity of leaving the

Island, accompanied by my father and brothers, who would undoubtedly have been condemned to an ignominious death, if they had remained; as the active part which they had taken, in communicating intelligence to the American forces, was now discovered. They were accordingly compelled to abandon a valuable property, which was destroyed by the ruthless enemy. Houses, barns, orchards, fruit trees, fences, were all wantonly torn in pieces; and the whole farm left a barren waste,—the mere soil, which they could not destroy, alone remaining.[2]

The Taggarts, once affluent and comfortable, were now landless and impoverished.

The Taggart Cottage

The American forces then gave the family a confiscated estate in Sakonnet. Major Taggart commanded a force to land troops in Rhode Island, and William was appointed a captain, reporting to him. This expedition, too, failed, and father and son went to the Sakonnet farm. In July 1779, William and one of his brothers were taken prisoner. When his brother tried to escape, he was killed. William was imprisoned in Newport, but after two weeks he escaped through a cellar window and, with a companion, built a raft from fence rails and somehow managed to get home. In the fall, the British forces left Rhode Island.

Major Taggart died in 1798, and what remained of the property went to William. He built a home for his family, but with far more sisters than brothers, farming was difficult. William had married in 1791. He and his wife, Elizabeth Macomber, had five daughters: Patience, Ann, Betsey, Cynthia, and Maria. In the cottage that he rebuilt, as he reported, "we have experienced a long scene of affliction."[3]

The cottage, on a large lot, was one and a half stories with a gambrel roof and a central chimney. It had four front windows on the ground floor, and two gables on the east side. The grounds included a barn, a shed, and the family burying ground.[4]

The Scene of Affliction

In 1832, James C. Richmond and his brother were waiting for a ferry at Middletown, Rhode Island. They noticed an elderly man leaning over a fence in front of a cottage, and they struck up a conversation. He introduced himself as William Taggart and told them about his service in the Revolutionary War. Then he told them about his present state: "I have the

17. Cynthia Taggart

"The New England Cottage," the house where Cynthia Taggart wrote her poetry in an upstairs bedroom. *Frontispiece of James C. Richmond, The Rhode Island Cottage, 1st English edition (Newport, Isle of Wight: R.J. Denyer, 1849). Drawn by Lieutenant Harwood, engraved by A. Brannon.*

most afflicted family on this island. I have one daughter who has been lying on her bed in that house more than eleven years, and the physicians can do nothing for her. Her sister has worn herself out in watching over her, and now she is a cripple, and has to be moved about the house. Another daughter is deranged, and my wife is old and feeble, and troubled with a bad cough. She does all she can, Sir, but I cannot work as I used to do: and I have had very heavy doctors' bills to pay. It is but a little while since I paid more than four hundred dollars. I have been obliged to mortgage my little farm; and it is almost gone. I hope it will be enough to carry me through this world to a better."[5]

Taggart invited the Richmond brothers into the house, and Mrs. Taggart served tea, "not a little disturbed, when it was discovered that her insane daughter, Maria, had hidden the tea-spoons." Richmond then went to Cynthia's bedroom. He found an emaciated woman, lying on a couch. She told him that she never slept and described excruciating pain that doctors had been unable to alleviate, except with opiates. When the men returned to the parlor, Richmond asked how Cynthia spent her time. Taggart handed him some manuscript poems. "At first we read a few of them," Richmond wrote, "through mere kindness to the father; not thinking that so pure a gem had been hidden among these barren rocks ... they are the poetry of truth and are peculiar, because her sufferings are peculiarly her own."⁶ Richmond decided that the poems should be published, and he gave William "a small sum ... as the first subscription for the poems of his daughter, of whose gifts the fond father was justly proud."⁵

The Poems

Cynthia had attended school occasionally until she was nine, but most of her education came from her parents, who were both well read. She wrote that as a child she enjoyed making up stories and living in her imagination. When her health permitted, she read avidly—religious works, astronomy, stories, and poetry. She composed her poems at night, when she could not sleep, and memorized them. Many of her poems are several pages long; perhaps the mental effort required to compose and memorize them provided some distraction from her sleeplessness and pain. She later dictated them to her father.

Once Cynthia became ill, her world was limited to the cottage, the garden next to her window, her view of the ocean, the sun, and the wind. Insomnia gave her an unusual slant on the passage of time:

> Thus anxiously why watch the dawn
> And hope for morning light?
> When day to me is still the same
> As sad and dreary night ["A Solace," 1822, pp. 3–4].

But in a brighter moment:

> Can aught be brighter than the ray
> That bears the orient smile of day
> When the first beams of sunlight play
> On dew-bespangled flowers? ["Health," 1823, p. 16]

She was very much aware of the ocean and the winds and storms that so often beset the coastline. At night the wind "through the darkling branches sounds / an unremitting moan," while "the blue wave, swelling heaves,— / Its mournful murmurs tell" ("The Starry World," p. 23). Despite their ferocity, storms did not frighten her:

> Yet ocean doth no fear impart,
> But soothes my anguish-swollen heart,
> And calms my feverish brain.
> It seems a sympathizing friend
> That doth with mine its troubles blend,
> To mitigate my pain ["On a Storm," 1825].

Cynthia was not completely isolated. Her family was important to her—especially her parents. In addition to Betsey and Maria, who lived with her, she had two married sisters. Patience had married Thomas Rogers, and when she died, Rogers married her sister Ann. Patience had three daughters: Amarintha, Sarah, and Martha; Ann had a son John. Cynthia wrote poems for each of them, though twins Sarah and Martha had to share. The poems for the girls were written as if the child were speaking, while the poem for John was in the poet's voice.

At one time, friends had visited, but that did not continue. She was fully aware of the way others reacted to her pain:

> How sweetly friends in kindness smile,
> And boast affection true;
> But long attention weans their love,
> And makes their number few.
> When first affliction prostrates low,
> They weep, and wish relief;
> But should it prove beyond their power,
> Deny the hopeless grief.
> The sleepless night, the wretched day,
> To months and years prolonged
> Drive all one's pitying friends away,
> That once benignant thronged [pp. 42–43].

The poem that best shows her double approach to the outside world and her own physical suffering is "Ode to the Poppy." After describing its beauty and fragrance, she turns to the special meaning the poppy has for her:

> This magic flower
> In desperate hour
> A balsam mild shall yield,
> When the sad, sinking heart
> Feels every aid depart
> And every gate of hope forever sealed:
> Then still its potent charm
> Each agony disarm,
> And its all-healing power shall respite give,
> The frantic sufferer, then
> Convulsed and wild with pain,
> Shall own the sovereign remedy, and live.
> The dews of slumber, now,
> Rest on her aching brow;
> ....
> Then will Affection twine
> Around this kindly flower;
> And grateful memory keep,
> How, in the arms of sleep,
> Affliction lost its power [pp. 34–36].

Publication

James Richmond was true to his word. The first edition of Cynthia's poems appeared in 1834; a second edition was published later that year; and a third in 1848. By 1833, the family's fortunes had deteriorated further. William Taggart had sold the cottage, and the family was living in a small house purchased with his military pension (which would soon expire) and the charity of Samuel Ward, a New York banker. William died in 1833. His death was difficult for Cynthia: for a month, he had been unable to climb the stairs to visit her, and she could not leave her room. She wrote a poem, "To her father, supposed to be Dying," which she read to Richmond when he visited.

It is not clear who paid for the book's publication. The preface says only that publication was "undertaken at the suggestion of her friends," in the hope that it "will be the means,—not of ministering to the love of fame, but of affording to the afflicted daughter, in the way most grateful to her fine feelings, and, through her, to the other portions of the family, a very needful relief from the pressure of adverse fortune." Richmond was at pains to assert that the poems had value beyond charity: "Had the author been favored with but a common share of that most essential blessing, health, she would not now need a preface to commend her to the public attention, but would, in all probability, be enjoying that home of consideration and esteem for eminent talent and personal excellence, which we delight to manifest towards the distinguished female writers of our country."[7]

Nor do we have any information about the number of copies sold, although the fact of second and third editions suggests that it did well. The *American Ladies' Magazine* published a long review of the book in March 1835, which would have brought national attention. In any case, publication made many people aware of Cynthia and the Taggart family, and brought financial help beyond the sales of the book. One of the sisters told James Richmond's brother, "Since you and your brother were first at our dear cottage on the sea shore, we have been supplied as if the ravens had been sent to feed us."[8] One benefactor paid for Maria to live at the Bloomingdale Asylum, a private institution for the mentally ill in New York City.

Cynthia's mother died in 1841; Cynthia died in 1849; and Betsey lived until 1880. They were buried in the family cemetery on the cottage grounds. There is no record of Maria's death.

Vermont

18

Shirley Jackson

It was no accident that the dustjackets of Shirley Jackson's best-known books featured pictures of houses. In her stories and novels, houses are sometimes settings and sometimes characters, but they are always important. She used her own home as the setting for her stories about the joys and trials of family life, while her fiction took place in the kinds of houses that had fascinated her from childhood.

Heritage

Houses were in Shirley Jackson's genes. Her great-great-grandfather, Samuel C. Bugbee, designed four lavish houses on Nob Hill for San Francisco's robber barons. Built in the 1870s, each had a distinctive style, and all were the scenes of drama: the Leland Stanfords abandoned their mansion after the death of their fifteen-year-old son; David Colton died after falling off a horse, and the house was abandoned after his daughter was twice widowed; after a dispute with a neighbor, Charles Crocker built a forty-foot spite wall; Richard Tobin's mansion burned down. Then the remaining houses burned in 1906, after the San Francisco earthquake. When she was working on *The Haunting of Hill House,* Jackson asked her mother to send photos of the houses Samuel Bugbee had designed. Her only comment on the Crocker house was that she was glad it hadn't survived the earthquake. Jackson's grandfather, Maxwell Bugbee, also practiced in the Bay Area, designing Beaux-Arts apartment buildings and suburban homes more on the scale of the houses in her novels. Shirley's mother sent her a photo of one of them, the Gray house in Ross, California, and it may have provided ideas for Hill House.[1]

Shirley grew up in the area where her grandfather worked, near Burlingame, in a house that he designed.[2] Her parents were affluent, and her mother was very conscious of appearances. She fretted about Shirley's weight, hair, clothes, friends, and manners. She let her daughter know that she did not live up to expectations. She was not dainty, or stylish, or even tidy. As Shirley's daughter Joanne explained, "Geraldine wanted a pretty little girl, and what she got was a lumpish redhead."[3] Shirley's brother Barry, two years younger, was handsome, blond, and athletic—and immediately their mother's favorite. Her mother's criticism, constant and harshly phrased, continued throughout her life. Shirley once told her daughter Sarah, "The first book you have to write to get back at your parents; the book you always had in you. Once you get that out of your way, you can start writing books." Her first novel, *The Road Through the Wall*, is set in a community like Burlingame, full of prejudice and spiteful gossip. In her notes for the book, Jackson drew a map of the community and put the names of real neighbors in parentheses after the names of the characters.[4]

Moving East

In 1932, when Shirley was 16 and about to enter her senior year in high school, the family moved to Rochester, New York. It was the worst possible time for her to move. Brighton High School was small, with only sixty students in each class. She was the new girl—overweight, with unruly hair, and eccentrically dressed. She was rejected by a sorority but made friends among the other girls who didn't quite fit in. Despite mediocre grades, she was accepted at the women's campus of University of Rochester, where she lived in a dormitory and published her first short story. She neglected her classes, preferring to write and spend time with friends. She was, unsurprisingly, excessively self-critical and began to experience the mood swings that would plague her throughout her life. During her sophomore year, she lived at home, subject to her mother's carping about her weight and appearance. She failed several courses and in June was asked to leave the university. She spent the next year at home severely depressed, but writing a thousand words a day.

Committed to a literary career, Jackson applied to Syracuse University, which had an excellent reputation for journalism and creative writing. She quickly made friends among her fellow writers, including Stanley Edgar Hyman. He was two years younger than she, and a Jew from New York City with left-wing political views, guaranteed to displease her parents (as she would displease his). They met in 1938 and were married in 1940 at a friend's apartment in New York. Hyman had won the *New Republic* college writing contest, earning a summer job in the magazine's New York office. They rented an apartment at 215 West 13th Street in Greenwich Village.[5]

Money was scarce. Hyman wrote short pieces for *The New Yorker* and book reviews for several other magazines, none of which paid well. At one point, he collected unemployment. Jackson took odd jobs, including a stint at Macy's department store at Christmas—an experience that she wrote about in the *New Republic*. In 1941 they rented a cabin in New Hampshire for only $100 a year, which was probably its greatest attraction. They had no gas or electricity, and the only running water was in the kitchen sink. It was a cold walk to the outhouse. In January 1942, the winter weather drove them back to Syracuse.

Hyman was unfaithful and was untouched by the pain he caused Jackson. She told him: "We should never have gotten married and I keep thinking that now we are we have to make the best of it—but doesn't a man ever get ashamed to think that the only way he can look like a man before his wife is to say cruel things to her until she cries." And Jackson was pregnant. In her journal she wrote, "Maybe when I have my baby, I can talk to it and it will love me and it won't grow up mean."[6]

When Laurence (Laurie) Jackson Hyman was born, on October 3, 1942, his parents were living in Woodside, Queens, though a year later they would move to the second floor of a narrow three-story brick house at 36 Grove Street, in Greenwich Village.[7] Hyman was hired full-time at *The New Yorker* in July, and he failed his army physical because of poor eyesight, avoiding the draft. They were both beginning to make names for themselves in the New York literary scene. Jackson, busy with a new baby, got little writing done, but in December *The New Yorker* accepted two of her stories, paying her the equivalent of two months of Hyman's salary. In 1943, she sold eight stories to a variety of magazines, earning $800; in 1944, she sold ten, including six to *The New Yorker*.

Domesticity

In the spring of 1945, Hyman was offered a teaching job at Bennington College in Vermont. Founded in 1932 as a small women's college, Bennington emphasized creativity and the arts. Most faculty families lived near the campus, but Jackson and Hyman rented an 1835 Greek Revival house at 12 Prospect Street in the village of North Bennington. Even though they were expecting a second child that fall, its 16 rooms were more than they needed. Jackson told a friend that "just mapping it out for the quickest route to the bathroom has been a problem."[8] The rent was low because it had sat vacant for several years. When the previous owner died, it had been left untouched, down to the doughnuts on the breakfast table. The house—with its four columns rising two stories from the porch—became identified with Jackson when a drawing based on it appeared on the dust-jacket for *Life Among the Savages*.

The house would have been a challenge for anyone, but although Jackson had learned to cook, she had no other domestic skills and little interest in developing them. Hyman complained but did not help. Friends remembered that the babies' diapers were changed infrequently, the cats left puddles, and the house was dirty and cluttered. Their neighbors were critical of Jackson's housekeeping, and they were uncomfortable about having a Jewish neighbor who invited a Black man to visit. Hyman and Jackson had become friendly with Ralph Ellison when they lived in New York, and he often stayed with them. He wrote parts of *Invisible Man* at their house. Ellison likely was the first Black person their neighbors had ever seen, and Hyman may have been the first Jew. Many of the stories that Jackson wrote in the 1940s dealt at some level with antisemitism, racism, and intolerance of any sort of difference. Her parents and their friends had displayed all of these biases; since her marriage she had been on the receiving end. She always identified with the outsider.

Housekeeping was a source of friction. Although he did not help

Shirley Jackson's house at 12 Prospect Street in North Bennington, where she lived from 1945 to 1949, and where she wrote "The Lottery." *Photograph by Rob Woolmington, the Fund for North Bennington.*

around the house, Hyman was fussy about his surroundings. His desk had to be immaculate, with his typewriter, pencils, paper, and books in exactly the right places. Jackson once told a friend, "Whenever I am very mad at Stanley, I go into his study and move one of his ashtrays one quarter inch to the side."[9] Hyman, for his part, refused to enter Jackson's study because her pictures were crooked and her books were not alphabetized.

Teaching at a women's college presented temptations to a man accustomed to infidelity. Although he apparently avoided sexual relationships with current students, he enjoyed the company of admiring young women. In *Raising Demons* Jackson wrote, "By the end of the first semester, what I wanted to do most in the world was invite a few of my husband's students over for tea and drop them down the well."[10] Hyman's contract was not renewed, and in spring of 1946 he was unemployed.

Minimizing both housekeeping and the responsibilities of a traditional faculty wife gave Jackson time to write. By 1947 she had completed *The Road Through the Wall,* a novel set in the California town of her childhood, fulfilling the first part of a two-book contract with Farrar, Straus that included a $1,500 advance. Having gotten back at her parents, she did indeed start writing books.

She also got back at her parents by being a very different kind of mother. Each of her children was temperamentally unlike the others: their individual personalities show up clearly in *Raising Demons*. Each was creative, articulate, and outspoken. Jackson loved them, and they knew they were loved. When necessary, she defended them ferociously against the outside world—when Laurie got into a fight or was hit by a car, when Sarah was abused at school, and on countless minor occasions. Their clothes might not always have been ironed properly, but they were well fed, much loved, and encouraged in whatever they wished to do. The family ate dinner together and read afterwards—for some time, the reading was a nightly Bible chapter, undoubtedly discussed as literature rather than gospel. Jackson read to the children at bedtime—usually stories of fantasy—and on Sunday afternoons they played poker. Their family life was far from perfect: Hyman was absorbed in his teaching, and Jackson's emotional volatility did not provide the kind of stability that children often need. But the children's interests, imaginations, and explorations were encouraged, not only by their parents but also by their parents' many friends.

Fame

In April 1948, Jackson sent a story to *The New Yorker.* No one at the magazine claimed to understand it, but they all agreed that they should publish it. They sent Jackson a check for $675, and "The Lottery" appeared in the June 26 issue. Within a month, more than a hundred readers had sent letters expressing dismay or puzzlement, canceling their subscriptions, or asking bizarre questions. Jackson later offered a sample of the queries she received: "Will you please tell me the locale and the year of the custom?" "As a psychiatrist I am fascinated by the psychodynamic possibilities suggested by this anachronistic ritual." "Other strange old things happen in the Appalachian mountain villages, I'm told." She told one journalist, "I suppose I hoped, by setting a particularly brutal ancient rite in the present and in my own village, to shock the story's readers with a graphic dramatization of the pointless violence and general inhumanity in their own lives"—an explanation that could not have sat well with her neighbors.[11]

Shirley Jackson reading *Life Among the Savages* to two of her children, Joanne and Barry, in the living room of the house at 66 Main Street. *Photograph © Laurence Jackson Hyman, ca. 1956.*

Only a month after "The Lottery," *Mademoiselle* published "Charles," her first—and very successful—attempt at domestic humor. Her stories of family life—later collected in *Life Among the Savages* and *Raising Demons*—might be thought of as Erma Bombeck with an edge. *Mademoiselle, Good Housekeeping,* and other popular magazines paid much higher fees than literary magazines, and the two collections sold better than almost all her novels. A third child, Sarah, was born that fall, her delivery described in "The Third Baby's the Easiest," published in *Harper's*.

To meet the obligations of her Farrar, Straus contract—and to capitalize on the notoriety of "The Lottery"—Jackson completed a short story collection, *The Lottery; or, The Adventures of James Harris,* published in April 1949. That fall, wanting to be closer to New York, and to have better schools for their children, the family moved to Saugatuck, Connecticut, near Westport. *Good Housekeeping* was paying Jackson a $1,500 advance each quarter for short stories, and Farrar, Straus advanced $3,000 for her next novel, *Hangsaman*. They could now afford to rent a five-bedroom Victorian house with a turret, a basement playroom for the children, and a garden with a playhouse, sandbox, and wading pool.[12] It was a great relief from the isolation of Vermont, with other writers—Peter DeVries, J.D. Salinger, Malcolm Cowley, and Ralph Ellison—living nearby and visiting. Jackson bought a 1940 Buick. Hyman, a true New Yorker, never learned to drive. Jackson learned, and driving gave her independence and, occasionally, an escape mechanism. She also hired household help, giving her more time for writing.

The publicists at Farrar, Straus presented Jackson as a busy homemaker who somehow found time to write stories, and she played along. Certainly that made sense for her women's magazine stories, but as a way of promoting her novels, it is misleading. It was probably true to the extent that, as she said, "all the time that I am making beds and doing dishes and driving to town for dancing shoes, I am telling myself stories." But another claim, that "fifty per cent of my life is spent washing and dressing the children, cooking, washing dishes and clothes, and mending," is surely an exaggeration. To present an acceptable public image, she was, in the words of her biographer Ruth Franklin, "bowing to stereotypes of the period."[13]

Jackson never became a typical suburban housewife, but she fell victim to one pitfall of the role. Concerned about her lifelong depression and anxiety, as well as her weight, she consulted a popular doctor who prescribed amphetamines (which controlled eating but aggravated anxiety) and tranquillizers (Miltown and, later Librium) to counter the anxiety. She continued to use and misuse prescription drugs for the rest of her life.

Hangsaman, published in April 1951, was not a critical or commercial success. Jackson continued to publish stories, and she received $1,000 for a television adaptation of "The Lottery," but Hyman had no reliable income. Their fourth child, Barry, was born that fall. When their lease was up, in spring 1952, they decided to move back to North Bennington. In 1953, Bennington offered Hyman a full-time teaching position, providing a stable income. But the money to buy the house where they would spend the rest of their lives came from *Life Among the Savages,* a collection of the magazine stories Jackson had written about her family. *Savages* was published in June 1953 and was on the *New York Times* best-seller list for 11 weeks. It was a selection of the Family Book Club and *Reader's Digest,* which together brought Jackson more than $8,000. The stories had taken place in the Prospect Street and Connecticut houses, but future adventures would take place at 66 Main Street.

Home

The new Vermont house, with 17 rooms and two staircases, was even larger than the old. It had been divided into four apartments, but the two sets of remaining tenants soon left. The attic became a library that held some of the family's thousands of books. Laurie, now 11, was developing impressive woodworking skills, and he built bookshelves in any space that could accommodate them. An ornate front porch ran across the front of the house; the kitchen ran the entire width of the house in back. Jackson described the house in a letter to a friend: "We have two magnificent rooms on one side which will be filled with bookcases, and make a lovely study, and a pleasant living room with a bay window, and a dining room and kitchen; upstairs, four bedrooms. Off the kitchen is a splendid pantry and utility room." To her parents, she explained, "We have two and a half acres of grounds, with nice old trees and a nice lawn, an enormous two-story barn full of pigeons ... the barn is our greatest blessing. It's almost as big as the house, and the kids have the whole upstairs for a play-room."[14]

It was a great house for parties, whether faculty gatherings where large amounts of alcohol were consumed, poker games for Hyman's friends, or dinner parties for local friends and visitors. Jackson was a good cook, but she did not allow either her cooking or her guests to distract her from her writing. One friend recalled, "We'd all be sitting at dinner and Shirley would excuse herself ... and retire to her room. Whenever she needed to write she wrote.... The ideas were churning, churning all the time. I had the sense she felt that if she didn't write them, she was going to lose them."[15]

The first book that Jackson wrote in the new house was *The Bird's Nest*, about a young woman with multiple personality disorder. After she finished it, she suffered a severe bout of depression, which did not lift despite the favorable reviews and the sale of movie rights. Her next project was a young adult book about the Salem witch trials commissioned by Random House. She was well read in the field, knew how to read the Tarot, and often suggested that she was a practicing witch. Her interpretation of the trials in *The Witchcraft of Salem Village* was not grounded in the supernatural, though: she saw the persecution as growing out of community conflict and the human impulse to find scapegoats. In "The Lottery," the scapegoat was chosen at random. In Salem, the targets were women who did not conform.

The house on Main Street next became the scene of *Raising Demons*, the sequel to *Life Among the Savages*. That first book of family stories had been a best seller at home and had been translated into French, German, Spanish, Italian, Polish, Norwegian, and Swedish. *Demons* was favorably

Shirley Jackson's house on Main Street, North Bennington, where she wrote her later novels. *Photograph by Rob Woolmington, the Fund for North Bennington.*

reviewed and sold well, though not at best-seller levels. Nevertheless, with royalties, magazine sales, and advances, Jackson's income for 1956 was nearly $15,000. Hyman's income was just under $10,000. Although she had been earning more than he for some time, it was Hyman who handled the money. Stories in *Demons* hinted not too subtly that he was stingy.

Haunted Houses

In 1957, Jackson completed her first novel in which a house is central. The house in *The Sundial* is surrounded by a stone wall to protect it from the expected apocalypse. If not literally haunted, it is eerie and afflicted with evil. Inside, a dysfunctional family and its hangers-on prepare for the end of the world by stocking up on increasingly bizarre supplies. At the end, it is unclear whether they survive—or indeed, whether the world does. Jackson may have been thinking about protecting her real home. She discovered that their younger daughter, Sarah, had been physically punished and threatened by her teacher. Jackson, together with some of the other parents whose children had been mistreated, demanded that the teacher be fired. Parents who had known the teacher for decades supported her, and they prevailed. She was allowed to finish out the school year and retire on schedule. Jackson and her family received hate mail, found swastikas drawn on their windows, and had garbage dumped in their yard. A wall would have seemed a desirable feature.

The Sundial was the last novel that Jackson had published by Farrar, Straus. She had become increasingly dissatisfied with their editing and marketing. Just before retiring, her agent, Bernice Baumgarten, arranged a contract with Viking Press. Her new publisher paid her a $15,000 advance for two novels and a collection of short stories. She immediately began researching haunted houses, amassing newspaper accounts of ghosts and poltergeists. She remembered a house not far from Burlingame that belonged to the Winchester Firearms heiress. It was rumored to be haunted by the ghosts of people who had been killed by their guns. On January 14, 1958, she wrote to her parents:

> Do you remember the Winchester house? and can you, do you think, get me any information about it? or pictures and information (particularly pictures) of any other big old California gingerbread houses?
> The reason for this is my new book; it is to be about a haunted house, and I can't seem to find anything around here; all the old New England houses are the kind of square, classical type which wouldn't be haunted in a million years....
> I am all wound up in houses right now, and spent yesterday in the library reading old architecture books. It occurred to me that perhaps mother might have, somewhere, some of my grandfather's old books, but I suppose it isn't likely.[16]

A month later, she told her new agent, Carol Brandt, "Local people tell me that there is a house in a little town about fifty miles away which is haunted. The people there see the ghost and talk to her. They do not ordinarily encourage visitors but everyone thinks that if I wrote them and told them I was doing a book they would invite me to come and meet their ghost. I am not going to do it because I am scared."[17]

Jackson's research had given her ideas about what a haunted house should look like, but Hill House was architecturally unique. Unlike those early New England houses, with their neat right angles and predictable layouts, it is off-kilter: "a maniac juxtaposition, a badly turned angle, some chance meeting of roof and sky, turned Hill House into a place of despair."[18] The rooms are arranged oddly, so that it is difficult to find even those rooms that you have already visited. Some rooms are surrounded entirely by other rooms, with no windows or doors to the outside. Even the rooms with windows are dark. Many of the rooms have no clear purpose. The doors close unpredictably. And of course, it has been the scene of many deaths. The novel has eight human characters (including two sinister servants), but the main character is the house itself. Terrifying noises, unexplained cold, mysterious writing on the wall, an overwhelming sense of menace—all these are attributable to the house, not to any visiting specters or poltergeists. And what perhaps makes the book truly a horror story is the lack of resolution: we are left with no explanation of the phenomena we have witnessed.

Hill House paid off the mortgage on 66 Main Street, as well as all the couple's debts. With the support of Carol Brandt and the Viking publicity team, the novel had advance sales of 8,000 copies before its October 1959 publication. Jackson received $17,500 for the *Reader's Digest* edition and $67,500 for the movie rights. The novel was a National Book Award finalist. Jackson bought a new washer and dryer, drapes, and a player piano. At the beginning of the new year, she began work on *We Have Always Lived in the Castle.*

The castle—in reality, just a large house—is the ancestral home of two sisters, an elderly uncle, and a cat. In the sisters' imagination, though, it *is* a castle: a secure defense against enemies. The rest of the family is dead—poisoned at dinner some years earlier. The older sister, Constance, was acquitted of the crime; the younger, Mary Catherine, "Merricat," was only 12 at the time. Like Hill House, the Castle is the source of fear and rumors, its inhabitants hated and taunted. There is no suggestion of the supernatural, but it is not a house where any reader would choose to spend the night or, probably, eat dinner. Jackson doesn't provide a detailed description of the house, emphasizing instead its contents: layer upon layer of china, silver, furniture, linens, even preserves brought by generations of brides, with nothing ever discarded. Meals, too, are described—including tea offered to visitors—and it is hard not to wonder whether everyone will rise from the table. Even more than *The Haunting of Hill House, Castle* is a novel of terror and suspense.

It took Jackson more than two years to write *We Have Always Lived in the Castle,* years fraught with physical and mental anguish. She had frequent attacks of colitis, debilitating and painful, which made it uncomfortable for her to travel. She also developed agoraphobia, which added to the difficulty of leaving the house. Yet when she finished the book, she found the strength to participate in the extensive publicity campaign that Viking had planned, giving newspaper and radio interviews. The reviews were glowing, and the book spent 11 weeks on the *New York Times* best-seller list between November 1962 and January 1963. The *New York Times* reviewer said that "most people will succumb at once to its dark enchantment. Dinner, phone calls and duties can't seem very important until it's all over and one can relax and worry about what it all means." Writing for *Esquire,* Dorothy Parker described Jackson as a "leader in the field of beautifully written, quiet, cumulative shudders. This novel brings back all my faith in terror and death. I can say no higher of it and her."[19]

The novel found its way into a local newspaper when the F.B.I. arrested one of their ten most wanted at a nearby inn. As Jackson wrote to her daughter Sally, "What they found was a copy of Merricat on his bedside table, with a bookmark showing that he was about halfway through. It belonged to the owners of the inn, who refused to let the F.B.I. take it away with his other stuff, so the poor book was tested for fingerprints and given back. Many people in Arlington think it would be a nice gesture if I sent him another copy, autographed, and I think I will, as soon as I find out which prison he is in, and which alias to autograph it to." She also wrote, "I no longer go out of the house."[20]

Time named *Castle* one of the ten best novels of the year and published an article about Jackson with a photograph. Her mother wrote perhaps the cruelest letter she could devise. Rather than congratulate her daughter on her success, she criticized the photograph: "If you don't care what you look like or care about your appearance why don't you do something about it for your children's sake—and your husband's.... I have been so sad all morning about what you have allowed yourself to look like.... You were and I guess still are a very wilful child." Jackson wrote: "I wish you would stop telling me that my husband and children are ashamed of me. If they are, they have concealed it very skillfully.... I have a happy and productive life, I have many good friends, I have considerable stature in my profession, and if I decide to make any changes in my manner of living, it will not be because you have nagged me into it. You can say this is 'wilful' if you like, but surely at my age I have a right to live as I please, and I have just had enough of the unending comments on my appearance and my faults." She never mailed the letter.[21]

For the next year, Jackson wrote only a diary. Agoraphobia, nightmares, and panic attacks sent her to a psychiatrist, who helped her gradually to leave the house, one destination at a time. By the beginning of 1964, she was able to write again: three short stories about houses and home were finished by the end of the year. She even began a comic novel, *Come Along with Me*. In February 1965, she became ill with pneumonia but recovered well enough to undertake a spring lecture tour. Exhausted, she spent June and July at home.

On August 6, 1965, Shirley Jackson wrote to Carol Brandt that she would soon be leaving on a wonderful journey.[22] Two days later, when Hyman went upstairs where she was taking her usual afternoon nap, he could not wake her. She had died in her sleep of a coronary occlusion. The *New York Times* obituary acknowledged the duality of her work: "She could describe the delights and turmoils of ordinary domestic life with detached hilarity; and she could, with cryptic symbolism, write a tenebrous horror story in the Gothic mold in which abnormal behavior seemed perilously ordinary. In either genre she wrote with remarkable tautness and economy of style, and her choice of words and phrases was unerring in building a story's mood." But the newspaper took her at her word when she portrayed herself as an ordinary housewife who took time out from washing dishes to dash off a story, with the subheading "Housework Came First." No one who knew her, whether close friend or suspicious neighbor, would have believed that.

19

Grace Paley

For most of her life, Grace Paley lived in New York City—in the Bronx and later Greenwich Village. In middle age, she began dividing her time between her apartment in the Village and a house in rural Thetford, Vermont, that she shared with her second husband. The city—its people and their voices—are at the heart of her stories. The country finds its way into her poetry. The stories set in those city apartments are not provincial. Characters' lives are affected by events and ideas far beyond the city limits, and their conversations delve into far-ranging topics. Paley herself quickly ventured beyond her home onto the street, into the neighborhood, the city, and eventually the world. Her political activism and her writing expanded together.

The Bronx

Grace Goodside was born into a trilingual, three-generation family. Her parents, Isaac and Manya Gutzeit, emigrated from Russia in 1906 and changed their name to Goodside. They were both 21, both recently released from exile as political dissidents, and expecting their first child. They settled in lower Manhattan and then moved to West 116th Street, where Isaac's mother and two sisters joined them. They spoke Russian at home, and Isaac's mother also spoke Yiddish. She was the only member of the family who attended synagogue. Isaac worked as a photographer, and Manya as a photo retoucher, and both soon learned English. Only eight years after arriving in the United States with little education, Isaac was admitted to medical school. Upon graduating in 1918, he moved the family to the Bronx, where he set up his practice. By then they had two children: Victor, born in 1907, and Jeanne, born a year later.

Their brick house at 1538 Hoe Avenue, between 172nd and 173rd streets, was divided between Isaac's first-floor office and 12 rooms above.[1] Manya was Isaac's receptionist, assistant, and nurse. They both worked long hours while his mother took care of the children. Isaac's sisters also worked. The Goodsides welcomed new immigrants, whether related or not. The house was always full, the dinner table crowded. Isaac and Manya both loved music, and as soon as they could afford it, they bought a Victrola and began to collect classical records. Friends and neighbors were invited to "musicales," where their collection provided the entertainment.

Born on December 11, 1922, Grace was a very late addition to the household. Victor was 16 and would leave home when Grace was a toddler; Jeanne married in 1929 and moved to her own home. From the age of seven, Grace was an only child, surrounded by adults. Her mother was no longer working and was able to spend more time with her than she had with the older children. Grace listened to conversations among family members, visiting friends and neighbors, and newly arrived immigrants—the voices that would find their way into her writing (she understood and spoke Russian as well as English). The neighborhood, too, was the setting of many of her stories: the mothers leaning out of their apartment windows to give orders to children playing on the sidewalk or to share news with neighbors, the children going to and from school, political discussions on stoops, the visible poverty of the Great Depression, and anxieties about the approaching world war: "There is a certain place where dumbwaiters boom, doors slam, dishes crash; every window is a mother's mouth bidding the street shut up, go skate somewhere else, come home. My voice is the loudest."[2]

Grace had learned to read by the time she was three and was always an avid reader. She wrote poetry, which her sister Jeanne saved. She was attractive, vivacious, and adventurous, popular with both girls and boys. But she hated school and was not a good student, performing poorly in every subject except English. Her parents were unhappy about her attitude toward school and her radical political views. As she explained, "In this country, they seemed to believe, education, once struggled for, came first—then socialism." Their political differences were to some extent generational. Manya and Isaac had been revolutionaries in Russia, but, as Grace wrote, "despite its adherence to capitalism, prejudice, and lynching, my father said we were lucky to be here in this America."[3] Her parents were reluctant to criticize the country that had given them asylum, opportunity, and success. Their American-born daughter felt no such constraints.

Grace continued to write poetry. Despite her poor grades, she was admitted to Hunter College, but she didn't stay long. Later she enrolled in a poetry class at the New School for Social Research, founded in 1919 as a center for progressive thought. The class was taught by the poet W.H. Auden, whose advice transformed her writing. He pointed out that she was writing like an Englishman, with vocabulary and cadences that were not hers. He urged her to use the language she spoke and heard around her. He gave her permission to write like herself and to see the world she lived in as a worthy subject. She heard that, too, as permission to write about women and their life experiences.

One talent that Grace did not inherit from her parents was an ear for music. When she was nine, she was practicing a song that she was to perform in a play put on by her Socialist youth group. Her mother, who had perfect pitch, stopped her: "Gracie, darling, you can't sing. You know you can't hold the tune…. You'll make a fool of yourself. People will laugh." Grace skipped the performance.[4] She did have piano lessons, though, and enjoyed the family musicales. One of the music lovers who attended those evenings was Jess Paley. They fell in love and married in 1942, when Grace was 19.

War and Work

Jess Paley joined the U.S. Signal Corps, and Grace traveled with him around the country—to New Jersey, Illinois, Florida, and North Carolina. In each place, she found work of some sort—"door opener and telephone answerer," typist, payroll clerk, babysitter, secretary. When Jess was sent to the South Pacific for eighteen months, she returned to New York to live with her family and took on secretarial jobs. In the 1960s, she summarized her feelings about this work: "But during all those jobs, once I was married and after I had children, most of the day I was a housewife. That is the poorest-paying job a woman can hold. But most women feel gypped by life if they don't get a chance at it. And all during those jobs and all the time I was a housewife, I was a writer. The whole meaning of my life, which was jammed until midnight with fifteen different jobs and places, was writing. It took me a long time to know that, but I know it now."[5]

Manya Goodside had been diagnosed with breast cancer in 1935, but she had not told her children. She died in 1944, only a few months after Grace returned home. Isaac sold his practice and the house, and he, his mother, and his sister moved to the West Bronx. He lived there until his death in 1973. Grace, always fond of her father, visited often. Jess returned from the war and began to work as a freelance photographer. He and Grace moved to Greenwich Village to restart their married life, their careers, and a family.

The Village

Their first apartment was on 11th Street between Sixth and Seventh avenues. It was only one and a half rooms on the first floor of a three-story building. Wrought-iron railings across the windows created a tiny balcony where their first child, Nora, born in 1949, learned to walk. In 1951, when Danny was born, they moved across the street to the grandly named Rhinelander Gardens, where they were the building's "supers," in charge of maintenance. It was an old, decrepit building. The children slept on a screened porch with a cement floor that filled with water when it rained unless they pulled the plug from a central drain. When the Rhinelander was torn down, they moved to a building at 15th Street and Ninth Avenue. During the day, the street was busy with truck traffic, but on the weekends and at night it was empty, so the children could roller skate and ride their bikes. The building was rundown, but it was all they could afford. They lived there for five years until 1960, when the family's fortunes began to improve.

Jess was getting more assignments, and though that meant a lot of traveling it also meant more income. And Grace had what she called "two small lucks": "I became sick enough for the children to remain in Greenwich House After School until suppertime for several weeks, but not so sick that I couldn't sit at our living-room table to write or type all day." She finished three stories. The second "small luck" came when a neighbor came to pick up his children. He said that his ex-wife, a friend of Grace's, had asked him to read her stories. The neighbor was Ken McCormick, editor-in-chief at Doubleday. "A couple of weeks later," she wrote, "he came for the children again. This time he sat down at our kitchen table (in the same room as our living-room table). He asked if I could write seven more stories like the three he'd read. He said he'd publish the book."[6] Grace did not usually write quickly, and she always rewrote several times. But she turned out seven more stories, and in 1960 Doubleday published *The Little Disturbances of Man*. Reviews were glowing, and Grace's family began to take her writing seriously. Many of the characters in these stories would reappear in later collections, growing and changing, creating their own world.

The Paleys could now afford to move back to their old block on Eleventh Street, this time to a lovely old building called the Unadilla. Their apartment was on the second floor of the six-story building. There were tall trees behind, and a new grammar school next door. The apartment was big enough for each child to have a bedroom. Grace's sister Jeanne said that "she had a very disorganized household. Very disorganized. Nothing was in its place. Everything—even the children—was out of order. There were always a million people in the house."[7] They weren't there because Grace was a writer. They were there because, like her, they had become involved in the affairs of the neighborhood and the nation. It was, after all, the sixties.

Activism

Paley's stories grew out of her family and neighborhood. So did her activism. Washington Square Park was the center of Greenwich Village life, where children played, mothers gathered with strollers and toddlers, and apartment dwellers socialized. City buses used the square as a place to turn around and gradually moved farther and farther into the park. Paley was among the neighbors who mobilized to protect their shared space, and by 1964 the park had been closed to traffic. The city next decided to ban singing in the park. Paley's children joined her and guitar-playing folk singers in a protest that turned violent, and a police officer grabbed Danny. He remembered: "My mother, who was about half of his height, pulled me away, pushed the cop and said, 'Don't you ever touch my kid!' And she said it in such a way that he backed off immediately ... and then she gathered together with other people and they defeated that ordinance."[8] When the park was redesigned in 1970, it included performance spaces and open areas that hosted numerous protests.

Nora Paley, too, protested. For her, the issue was civil defense drills. In the 1950s, children were taught to "duck and cover," hiding under desks in school basements to prepare for atomic war. Nora "refused to do it. It was the first action I ever initiated.... That was something I decided to do myself, but it came out of my knowing something that the other kids maybe didn't know—I knew about it because it was talked about in my house."[9]

Paley was soon involved in protests that took on issues beyond the Village: the war in Vietnam, civil rights, women's rights, pacifism, and environmentalism. All these issues were connected to the basic values she believed in: peace, justice, and human rights. For the rest of her life, she showed up for marches, sit-ins, conferences, and fact-finding missions. She was arrested often and spent six days in the New York Women's House of Detention for an offense that a fellow inmate described: "You got six days for sitting down front of a horse? Cop on the horse? Horse step on you? Jesus in hell, cops gettin crazier and stupider and meaner." The worst part of that imprisonment was not being allowed paper, pen, or pencil. She "was suffering a kind of frustration, a sickness in the way claustrophobia is a sickness—this paper-and-penlessness was a terrible pain in the area of my heart, a nausea."[10]

Paley was a highly visible activist. She was a charismatic speaker, and despite her diminutive size she was easily recognized. Her prominence led to a trip to Vietnam in 1969, as one of several nonviolent antiwar activists sent by the U.S. State Department to bring home three prisoners of war. In 1973, she was a delegate to the World Peace Congress in Moscow, where she spoke Russian with dissidents. She later traveled to China, Nicaragua, and El Salvador. At a dinner given by the War Resisters League in honor of her 65th birthday in 1987, she reminded her audience that "the world still has to be saved—every day."[11]

Teaching and Writing

Paley also needed to earn a living. She began teaching, first at Columbia and then at Sarah Lawrence. Teaching responsibilities, children, and activism inspired her imagination, and those experiences would find their way into her stories. But they left little time to write those stories. Her sister, Jeanne, hoped that someday Grace would have time "to sit down, alone every day, to write," and Nora felt that "she should have had a door to close and be behind it."[12] Instead, she wrote during meetings, between classes, on trains and buses, in spare moments here and there. A few stories appeared in the *Atlantic, Esquire,* and literary magazines, but her second collection of stories, *Enormous Changes at the Last Minute,* was not published until fifteen years after her first, and *Later the Same Day* appeared ten years later, along with *Leaning Forward,* her first published collection of poems.

The Little Disturbances of Man had earned Paley national recognition in the form of a coveted Guggenheim Award in 1961 and a grant from the National Endowment for the Arts in 1966. In 1980, with two critically praised collections, she was elected to the American Academy of Arts and Letters. In 1985, her third collection, *Later the Same Day,* won the PEN/Faulkner Prize. In 1987 she was awarded a senior fellowship in the Literary Program of the National Endowment for the Arts. National recognition did not change her loyalty to her neighborhood. When in 1986 she was named the first State Author of New York, she said, "The only nicer thing maybe for me would be if I got an award from my block."[13] In 2003, this quintessentially New York writer was named Poet Laureate of Vermont—a result of enormous changes in her personal life.

Life in the Country

In the late 1960s, the Paleys' marriage began to fall apart. Grace was busy with teaching and demonstrations, and Jess, who disapproved of Grace's activism, was traveling a lot. The children were nearly grown. In 1972, Grace divorced Jess and married Bob Nichols, a fellow writer and Village activist. They had known each other since the fight with the city over Washington Square Park, in which Nichols—a landscape architect—had played a leading role. Although she kept her apartment on 11th Street, Paley began spending more time in the country. Nichols had a small two-story house in Thetford, Vermont, that had belonged to his parents. The house had wide-plank wood floors, and the living room was heated by a coal-burning stove. The views of woods and mountains were spectacular. Paley wrote downstairs, and Nichols wrote upstairs in a workroom that included a bathtub. For a New York apartment dweller, living in a house meant a new kind of responsibility. Instead of calling the "super" when something breaks, Paley noted, you are left on your own to worry about freezing pipes, "keeping the mud and hay out of the house, and stacking the wood in the woodshed. There is also stuffing newspapers and rags into the cracks and chinks that each new descent of temperature exposes."[14]

Paley's stories stayed in the city. She couldn't write Vermont stories, she explained: "I don't have the lingo for it. I don't have the language for it." There was no streetscape. In fact, there was no street. The house was at the end of a dirt road, off a numbered state road, and at 55 she had to learn

Grace Paley writing in the kitchen of the house in Thetford, Vermont, that she shared with her second husband, Bob Nichols, from 1972 until her death. *Photograph by Matthew Thorsen.*

to drive. She did write poetry, though, and she of course involved herself in local and national affairs, including demonstrations against the Gulf War and against the Seabrook Nuclear Power Plant in New Hampshire. She conceded, though, that she missed New York demonstrations: "Vigiling in a shopping center in New Hampshire is not quite the same."[15]

In 1998, Paley published a collection of essays, *Just as I Thought*, which is the closest she came to autobiography or memoir. In one of the essays, "Upstaging Time," she approaches the question of aging. Her mirror tells her that she is older, but not *old*. And if being old means stepping back, bowing out, or not paying attention, she was never old. In 2002, she was diagnosed with breast cancer, which she fought for five years. In an interview given the year she died, she was railing against the war in Iraq and getting ready for a sit-in in her congressman's office. Asked what she hoped for her grandchildren, whose pictures were on the wall, she said, "It would be a world where all of my grandchildren—you saw two of them are black, not white—could feel at home in their world. I know when those children grow up, they're going to face some hard things. So it would be a world without militarism and racism and greed—and where women don't have to fight for their place in the world." Asked for advice, she just said, "It's important to pay attention to what's going on in the world."[16]

Chapter Notes

Chapter 1

For the details of Keller's life, I have relied on Dorothy Herrmann, *Helen Keller: A Life* (New York: Knopf, 1998), and Keller's own writings: *The Story of My Life: The Restored Edition*, ed. James Berger (1903; New York: Modern Library, 2003), which includes letters and other materials; *Selected Writings*, ed. Kim E. Nielsen (New York: New York University Press, 2005); and *The World I Live In & Optimism* (1908, 1903; Mineola, N.Y.: Dover, 2009).

1. The house and gardens, 300 North Commons Street West, Tuscumbia, AL 35674, have been restored and are open to visitors.
2. Quoted in Herrmann, *Helen Keller*, 31.
3. Evaline H. Keller to Alexander Graham Bell, Apr. 20, 1887, images at www.loc.gov. This account differs from Helen Keller's version in *The Story of My Life*, 15–16. Evaline's version, a contemporary account by an adult, is probably more accurate.
4. Keller, *Story of My Life*, 20.
5. Quoted in Herrmann, *Helen Keller*, 53.
6. Sullivan to Anagnos, quoted in Herrmann, *Helen Keller*, 82; Keller, *Story of My Life*, 51–52.
7. Keller, *Story of My Life*, 54–55.
8. Keller, *Story of My Life*, 59; *The Youth's Companion*, January 4, 1894, 3.
9. Gilman quoted in Herrmann, *Helen Keller*, 116.
10. Copeland quoted in Herrmann, *Helen Keller*, 131.
11. Keller and Sullivan sold the house in 1917 to the Jordan Marsh department store, for the use of female employees in need of rest. A residence for men was added later. It has since been divided into apartments.
12. Helen Keller, *Midstream: My Later Life* (1929), excerpted in *Selected Writings*, 137; Nella Braddy Henney, quoted in Herrmann, *Helen Keller*, 150; Macy quoted in Herrmann, 155.
13. Keller, *Midstream*, 138.
14. Keller, *The World I Live In*, in *The World I Live In & Optimism*, 1, 28, xi.
15. Keller, *Midstream*, 144, 145.
16. In the 1920s the address was changed to 71–11 112th Street; the house burned down after Keller's death.
17. In 1921, Polly Thomson took Sullivan's place in the performances. See Herrmann, *Helen Keller*, 221–28, for a full account of the vaudeville act. Quotations on 222, 223.
18. Quoted in Herrmann, *Helen Keller*, 257.
19. Clark to Keller, November 20, 1939, quoted in David Serlin, "'Yours Is a Different Understanding of Architecture': Helen Keller's House in Easton, Connecticut," afb.org. The house is a private residence.

Chapter 2

For the facts of Stowe's life I have relied on Milton Rugoff, *The Beechers: An American Family in the Nineteenth Century* (New York: Harper & Row, 1981); Joan D. Hedrick, *Harriet Beecher Stowe: A Life* (New York: Oxford University Press, 1994); Barbara A. White, *The Beecher Sisters* (New Haven, CT: Yale University Press, 2003); and Philip McFarland, *Loves of Harriet Beecher Stowe* (New York: Grove Press, 2007).

Notes—Chapter 3

1. The house, at 2950 Gilbert Avenue, is being restored to its appearance at the time of the Beechers' residence and is open to visitors by appointment. For a detailed account of the house, from its construction through its many alterations and current restoration, see "Discover the History—Harriet Beecher Stowe House," stowehousecincy.org.

2. Calvin to Harriet, spring 1842, Harriet to Calvin, n.d., quoted in Charles Edward Stowe, *Life of Harriet Beecher Stowe Compiled from Her Letters and Journals* (Boston: Houghton Mifflin, 1889), 102, 104.

3. Quotation in C. E. Stowe, *Life*, 72.

4. Charles Dudley Warner, "The Story of *Uncle Tom's Cabin*," *Atlantic Monthly* 78 (Sept. 1896): 312–13; quotations from C. E. Stowe, *Life*, 145.

5. The house is now used for college offices, but one room features an exhibit about Harriet and is open to the public. For the history of the house from its construction to the present, see "History of the House" at www.bowdoin.edu. Harriet's own account of the installation of the sink can be found in C. E. Stowe, *Life*, 138–39. Quotation from Harriet to Calvin, December 29, 1850, in C. E. Stowe, *Life*, 147.

6. Harriet to Calvin, quoted in Hedrick, *Harriet Beecher Stowe*, 194.

7. John Andrew Jackson, *The Experience of a Slave in South Carolina* (London: Passmore & Alabaster, 1862), 32; C. E. Stowe, *Life*, 149.

8. Catharine Beecher to Mary Beecher Perkins, September 27, 1851, quoted in Hedrick, *Harriet Beecher Stowe*, 221.

9. David S. Reynolds, *Mightier Than the Sword:* Uncle Tom's Cabin *and the Battle for America* (New York: W. W. Norton, 2012), 126; Thomas Desjardin, *Joshua L. Chamberlain: The Life in Letters of a Great Leader of the American Civil War* (Oxford, U.K.: Osprey Publishing, 2012), 10.

10. Henry Wadsworth Longfellow, Journal, February 24, 1853, in Samuel L. Longfellow, *Life of Henry Wadsworth Longfellow*, 3 vols. (Boston: Ticknor, 1886), 2:233; Rugoff, *The Beechers*, 318.

11. Andover Historic Preservation, "80 Bartlet Street," https://preservation.mtl.org. The house has since been altered several times and moved. It is now used as faculty and student housing.

12. Hedrick, *Harriet Beecher Stowe*, 300–05. For the genesis and debunking of the Lincoln story, see Daniel R. Vollaro, "Lincoln, Stowe, and the 'Little Woman/Great War' Story: The Making, and Breaking, of a Great American Anecdote," *Journal of the Abraham Lincoln Association* 30, no. 1 (Winter 2009): 18–34.

13. Rugoff, *The Beechers*, 102, 394, 405, 417, 442–50; White, *Beecher Sisters*, 59, 60, 71–75.

14. For a complete history of Nook Farm, see Kenneth R. Andrews, *Nook Farm: Mark Twain's Hartford Circle* (1950; Hamden, CT: Archon Books, 1967).

15. Harriet to James Fields, November 3, 1863, quoted in Hedrick, *Harriet Beecher Stowe*, 311–12.

16. Rugoff, *The Beechers*, 361; Hedrick, *Harriet Beecher Stowe*, 310, 327–28. Both Oakholm and the Florida house have been demolished.

17. Harriet to Howells, n.d. [1869], quoted in Hedrick, 362.

18. Dickens to Fields, October 1869, quoted in McFarland, *Loves*, 187; Twain quoted in McFarland, 190; Hedrick, *Harriet Beecher Stowe*, 369. The truth of Harriet's accusation of incest is now generally accepted.

19. Author's visit, July 19, 2019.

20. The best account of the scandal is that of Debby Applegate, *The Most Famous Man in America: The Biography of Henry Ward Beecher* (New York: Doubleday, 2006), chapters 12, 13, and epilogue.

21. Thomas K. Beecher to Isabella Hooker, November 5, 1872, in J. E. P. Doyle, *Plymouth Church and Its Pastor* (St. Louis: Bryan, Brand & Company, 1875), 511–12.

22. "Harriet Beecher Stowe" (obituary), *New York Times*, July 2, 1896.

Chapter 3

For Tarbell's life, I have relied on her autobiography, *All in the Day's Work* (New York: Macmillan, 1939), and Kathleen Brady, *Ida Tarbell: Portrait of a Muckraker* (New York: Seaview/Putnam, 1984). Most of her books are available online.

1. Tarbell, *All in the Day's Work*, 1.

2. The house is at 324 East Main Street. The family expanded the house twice,

adding a second floor over the kitchen as well as a one-story addition behind the kitchen. They also added a second-floor artist's studio at the back of the home prior to 1912.
   3. Quoted in Brady, *Ida Tarbell*, 35.
   4. The house is still standing, with a bookshop on one side and a fabric shop on the other.
   5. The stone house, with balconies at all the front windows, is still standing in an elegant residential neighborhood.
   6. Since 1937, Twin Oaks has been owned by the Republic of China (Taiwan).
   7. Quoted in Brady, *Ida Tarbell*, 91.
   8. The house is no longer standing.
   9. The building is still standing, divided into apartments.
   10. Tarbell to John Siddell, September 11, 1901, quoted in Brady, *Ida Tarbell*, 125.
   11. Tarbell, *All in the Day's Work*, 206–7.
   12. Tarbell, *All in the Day's Work*, 213–14.
   13. Stephanie Gorton, *Citizen Reporters: S. S. McClure, Ida Tarbell, and the Magazine That Rewrote America* (New York: Ecco, 2020), 271.
   14. Review quoted in Brady, *Ida Tarbell*, 152; Dr. Paul Giddens to Brady, quoted on 160; "The Top 100 Works of Journalism of the Century—NYU Journalism," https://journalism.nyu.edu.
   15. Tarbell, *All in the Day's Work*, 263. The house, at 320 Valley Road, Easton, is a private residence.
   16. Tarbell, *All in the Day's Work*, 359.
   17. Quoted in Paula Treckel, "Ida Tarbell and the Business of Being a Woman," https://sites.allegheny.edu/tarbell/ida-tarbell-and-the-business-of-being-a-woman/.
   18. Quoted in Brady, *Ida Tarbell*, 225.
   19. Tarbell, *All in the Day's Work*, 399, 405.

Chapter 4

For the details of Jewett's life, I have relied on Paula Blanchard, *Sarah Orne Jewett: Her World and Her Work* (Reading, MA: Addison-Wesley, 1994), and F. O. Matthiessen, *Sarah Orne Jewett* (Gloucester, MA: Peter Smith, 1965). For her works, I have used Sarah Orne Jewett, *Novels and Stories* (New York: Library of America, 1994). Jewett's letters, diaries, stories and poems, as well as scholarship about her, are available online at Sarah Orne Jewett Text Project.
   1. Historic New England's website provides a history of the house and many photographs of the interior: Sarah Orne Jewett House Museum and Visitor Center (historicnewengland.org).
   2. "Looking Back on Girlhood," in *Novels and Stories*, 755–58.
   3. Jewett to Sara Norton, October 28, 2897, in *Letters of Sarah Orne Jewett*, ed. Annie Fields (Boston: Houghton Mifflin, 1911), 132.
   4. *Sarah Orne Jewett*, 17.
   5. "Looking Back," 7.
   6. Jewett to Annie Fields, July 5, 1889, in *Letters*, 46–47.
   7. Jewett Text Project.
   8. Jewett to Scudder, July 1 and 13, 1873, Jewett Text Project.
   9. In *Novels and Stories*, 135–36.
   10. Jewett to Horace Scudder, July 13, 1873, Jewett Text Project.
   11. David Bonnell Green, "The World of Dunnet Landing," *New England Quarterly* 34, no. 4 (Dec. 1961): 515.
   12. Charles Johanningsmeier, "Sarah Orne Jewett and Mary E. Wilkins (Freeman): Two Shrewd Businesswomen in Search of New Markets," *New England Quarterly* 70, no. 1 (1997): 65. The Howells quotation is from "The Man of Letters as a Man of Business," *Scribner's Magazine* 14 (1893): 441.
   13. Johanningsmeier, "Sarah Orne Jewett," 71.
   14. Blanchard, *Sarah Orne Jewett*, 117, 315–16; Margaret Roman, *Sarah Orne Jewett: Reconstructing Gender* (Tuscaloosa: University of Alabama Press, 2017), 143.
   15. Richard Brodhead, *Cultures of Letters: Scenes of Reading and Writing in Nineteenth-Century America* (Chicago: University of Chicago Press, 1993), 153.
   16. Whittier to Jewett, 1879, in *The Letters of John Greenleaf Whittier*, ed. John B. Pickard (Cambridge: Harvard University Press, 1975), 2:654.
   17. Blanchard, *Sarah Orne Jewett*, 134.
   18. Blanchard, *Sarah Orne Jewett*, 357.

Chapter 5

For Mary McCarthy's life, I have relied on two excellent biographies: Carol Brightman, *Writing Dangerously: Mary McCarthy and Her World* (New York: Clarkson Potter, 1992); and Carol Gelderman, *Mary McCarthy: A Life* (New York: St. Martin's, 1988). McCarthy's memoirs have also been useful: *Memories of a Catholic Girlhood* (New York: Harcourt Brace, 1957), *How I Grew* (New York: Harcourt Brace Jovanovich, 1987); and *Intellectual Memoirs: New York, 1936–1938* (New York: Harcourt Brace, 1992). For Elizabeth Hardwick I have used Cathy Curtis, *A Splendid Intelligence: The Life of Elizabeth Hardwick* (New York: Norton, 2022), which includes interviews, correspondence, and other archival material. All issues of *Partisan Review* are online at www.openculture.com/2014/09/partisan-review-now-free-online.html.

1. The grandparents' house, at 2214 Blaisdell Avenue South, is three stories, with 14 rooms and six bedrooms, built in 1900. It is a private residence. The smaller house is no longer standing.
2. Mary McCarthy, *Memories of a Catholic Girlhood*, 64.
3. The house, privately owned, is still standing.
4. *Partisan Review* 8, no. 4 (July–August 1941): 279–88, 324–43.
5. The series ran in the issues of October 22, November 6 and 20, and December 4 and 18, 1935.
6. Hardwick to McCarthy, June 28, 1949, quoted in Curtis, *Splendid Intelligence*, 55.
7. Deirdre Carmody, "Mary McCarthy, '33, Sends Papers to Vassar," *New York Times*, May 1, 1985, p. B1.
8. McCarthy quoted in Gelderman, *Mary McCarthy*, 185.
9. McCarthy to Hardwick, June 24, 1949, quoted in Gelderman, *Mary McCarthy*, 156–57.
10. Hardwick to John McCormack, October 26, 1952, quoted in Curtis, *Splendid Intelligence*, 92.
11. "The Subjection of Women," *Partisan Review* 20, no. 3 (May–June 1953): 321–31; 20, no. 5 (September–October 1953): 527–39; 20, no. 6 (November–December 1953): 690–96.
12. Hardwick to Susan Turner, July 7, 1953, quoted in Curtis, *Splendid Intelligence*, 113.
13. *The Selected Letters of William James* was published by Farrar, Straus and Cudahy in 1961.
14. The house is still standing. For a complete history of its ownership, see https://backbayhouses.org/239-marlborough/.
15. Hardwick to Tate, June 1, 1959, quoted in Curtis, *Splendid Intelligence*, 146.
16. The building is still standing, but the large duplexes have been divided into smaller apartments.
17. Hardwick to Lowell, June 1961, quoted in Curtis, *Splendid Intelligence*, 161.
18. Hardwick to McCarthy, November 30, 1963, quoted in Curtis, *Splendid Intelligence*, 172.
19. McCarthy to Doris Grumbach, quoted in Grumbach, *The Company She Kept* (New York: Coward, McCann, 1967), 184; McCarthy to Hannah Arendt, November 23, 1960, quoted in Gelderman, *Mary McCarthy*, 233.
20. April 22, 1965, May 9, 1968, November 7, 1968, and March 3, 1966, all in *NYRB*.
21. The house is a private residence.
22. Lowell to Bishop, July 30, 1968, quoted in Brightman, *Writing Dangerously*, 558.
23. Interview with Deborah Pulliam in *Maine Times*, September 17, 1983, quoted in Curtis, *Splendid Intelligence*, 247.
24. Rich, "Caryatid: A Column," *American Poetry Review* 2 (September–October 1973): 3442–43; Hardwick to McCarthy, June 15, 1977, quoted in Curtis, *Splendid Intelligence*, 243. The letters were published as *The Dolphin Letters, 1970–1979*, ed. Saskia Hamilton (New York: Farrar, Straus & Giroux, 2019).
25. Transcript of interview quoted in Brightman, *Writing Dangerously*, 600.
26. Brightman, *Writing Dangerously*, 613. Brightman's excellent analysis of the longstanding feud between the two women and the issues at stake appears in chapter 38, pp. 597–620.
27. *New York Times*, August 27, 1984.
28. *A View of My Own* (New York: Farrar, Straus and Cudahy, 1962), 35.

29. Constance Hunting, "The Experience of Art," *Peckerbrush Review*, n.d., 5, quoted in Curtis, *Splendid Intelligence*, 279.

30. Jon Jewett, *The Castine Visitor* 18, no. 1 (Spring 2008), 8.

Chapter 6

For Millay's biography I have relied on Daniel Mark Epstein, *What Lips My Lips Have Kissed: The Loves and Love Poems of Edna St. Vincent Millay* (New York: Henry Holt, 2001), and Nancy Milford, *Savage Beauty: The Life of Edna St. Vincent Millay* (New York: Random House, 2002). All quotations of Millay's poetry are from *Edna St. Vincent Millay: Collected Poems*, ed. Norma Millay (New York: Harper & Row, 1982).

1. Milford, *Savage Beauty*, 26.
2. 2 Epstein, *What Lips*, 6; *Collected Poems*, 180.
3. Edna St. Vincent Millay, undated memoir written in the third person, quoted in Epstein, *What Lips*, 10.
4. *Collected Poems*, 90, 494.
5. Millay, diary, July 19, 1908, quoted in Epstein, *What Lips*, 11–12.
6. Millay, diary, April–October 1911, quoted in Epstein, *What Lips*, 3–4.
7. Ficke to Ferdinand Earle, quoted by Earle in a letter to Millay, December 3, 1912, quoted in *Letters of Edna St. Vincent Millay*, ed. Allan Ross Macdougall (New York: Harper & Brothers, 1952), 18, 20.
8. "Renascence," in *Collected Poems*, 3.
9. Epstein, *What Lips*, 64–65; "Edna St. Vincent Millay," *Vassar Encyclopedia*, vcencyclopedia.vassar.edu.
10. Millay to Arthur Davison Ficke, 1914, in *Letters*, 49; Epstein, *What Lips*, 83.
11. Sonnet xi, *Collected Poems*, 571.
12. Bishop quoted in Epstein, *What Lips*, 149; Floyd Dell, "My Friend Edna St. Vincent Millay," *Mark Twain Journal* 12, no. 2 (Spring 1964): 2.
13. Millay to Cora and Norma Millay, 1917, in *Letters*, 76–77.
14. Millay to Witter Bynner, October 29, 1920, in *Letters*, 102.
15. See *Letters*, 113–69. On the Nancy Boyd stories, see Catherine Keyser, "Edna St. Vincent Millay and the Very Clever Woman in 'Vanity Fair,'" *American Periodicals* 17, no. 1 (2007): 65–96. Millay to Isobel Simpson, December 15, 1922, in *Letters*, 168.
16. Epstein, *What Lips*, 190.
17. For a recent update on the property, see Laura Mars, "Edna St. Vincent Millay's Steepletop," *Berkshire Magazine* 11, no. 4 (August 2022): 70–75.
18. Millay to Boissevain, January 1924, in *Letters*, 181.
19. Epstein, *What Lips*, 189; Boissevain to Arthur Ficke, December 1925, quoted in Milford, *Strange Beauty*, 279.
20. Epstein, *What Lips*, 191, 199, quotation on 210; J. D. McClatchy, "Introduction," *Edna St. Vincent Millay: Selected Poems* (New York: Library of America, 2003), xxvi; Boissevain to Dillon, 1929, quoted in Milford, *Strange Beauty*, 310. On *Fatal Interview*, see Ann K. Hoff, "'How Love May Be Acquired': Prescriptive Autobiography in Millay's 'Fatal Interview,'" *CEA Critic* 68, no. 3 (Spring and Summer 2006): 1–15.
21. *Fatal Interview*, in *Collected Poems*, 655, 676.
22. "First Fig," in *Collected Poems*, 127.
23. Millay to unnamed correspondent, September 1940, quoted in *Letters*, 282; McClatchy, "Introduction," xxviii; Epstein, *What Lips*, 258; "Edna St. Vincent Millay," poetryfoundation.org.
24. Millay to Eugene Saxton, March 10, 1941; to Amy Flashner, July 1943; to Cass Canfield, October 1947, June 1949, in *Letters*, 312–13, 320–21, 336, 353; Canfield to Millay, June 1949, quoted in *Letters*, 354.
25. Millay to Manuel Maria Mischoulon, December 10, 1949, in *Letters*, 362; quotation from Millay to Norma Millay, January 27, 1950, in *Letters*, 363–64.
26. Millay to Lena Ruesch, in *Letters*, 376.

Chapter 7

For the facts of Thaxter's life, I have relied on her granddaughter's biography: Rosamond Thaxter, *Sandpiper: The Life of Celia Thaxter* (Sanbornville, N.H.: Wake-Brook House, 1962); and *Letters of Celia Thaxter*, ed. A[nnie] F[ields] and R[ose] L[amb] (Boston: Houghton, Mifflin and Company, 1896). Celia Thaxter's prose works—*Among the Isles of Shoals* (Boston: James

R. Osgood and Col, 1873) and *An Island Garden* (1894; Boston: Houghton Mifflin, 1904)—are both available online, as are her poetry collections: *Poems*, 1872; *Drift-weed*, 1878; *Poems for Children*, 1884; *The Cruise of the Mystery and Other Poems* (1886); and *Idyls and Pastorals* (1886).

1. Celia Thaxter, *Among the Isles of Shoals*, 120–21. The lighthouse has not had a resident keeper since 1986, but it was restored in 2005 with a Save America's Treasures Grant. It is not open to visitors.
2. Higginson quoted in R. Thaxter, *Sandpiper*, 53; Longfellow quoted on 52.
3. The house, at 324 California Street, has been divided into two condominiums.
4. Quoted in R. Thaxter, *Sandpiper*, 86.
5. September 23, 1861, in *Letters*, 23.
6. Both letters quoted in R. Thaxter, *Sandpiper*, 121–23.
7. Annie Fields, diary entry for May 20, 1873, quoted in R. Thaxter, *Sandpiper*, 142; introduction, *Letters*, xiii.
8. Celia Thaxter to Samuel T. Pickard, in his *Life and Letters of John Greenleaf Whittier*, 2 vols. (Boston: Houghton, Mifflin, 1895), 2:520.
9. Celia Thaxter, *Among the Isles of Shoals*, 8, 14, 16–17.
10. The story appeared in the May 1875 issue of the *Atlantic Monthly* and was reprinted in *True Crime: An American Anthology* (New York: Library of America, 2008), 131–55. This quotation is on 132.
11. Celia Thaxter to Annie Fields, 1877, *Letters*, 84.
12. Roland quoted in R. Thaxter, *Sandpiper*, 184.
13. The hand-painted books are now collectors' items. One can be viewed at the Isabella Stewart Gardner Museum in Boston.
14. Quoted in R. Thaxter, *Sandpiper*, 184.
15. Subsequent research has determined that her garden, in fact, contained nearly one hundred varieties: www.shoalsmarinelaboratory.org.
16. Celia Thaxter, *An Island Garden*, 5, 6, 71, 112–13.

Chapter 8

For Alcott's biography, see Madelon Bedell, *The Alcotts: Biography of a Family* (New York: Clarkson Potter, 1980); Susan Cheever, *Louisa May Alcott: A Personal Biography* (New York: Simon & Schuster, 2010); Eve LaPlante, *Marmee and Louisa: The Untold Story of Louisa May Alcott and Her Mother* (New York: Free Press, 2012); and John Matteson, *Eden's Outcasts: The Story of Louisa May Alcott and Her Father* (New York: Norton, 2007).

1. Charles Strickland, "A Transcendentalist Father: The Child-Rearing Practices of Bronson Alcott," *History of Childhood Quarterly* 1, no. 1 (Summer 1973): 9–10.
2. A. Bronson Alcott, *Conversations with Children on the Gospels* (Boston: James Munroe, 1836), 1:68.
3. Abigail to Samuel May, October 3, 1839, quoted in Eve LaPlante, ed., *My Heart Is Boundless* (New York: Free Press, 2012), 80.
4. Abigail May Alcott, Journal, March 6, 1843, in *The Journals of Bronson Alcott* (Boston: Little Brown, 1938), 152; Abigail to Samuel May, August 1843, quoted in F. B. Sanborn and William T. Harris, *A. Bronson Alcott: His Life and Philosophy*, 2 vols. (Boston: Roberts Brothers, 1893), 1:309. Also known as the Hosmer Cottage, 572 Main Street was the model for The Dovecote in *Little Women*. The early 18th-century house was rebuilt in 1820 and later much altered.
5. Abigail's journal, November 29, 1842, quoted in Cheever, *Louisa May Alcott*, 56.
6. Fruitlands was remodeled in 1914 and is less primitive than it was in the Alcotts' time.
7. Hecker quoted in Richard Francis, *Fruitlands: The Alcott Family and Their Search for Utopia* (New Haven, CT: Yale University Press, 2010), 156, 195.
8. Lane quoted in Sears, *Alcott's Fruitlands*, 122; Abigail to Samuel May, January 6, 1844, quoted in Cheever, *Louisa May Alcott*, 73.
9. February 17, 1844, quoted in Bedell, *The Alcotts*, 232.
10. Hillside is now known as The Wayside, the name Nathaniel Hawthorne gave it when he purchased it from the Alcotts. It has been restored to the time of his residence.
11. Louisa to Abigail, 1845, in *The Selected Letters of Louisa May Alcott*, ed.

Joel Myerson and Daniel Shealy (Boston: Little Brown, 1987), 6; Louisa's journal, March 1846, in Cheney, *Louisa May Alcott*, 30.

12. Abigail to Samuel May, February 8, 1847, quoted in Eve LaPlante, ed., *My Heart Is Boundless* (New York: Free Press, 2012), 154.

13. Louisa's undated [1851] journal, quoted in Matteson, *Eden's Outcasts*, 197.

14. See Susan W. Bailey, "Louisa May Alcott's Walpole," https://louisamayalcottismypassion. The Walpole house is now the Alcott Apartments on High Street near the town center.

15. Matteson, *Eden's Outcasts*, 231–33.

16. Child quoted in Sanborn and Harris, *A. Bronson Alcott*, 2:437. The house has been restored to the time the Alcotts lived there, and most of the furniture and artifacts belonged to them.

17. Louisa to Alfred Whitman, 1861, quoted in Daniel Lester Shealy, "The Author-Publisher Relationships of Louisa May Alcott," Ph.D. dissertation, University of South Carolina, 1965, 11.

18. Shealy, "Author-Publisher Relationships," 47, journal quoted on 49.

19. Diary quoted in Shealy, "Author-Publisher Relationships," 58.

20. Journal, December 1868, quoted in Cheney, *Louisa May Alcott*, 141.

21. LaPlante, *Marmee and Louisa*, 228.

22. Louisa to Eden Conway, May 1, 1878, in Myerson and Shealy, *Selected Letters*, 230; Journal, May–June 1879, in Cheney, *Louisa May Alcott*, 231.

23. Harriet Reisin, *Louisa May Alcott: The Woman Behind Little Women* (New York: Macmillan, 2010), 366–69. Ten Louisburg Square is now a private residence valued at more than $10 million.

Chapter 9

For the details of Emily Dickinson's life, I have relied on Richard B. Sewall, *The Life of Emily Dickinson* (Cambridge, MA: Harvard University Press, 1980). Her letters are available in *The Letters of Emily Dickinson*, ed. Thomas H. Johnson and Theodora Ward (Cambridge, MA: Belknap Press of Harvard University Press, 1958), and other documents can be found in Jay Leyda, *The Years and Hours of Emily Dickinson* (New Haven, CT: Yale University Press, 1960). The most recent editions of her poems are by Ralph Franklin, *The Poems of Emily Dickinson*, a three-volume variorum edition (Cambridge, MA: Belknap Press of Harvard University Press, 1998) and a one-volume reading edition (Cambridge, MA: Harvard University Press, 2005). I have used *The Complete Poems of Emily Dickinson*, ed. Thomas H. Johnson (Boston: Back Bay Books/Little, Brown, 1961).

1. The house is no longer standing.

2. Emily Dickinson to Joel Warren Norcross, January 11, 1850, in *Letters*, 1:80.

3. Emily to Mary Haven, February 13, 1859, in *Letters*, 2:346.

4. Emily to Susan Gilbert, April 1851, in *Letters*, 1:201; poem 14, *Complete Poems*, 12.

5. Emily to Austin Dickinson, April 2, 1853, in *Letters*, 1:237.

6. Emily to Elizabeth Holland, ca. January 20, 1856, in *Letters*, 2:323–24.

7. Descriptions of the houses come from two visits by the author, in 2017 and 2019. The Homestead underwent a complete restoration in 2021. Both houses are owned by Amherst College and are open to visitors. The North Pleasant Street house is no longer standing.

8. John William Burgess, *Reminiscences of an American Scholar* (New York: Columbia University Press, 1934), quoted in Sewall, *Life*, 116.

9. Emily to Higginson in *Letters*, 2:460; Emily to Samuel Bowles, August 1860, in *Letters*, 2:366.

10. Emily to J. G. and Elizabeth Holland, autumn 1853, in *Letters*, 1:264.

11. Emily to Elizabeth Holland, late November 1866?, early March 1866, in *Letters*, 2:455, 449.

12. Mabel Todd to Austin, April 20, 1890; Austin Dickinson, diary; both quoted in Polly Longsworth, *Austin and Mabel: The Amherst Affair and Love Letters of Austin Dickinson and Mabel Loomis Todd* (New York: Farrar, Straus and Giroux, 1984), 356, 63.

13. Emily to Susan, ca. 1877, late 1885, in *Letters*, 2:598; 3:893.

14. Mabel Loomis Todd to her mother, quoted in Longsworth, *Austin and Mabel*, 111; to Eben and Mary Wilder Loomis,

September 29, 1881, in Leyda, *Years and Hours*, 2:353–54.
  15. Longsworth, *Austin and Mabel*, 173.
  16. Sewall, *Life*, 193; Longsworth, *Austin and Mabel*, 117.
  17. Millicent Todd Bingham, unpublished reminiscences, quoted in Sewall, *Life*, 297–98.

Chapter 10

For the facts of Sojourner Truth's life, I have relied on the biography by Margaret Washington, *Sojourner Truth's America* (Urbana: University of Illinois Press, 2009), which sets the events of her life in the context of her time and the movements in which she was involved. I have also used the two books that Truth wrote with white collaborators: *Fanaticism; its source and influence, illustrated by the Simple Narrative of Isabella...*, written with Gilbert Vale, 2 vols. (New York: G. Vale, 1835), generally referred to as *The Simple Narrative of Isabella*, online at https://catalog.hathitrust.org/Record/009732918; and *The Narrative of Sojourner Truth*, written with Olive Gilbert (Boston: The Author, 1850), online at https://digital.library.upenn.edu/women/truth/1850/1850html.

  1. The loss of the house is detailed in A. J. Schenkman, "Preservation Failures: The Hardenbergh House," *New York Almanack*, July 18, 2013 (https://www.newyorkalmanack.com).
  2. Frances W. Titus, "Sojourner Truth," *Daily Inter Ocean* (Chicago), September 24, 1893.
  3. Washington develops this argument in *Sojourner Truth's America*, 40–47.
  4. Truth, *Narrative*, 43–44. According to a note by Olive Gilbert, the misspelling of *Wagenen* as *Wagener* was a typographical error that she was unable to correct.
  5. Truth, *Narrative*, 53–54.
  6. Truth, *Narrative*, 54, 58.
  7. Washington, *Sojourner Truth's America*, 80.
  8. Washington, *Sojourner Truth's America*, 104.
  9. Truth, *Fanaticism*, 2:120, 1:62.
  10. Truth, *Fanaticism*, 1:61. Corporal Trim is a loquacious character in Laurence Sterne's *The Life and Opinions of Tristram Shandy, Gentleman*.
  11. Truth, *Fanaticism*, 2:116, 127.
  12. Truth, *Fanaticism*, 2:125.
  13. Truth, *Narrative*, 100.
  14. *Daily Inter Ocean*, August 13, 1879, quoted in Washington, *Sojourner Truth*, 165.
  15. Truth, *Narrative*, 14–15.
  16. Truth, *Narrative*, 30, 33.
  17. Truth, *Narrative*, 34, 38.
  18. *Commonwealth* (Boston), July 3, 1863, quoted in Washington, *Sojourner Truth's America*, 190.
  19. October 6, 1850, quoted in Washington, *Sojourner Truth's America*, 204.
  20. Lucy Stone's account of the meeting, quoted in Washington, *Sojourner Truth's America*, 269–270.
  21. Marilyn Creswell, "Sojourner Truth and the Power of Copyright Registration," https://blogs.loc.gov/copyright/2020/12; Truth to Gale, February 25, 1864, quoted in Matthew K. Samra, "Shadow and Substance: The Two Narratives of Sojourner Truth," *Midwest Quarterly* 38, no. 2 (January 1, 1997): 158. Many years later, President Ulysses S. Grant paid her $5 for a photograph.
  22. *National Anti-Slavery Standard*, December 17, 1864, quoted in Washington, *Sojourner Truth's America*, 315.
  23. The house is still standing but has been divided into three apartments.

Chapter 11

For Wharton's biography, I have relied on Eleanor Dwight, *Edith Wharton: An Extraordinary Life* (New York: Abrams, 1956); Hermione Lee, *Edith Wharton* (New York: Knopf, 2007); and R. W. B. Lewis, *Edith Wharton: A Biography* (New York: Harper & Row, 1975).

  1. Edith Wharton, *A Backward Glance*, in *Novellas and Other Writings* (New York: Library of America, 1990), 778, 805, 824. The house on 23rd Street was renovated as retail space in 1882 and underwent several other renovations. Its ground floor is now home to a Starbucks. Elizabeth Schermerhorn Jones's mansion, later known as Wyndcliffe, has been deserted since 1950. The current owner has applied for permission to demolish it. Photographs are available online at "Stepping Back in Time with a Pictorial Visit to the Wyndcliffe Mansion in Rhinebeck | GothamToGo."

2. Wharton, *Backward Glance*, 817, 824.
3. Wharton, *Backward Glance*, 833.
4. Wharton, *Backward Glance*, 853.
5. Land's End, 42 Ledge Road, recently sold for $8.6 million. Its nearly 11,000 square feet includes 11 bedrooms, and porches and balconies overlooking the ocean. It is privately owned but can be seen from the Cliff Walk. The Manhattan houses have been demolished.
6. Wharton, *Backward Glance*, 864, 865.
7. Edith Wharton and Ogden Codman, Jr., *The Decoration of Houses* (1897; rev. and expanded ed., New York: Norton, 1978).
8. Edith Wharton, *Italian Villas and Their Gardens* (1904; New York: DaCapo, 1988), 7, 147–48.
9. Edith Wharton, *The House of Mirth*, in *Novels* (New York: Library of America, 1985), 168–69; *Age of Innocence*, in *Novels*, 1280.
10. Wharton, *Age of Innocence*, 1118–19, 1056.
11. In *Novellas*, 760.
12. *Scribner's Magazine* 14, no. 6 (Dec. 1893): 700; *Decoration*, 25.
13. The descriptions of the house and gardens are based on a 1999 visit by the author (before the restoration); The Mount's well-illustrated website (www.edithwharton.org, especially "Facts about the Estate"); and the illustrations in Richard Guy Wilson, *Edith Wharton at Home* (New York: Monacelli Press, 2012).
14. "Background," www.edithwharton.org.
15. On Wharton's income from writing, see Gary Totten, "Selling Wharton," in *Edith Wharton in Context*, ed. Laura Rattray (New York: Cambridge University Press, 2012), 127–36.
16. Wharton, *Backward Glance*, 153.
17. "Pavillon Colombe," https://househistree.com; Lee, *Edith Wharton*, 529–30, 532. The house is now the home of the Prince and Princess of Liechtenstein.
18. "Sainte-Claire du Vieux Château," www.doaks.org; Lee, *Edith Wharton*, 546–47. The chateau now belongs to the city of Hyères.
19. Wharton, *Backward Glance*, 830.

Chapter 12

For biographical facts, I have relied on Gillian Gill, *Mary Baker Eddy* (Cambridge, MA: Perseus Books, 1998), and Eddy's memoir, *Retrospection and Introspection* (Boston: First Church of Christ, Scientist, 1891). All of Eddy's works are readily available in print and online. Sermons and many other documents are available online through the digitization efforts of the Mary Baker Eddy Library: https://mbepapers.org.

1. Abigail to George Baker, April 24, 1836, quoted in Gill, *Mary Baker Eddy*, 29.
2. Eddy, *Retrospection*, 20.
3. Eddy, *Retrospection*, 20.
4. Eddy, *Retrospection*, 90.
5. The houses in North Groton (29 Hall's Brook Rd.) and Rumney (58 Stinson Lake Rd.) have been restored by the Longyear Museum, which offers online tours as well as in-person visiting hours: www.longyear.org/visit/historic-houses/.
6. P.P. Quimby, "To the Sick in Body and Mind," ppquimby.com.
7. Letter quoted in Gill, *Mary Baker Eddy*, 131,
8. The house at 23 Paradise Road has been restored and can be visited or viewed at www.longyear.org/visit/historic-houses/.
9. Eddy, *Retrospection*, 24.
10. Daisette Stocking McKenzie, "Reminiscences of Daisette Stocking McKenzie, C.S.B., and William Patrick McKenzie, C.S.B., as recorded by Daisette D. S. McKenzie, C.S.B.," typescript, n.d., Mary Baker Eddy Library, Boston, MA, 27–28. Letters and Reminiscences, © The Mary Baker Eddy Collection. Used by permission.
11. To visit the Stoughton house virtually or in person, see www.longyear.org/visit/historic-houses/.
12. To visit the Lynn house virtually or in person, see www.longyear.org/visit/historic-houses/.
13. Eddy, *Retrospection*, 38–39.
14. *London Times,* May 26, 1885.
15. Eddy to James Ackland, January 21, 1880, L10638, marybakereddypapers.org © The Mary Baker Eddy Collection. Used by permission.
16. Both buildings are still standing.
17. For a detailed history of 385 Commonwealth Avenue, which is still owned by the church, see https://backbayhouses.org/ 385-commonwealth/.
18. Stephen Gottschalk, *The Emergence*

of Christian Science in American Religious Life (Berkeley: University of California Press, 1973), 176. A domed extension, in the Byzantine style, was added between 1903 and 1906, with a capacity of three thousand.

19. To visit the North State Street house virtually or in person, see www.longyear.org/visit/historic-houses/.

20. Gill, *Mary Baker Eddy*, 388–89. The house was demolished in 1917. Several images of the interior are available at https://longyear.org/learn/research-archive/sixteen-years-at-pleasant-view-1892-1908/.

21. Rev. Irving C. Tomlinson, *Twelve Years with Mary Baker Eddy* (Boston: Christian Science Publishing Association, 1945), 158.

22. Twain to Peabody, December 5, 1902, quoted in Gill, *Mary Baker Eddy*, 458.

23. The *McClure's* articles were published in 1909 as a book, *The Life of Mary Baker Eddy and the History of Christian Science*, supposedly written by Georgine Milmine but actually written by Ida Tarbell and Willa Cather.

24. Quoted in Gill, *Mary Baker Eddy*, 519.

25. For a virtual or in-person tour of 1125 Boylston Street, see www.longyear.org/visit/historic-houses/.

26. See M. Adelaide Still, "Reminiscences of the Time I Spent in Mrs. Eddy's Home May 1907 to December 1910," typescript, n.d., Mary Baker Eddy Library, Boston, MA, 23; Calvin C. Hill, "Reminiscences of Calvin C. Hill," typescript, 1943, Mary Baker Eddy Library, Boston, MA, 190, © The Mary Baker Eddy Library Collection. Used by permission; Gill, *Mary Baker Eddy*, 524–26.

27. Quoted in Gill, *Mary Baker Eddy*, 549.

Chapter 13

For the facts of Sarah Josepha Hale's life, I have relied on the biography by Ruth E. Finley, *The Lady of Godey's: Sarah Josepha Hale* (Philadelphia: J. B. Lippincott, 1931); and Melanie Kirkpatrick, *Lady Editor: Sarah Josepha Hale and the Making of the Modern American Woman* (New York: Encounter Books, 2021). Both *The Ladies' Magazine* and *Godey's Lady's Book* are available online, as are *Northwood* and the 1852 and 1876 editions of *Woman's Record: Sketches of all Distinguished Women from the Creation to A.D. 1854/1876* (New York: Harper Brothers, 1852, 1876).

1. Sarah Josepha Hale, *The Ladies' Wreath: A Selection From the Female Poetic Writers of England and America* (Boston: Marsh, Capen & Lyon; New York: D. Appleton, 1837), 384–85.

2. The house was later moved to Myrtle Street and was converted into a duplex. The Richards Free Library stands on the original site.

3. *Northwood, a Tale of New England* (Boston: Bowles & Dearborn, 1827). Quotations from Hale, *The Ladies' Wreath*, 387, and Hale's preface to the fifth edition of *Northwood* (New York: H. Long, 1852), iii.

4. *The Ladies Magazine* 1, no. 1 (1828): 1–2.

5. Hale to Messrs, Carey & Hart, November 19, 1835, in Finley, *Lady of Godey's*, 92.

6. *Godey's Lady's Book* 13 (September 1836): 144; (December 1836): 283.

7. *Godey's Lady's Book* 18 (April 1839): 192.

8. Hale, *Woman's Record*, 1876.

9. Hale's preface to the fifth edition, iv.

10. Hale, "Editor's Table," *Godey's Lady's Book* 59 (November 1859): 466; 63 (December 1861): 441.

11. The Spruce Street house still stands, with a historic plaque on the street in front of it. The Locust Street house has been torn down.

12. Hale, "Editor's Table," *Godey's Lady's Book* 95 (December 1877): 523.

Chapter 14

For Metalious's life, I have relied on Emily Toth, *Inside Peyton Place: The Life of Grace Metalious* (Garden City, NY: Doubleday, 1981) and Michael Callahan, "Peyton Place's Real Victim," *Vanity Fair* 48, no. 3 (2006): 332 et seq.

1. Grace Metalious, "All About Me and Peyton Place," *American Weekly*, May–June 1958, quoted in Toth, *Inside Peyton Place*, 208.

2. Toth, *Inside Peyton Place*, 62.
3. Grace quoted in Toth, *Inside Peyton Place*, 92; Louise Riegel quoted on 78.
4. Grace quoted in Toth, *Inside Peyton Place*, 80; Metalious, "All About Me," 11; interview with Pat Carbine, *Look*, March 1958.
5. Messner quoted in Toth, *Inside Peyton Place*, 94.
6. Toth, *Inside Peyton Place*, 119.
7. Quoted in Toth, *Inside Peyton Place*, 120, 122.
8. Quoted in Laura Lippman, "The Women of Peyton Place," *Baltimore Sun*, June 14, 1999.
9. David Carkhuff, "Gilmanton Winery's Serial-Killer Roots," *Laconia Daily Sun*, April 12, 2017. The house is now the Gilmanton Winery, 528 Meadow Pond Road.
10. Quoted in Toth, *Inside Peyton Place*, 244.
11. John Rees, "Grace Metalious' Battle with the World," *Cosmopolitan*, September 1964, 50, quoted in Toth, *Inside Peyton Place*, 315.
12. Ithaca, NY: Cornell University Press, 2015, 178.

Chapter 15

Elleanor Eldridge, *Memoirs of Elleanor Eldridge* (Providence: B.T. Albro, 1838) and *Elleanor's Second Book* (Providence, B.T. Albro, 1839), are the primary sources for Eldridge's story. They are not entirely accurate or reliable. The best account is that of Jacqueline Jones in *A Dreadful Deceit: The Myth of Race from the Colonial Era to Obama's America* (New York: Basic Books, 2013). Jones corrects many factual errors in the text and provides context for the narrative. I have relied on her book to evaluate the facts of Eldridge's life as presented in the *Memoirs*. Jane Lancaster has examined court records, and her article, "A Web of Iniquity? Race, Gender, Foreclosure, and Respectability in Antebellum Rhode Island," *Rhode Island History Journal* 69 (Summer–Fall 2011): 72–92, is invaluable for understanding Eldridge's legal entanglements.

1. Eldridge, *Memoirs*, 2nd ed. (Providence: B.T. Albro, 1843), 34.
2. Eldridge, *Memoirs*, 65.
3. For a detailed account of these riots, see Jones, *Dreadful Deceit*, 97–107.
4. Jones, *Dreadful Deceit*, 126.
5. Jones, *Dreadful Deceit*, 130.
6. Eldridge, *Memoirs*, 77.
7. Eldridge, *Memoirs*, 85, 82.
8. Eldridge, *Memoirs*, 14, 89–90.

Chapter 16

Although Gilman's last name was Stetson from 1884 to 1900, I have used Gilman throughout to avoid confusion. I have relied on two excellent biographies for the events of Gilman's life: Cynthia Davis, *Charlotte Perkins Gilman: A Biography* (Redwood City, CA: Stanford University Press, 2010) and Ann J. Lane, *To Herland and Beyond: The Life and Works of Charlotte Perkins Gilman* (New York: Pantheon, 1990). Gilman's autobiography, *The Living of Charlotte Perkins Gilman* (New York: Appleton-Century, 1935), is useful for her view of events at the end of her life. It is also available in an edition edited by Ann J. Lane (Madison: University of Wisconsin Press, 1991). For a complete account of Perkins' writings, see Gary Scharnhorst, *Charlotte Perkins Gilman: A Bibliography* (Metuchen, NJ: Scarecrow Press, 1985).

1. Quoted in Lane, *To Herland*, 362.
2. The house at 22 East Manning Street is a private residence.
3. Frederick B. Perkins, *Devil-Puzzlers and Other Stories* (New York: G. P. Putnam, 1877), 215; Gilman, *The Living*, 5.
4. Images of most of these trading cards can be found online, sometimes attributed to Gilman.
5. Gilman, *The Living*, 78.
6. Walter's oath quoted in Lane, *To Herland*, 85; Gilman to Grace Channing, February 28, 1884, quoted in Lane, *To Herland*, 92.
7. Gilman, *The Living*, 85. The building is no longer standing.
8. Gilman, *The Living*, 88–89.
9. Mary A. Hill, ed., *Endure: The Diaries of Charles Walter Stetson* (Philadelphia: Temple University Press, 1985), 282, entry for August 27, 1885.
10. Gilman, *The Living*, 96.
11. Gilman to Grace Channing Stetson, November 1887, quoted in Lane, *To Herland*, 123.

12. Horace Scudder to Gilman, quoted in Gilman, *The Living*, 119. The cottage is no longer standing.
13. Gilman, *The Living*, 121; "Why I Wrote 'The Yellow Wallpaper?'" *Forerunner* 4 (1913): 271.
14. Gilman, *The Living*, 140, 169. The house is no longer standing.
15. Gilman, *The Living*, 184.
16. Charlotte Perkins Gilman, *The Home: Its Work and Influence* (New York: McClure, Phillips, 1903), 58–59.
17. Davis gives an excellent account of her lecturing in *Charlotte Perkins Gilman*, 127–28. The quotation from the *Woman's Journal* is on 191–92.
18. Unnamed reviewer quoted in Davis, *Charlotte Perkins Gilman*, 212.
19. Gilman, *The Living*, 281.
20. Gilman, *The Living*, 310.
21. The house is now called Lathrop Manor and is available for short-term or event rental.
22. Gilman to Grace Channing Stetson, May 3, 1934, quoted in Davis, *Charlotte Perkins Gilman*, 360.
23. Gilman, *The Living*, addendum, 335, 331.

Chapter 17

There are only two sources for Cynthia Taggart's biography. The first is James C. Richmond, *The Rhode Island Cottage*, with U.S. editions in 1835, 1841, 1842, 1849, and 1861 and an English edition in 1849, based on the second American edition. The second is her *Poems*, which includes a memoir by her father and a good deal of biographical information.

1. William Taggart [the younger], "Memoir of William Taggart," in Cynthia Taggart, *Poems*, 3d ed. (New York: Barlow, 1848), xxxi.
2. William Taggart, "Memoir," xxxiii.
3. William Taggart, "Memoir," xxxviii.
4. "Another gambrel-roofed Taggart house was moved to West Main Road #106, probably in the early 19th century. In 1944, this house was left to St. Colomba's Church, the Berkeley Memorial Chapel; it was leased in 1946 by the present occupant, who made extensive renovations." State of Rhode Island and Providence Plantations, Preliminary Survey Report, Town of Middletown, June 1979, 40A. The house is either no longer standing or so changed as to be unrecognizable.
5. Richmond, *Rhode Island Cottage*, 5.
6. Richmond, *Rhode Island Cottage*, 25.
7. Richmond, preface to the first edition, *Poems*, viii–ix.
8. Richmond, *Rhode Island Cottage*, 143. For more on James Richmond's life, see Ben Maryniak, "Errant Chaplain of the Iron Brigade: Biography of the Reverend James C. Richmond, 2nd Wisconsin," *Military Images* 16, no. 4 (January–February 1995): 28–30.

Chapter 18

The most recent biography—*Shirley Jackson: A Rather Haunted Life*, by Ruth Franklin (New York: Liveright, 2016)—weaves together her life, her work, and her houses and sets them in the context of the social and political time in which she lived. Also indispensable is *The Letters of Shirley Jackson*, edited by her older son, Laurence Jackson Hyman (New York: Random House, 2021). Most of Jackson's work is available in two collections published by the Library of America: *Shirley Jackson: Four Novels of the 1940s and 1950s* (2020) and *Shirley Jackson: Novels and Stories* (2010). Jackson never used capital letters, and authors and editors disagree about retaining that practice in quotations. I found it distracting and have used normal capitalization.

1. Rae Alexandra, "A Grim History of Nob Hill's Mansions—And the Horror Novels They Inspired," KQED, July 13, 2020, www.kqed.org. The article includes photos of the mansions.
2. The house at 1609 Forest View Avenue is privately owned.
3. Quoted in Franklin, *Shirley Jackson*, 24.
4. Judy Oppenheimer, interview with Sarah Hyman Stewart, n.d., in *Private Demons: The Life of Shirley Jackson* (New York: Putnam, 1988), 125; Franklin, *Shirley Jackson*, 29.
5. The wide, six-story brick building is still standing.
6. Letter and journal entry quoted in Franklin, *Shirley Jackson*, 156, 157.
7. It is now a single-family home.
8. Jackson to Louise Harop, April 1,

1945, in *Letters*, 104. The house is a private residence.

9. Judy Oppenheimer, interview with Jean Krochalis, December 10, 1986, in *Private Demons*, 116.

10. *Raising Demons* (New York: Farrar Straus, 1957), 154.

11. Jackson, "Biography of a Story," in *Novels and Stories*, 787–801; Joseph Henry Jackson, "How a Story Puzzled Readers, Critics (and the Author)," *San Francisco Chronicle*, July 22, 1948, quoted in Franklin, 235.

12. The house at 18 Indian Hill Road has been restored and is privately owned.

13. Franklin, *Shirley Jackson*, 258, 172; "Shirley Jackson, Author of Horror Classic, Dies," *New York Times*, August 10, 1965. Grace Metalious' publicists used the same tactic; see chapter 14.

14. Jackson to Virginia Olsen, Sept. 2, [1953]; Jackson to Geraldine and Leslie Jackson, [Sept. 1953], in *Letters*, 250, 253. The house is privately owned.

15. Ruth Franklin, interview with Catherine Morrison, November 6, 2013, in *Shirley Jackson*, 330.

16. *Letters*, 356. The Winchester Mystery House (525 South Winchester Boulevard, San Jose) is a sprawling, ornate, 160-room Victorian mansion completed in 1922. The story of the haunting was promoted when the house was opened as a tourist attraction in 1923. (U.S. Department of Interior, National Park Service, "Winchester Mystery House," National Register of Historic Places Inventory Nomination, 1974.) It is open for tours and special events.

17. Jackson to Brandt, February 5, [1958], *Letters*, 361–62.

18. *The Haunting of Hill House*, in *Novels and Stories*, 265.

19. Orville Prescott, *New York Times*, October 5, 1962; Parker, *Esquire*, December 1962.

20. Jackson to Sally, December 5, 1962, *Letters*, 548–49.

21. Both letters quoted in Franklin, *Shirley Jackson*, 453, 455.

22. *Letters*, 600. The letter, seen by two people, has since been lost.

Chapter 19

For the facts of Grace Paley's life, I have relied on her collection of essays, *Just As I Thought* (New York: Farrar, Straus, and Giroux, 1998), and Judith Arcana, *Grace Paley's Life Stories: A Literary Biography* (Urbana: University of Illinois Press, 1993). Arcana's work is especially helpful because it includes her interviews with Paley and her children, as well as her thoughtful analysis of the relationship between Paley's experiences and those of her characters. For her prose, I have used *The Collected Stories* (New York: Farrar, Straus, and Giroux, 1994), which contains all of her short-story collections: *The Little Disturbances of Man* (1959), *Enormous Changes at the Last Minute* (1974), and *Later the Same Day* (1985).

1. The house, on a block with single-family and apartment houses, is no longer standing.

2. "The Loudest Voice," in Paley, *Collected Stories*, 34.

3. "Introduction," "Injustice," in Paley, *Just As I Thought*, xiii, 6.

4. "Injustice," 7.

5. "Jobs," in Paley, *Just As I Thought*, 23.

6. "Two Ears, Three Lucks," in Paley, *Collected Stories*, ix–x.

7. Jeanne Goodside Tenenbaum, quoted in Arcana, *Grace Paley's Life Stories*, 76. The Unadilla is still standing.

8. Danny Paley quoted in Arcana, *Grace Paley's Life Stories*, 98.

9. Nora Paley quoted in Arcana, *Grace Paley's Life Stories*, 96.

10. Paley, "Six Days: Some Rememberings," in *Just As I Thought*, 25, 29.

11. Quoted in Arcana, *Grace Paley's Life Stories*, 218.

12. Jeanne Goodside Tenenbaum quoted in Arcana, *Grace Paley's Life Stories*, 89; Nora Paley quoted in Arcana, 81.

13. Paley quoted in Arcana, *Grace Paley's Life Stories*, 93.

14. Paley, "Life in the Country: A City Friend Asks, 'Is it Boring?'" in *Just As I Thought*, 300.

15. "Interview by Juniper Institute Participants," June 2005, *Massachusetts Review* 49, no. 4 (Winter 2008): 509; "Upstaging Time," in *Just As I Thought*, 298.

16. Rickey Gard Diamond, "The Amazing Grace Paley: Vermont's Poetic Conscience," *Vermont Woman* (www.vermontwoman.com/articles/2007/0507/GracePaley.html).

Bibliography

Alcott, A. Bronson. *Conversations with Children on the Gospels.* Boston: James Munroe, 1836.
_____. *The Journals of Bronson Alcott*, ed. Odell Shephard. Boston: Little Brown, 1938.
_____. *Record of a School.* New York: Peabody, 1835.
Alcott, Louisa May. *Flower Fables.* Boston: George W. Briggs, 1854.
_____. *Hospital Sketches.* Boston: Roberts Brothers, 1863.
_____. *Little Men.* Boston: Roberts Brothers, 1871.
_____. *Little Women.* Boston: Roberts Brothers, 1868.
_____. *Moods.* Boston: Loring, 1864.
_____. *An Old-Fashioned Girl.* Boston: Roberts Brothers, 1870.
_____. *Under the Lilacs.* Boston: Roberts Brothers, 1878.
Alexandra, Rae. "A Grim History of Nob Hill's Mansions—And the Horror Novels They Inspired." KQED, July 13, 2020, www.kqed.org.
Andrews, Kenneth R. *Nook Farm: Mark Twain's Hartford Circle.* 1950. Hamden, CT: Archon Books, 1967.
Applegate, Debby. *The Most Famous Man in America: The Biography of Henry Ward Beecher.* New York: Doubleday, 2006.
Arcana, Judith. *Grace Paley's Life Stories: A Literary Biography.* Urbana: University of Illinois Press, 1993.
Bailey, Susan W. "Louisa May Alcott's Walpole," https://louisamayalcottismypassion.
Bedell, Madelon. *The Alcotts: Biography of a Family.* New York: Clarkson Potter, 1980.
Blanchard, Paula. *Sarah Orne Jewett: Her World and Her Work.* Reading, MA: Addison-Wesley, 1994.
Brady, Kathleen. *Ida Tarbell: Portrait of a Muckraker.* New York: Seaview/Putnam, 1984.
Brightman, Carol. *Writing Dangerously: Mary McCarthy and Her World.* New York: Clarkson Potter, 1992.
Brodhead, Richard. *Cultures of Letters: Scenes of Reading and Writing in Nineteenth-Century America.* Chicago: University of Chicago Press, 1993.
Burgess, John William. *Reminiscences of an American Scholar.* New York: Columbia University Press, 1934.
Callahan, Michael. "Peyton Place's Real Victim." *Vanity Fair* 48, no. 3 (2006): 332 et seq.
Cameron, Ardis. *Unbuttoning America: A Biography of Peyton Place.* Ithaca, NY: Cornell University Press, 2015.
Cheever, Susan. *Louisa May Alcott: A Personal Biography.* New York: Simon & Schuster, 2010.
Creswell, Marilyn. "Sojourner Truth and the Power of Copyright Registration," https://blogs.loc.gov/copyright/2020/12.
Curtis, Cathy. *A Splendid Intelligence: The Life of Elizabeth Hardwick.* New York: Norton, 2022.
Davis, Cynthia. *Charlotte Perkins Gilman: A Biography.* Palo Alto, CA: Stanford University Press, 2010.

Dell, Floyd. "My Friend Edna St. Vincent Millay." *Mark Twain Journal* 12, no. 2 (Spring 1964): 1–2.
Desjardin, Thomas. *Joshua L. Chamberlain: The Life in Letters of a Great Leader of the American Civil War.* Oxford, U.K.: Osprey Publishing, 2012.
Diamond, Rickey Gard. "The Amazing Grace Paley: Vermont's Poetic Conscience." *Vermont Woman*, www.vermontwoman.com/articles/2007/0507/GracePaley.html.
Dickinson, Emily. *The Complete Poems of Emily Dickinson*, ed. Thomas H. Johnson. Boston: Back Bay Books/Little, Brown, 1961.
_____. *The Poems of Emily Dickinson*, ed. Ralph Franklin. Reading edition. 1 vol. Cambridge, MA: Harvard University Press, 2005.
_____. *The Poems of Emily Dickinson*, ed. Ralph Franklin. Variorum edition. 3 vols. Cambridge, MA: Belknap Press of Harvard University Press, 1998.
Doyle, J.E.P. *Plymouth Church and Its Pastor.* St. Louis: Bryan, Brand & Company, 1875.
Dwight, Eleanor. *Edith Wharton: An Extraordinary Life.* New York: Abrams, 1956.
Eddy, Mary Baker. *Retrospection and Introspection.* Boston: First Church of Christ, Scientist, 1891.
_____. *Science and Health.* Boston: Christian Science Publishing Company, 1875.
_____. *The Science of Man.* Boston: Christian Science Publishing Company, 1876.
"Edna St. Vincent Millay." *Vassar Encyclopedia*, vcencyclopedia.vassar.edu.
Eldridge, Elleanor. *Elleanor's Second Book.* Providence, RI: B.T. Albro, 1839.
_____. *Memoirs of Elleanor Eldridge.* Providence, R.I.: B.T. Albro, 1838.
Epstein, Daniel Mark. *What Lips My Lips Have Kissed: The Loves and Love Poems of Edna St. Vincent Millay.* New York: Henry Holt, 2001.
Fields, Annie, ed. *Letters of Sarah Orne Jewett.* Boston: Houghton Mifflin, 1911.
_____, and Rose Lamb, eds. *Letters of Celia Thaxter.* Boston: Houghton, Mifflin and Company, 1896.
Finley, Ruth E. *The Lady of Godey's: Sarah Josepha Hale.* Philadelphia: J.B. Lippincott, 1931.
Francis, Richard. *Fruitlands: The Alcott Family and Their Search for Utopia.* New Haven, CT: Yale University Press, 2010.
Franklin, Ruth. *Shirley Jackson: A Rather Haunted Life.* New York: Liveright, 2016.
Gelderman, Carol. *Mary McCarthy: A Life.* New York: St. Martin's, 1988.
Gill, Gillian. *Mary Baker Eddy.* Cambridge, MA: Perseus Books, 1998.
Gilman, Charlotte Perkins. *Concerning Children.* Boston: Small, Maynard & Company, 1900.
_____. *Herland. The Forerunner*, 1915.
_____. *The Home: Its Work and Influence.* New York: McClure, Phillips, 1903.
_____. *Human Work.* New York: McClure, Phillips, 1904.
_____. *In This Our World.* Boston: Small, Maynard & Company, 1893.
_____. *The Living of Charlotte Perkins Gilman.* New York: Appleton-Century, 1935.
_____. *The Man-Made World; or, Our Androcentric Culture.* New York: Charlton, 1911.
_____. *Unpunished.* 1920s. New York: Feminist Press, 1989.
_____. *With Her in Ourland. The Forerunner*, 1916.
_____. *Women and Economics: A Study of the Economic Relation Between Men and Women as a Factor in Social Evolution.* Boston: Small, Maynard & Company, 1898.
_____. *The Yellow Wallpaper.* Boston: Small, Maynard & Company, 1899.
_____. "The Yellow Wallpaper: A Story." *The New England Magazine* 11, no. 5 (January 1892): 647–656.
Gorton, Stephanie. *Citizen Reporters: S.S. McClure, Ida Tarbell, and the Magazine That Rewrote America.* New York: Ecco, 2020.
Gottschalk, Stephen. *The Emergence of Christian Science in American Religious Life.* Berkeley: University of California Press, 1973.
Green, David Bonnell. "The World of Dunnet Landing." *New England Quarterly* 34, no. 4 (December 1961): 514–17.
Green, Frances Harriet Whipple. *Elleanor's Second Book.* Providence, RI: B.T. Albro, 1839.
_____. *The Envoy: From Free Hearts to the Free.* Pawtucket, RI: Juvenile Emancipation Society, 1840.

———. *The Mechanic: Responsibility*. Providence, RI: Burnett & King, 1842.
———. *Memoirs of Elleanor Eldridge*. Providence, RI: B.T. Albro, 1838.
———. *Shahmah in Pursuit of Freedom, or The Branded Hand*. New York: Thatcher & Hutchinson, 1858.
Grumbach, Doris, *The Company She Kept*. New York: Coward, McCann, 1967.
Hale, Sarah Josepha. *The Ladies' Wreath: A Selection from the Female Poetic Writers of England and America*. Boston: Marsh, Capen & Lyon; New York: D. Appleton, 1837.
———. *Liberia; or, Mr. Peyton's Experiments*. New York: Harper & Brothers, 1853.
———. *Northwood, a Tale of New England*. Boston: Bowles & Dearborn, 1827. Rev. ed., *Northwood, or Life North and South*. New York: H. Long and Brother, 1852.
———. *Traits of American Life*. Philadelphia: Carey & Hart, 1835.
———. *Woman's Record: Sketches of all Distinguished Women from the Creation to A.D. 1854/1876*. New York: Harper Brothers, 1852, 1876.
Hamilton, Saskia, ed. *The Dolphin Letters, 1970–1979*. New York: Farrar, Straus & Giroux, 2019.
Hardwick, Elizabeth. *The Ghostly Lover*. New York: Harcourt, Brace, 1945.
———. *Herman Melville*. New York: Viking, 2000.
———. *The Simple Truth*. New York: Harcourt Brace, 1955.
———. *Sleepless Nights*. New York: Random House, 1979.
———. *A View of My Own*. New York: Farrar, Straus and Cudahy, 1962.
Hedrick, Joan D. *Harriet Beecher Stowe: A Life*. New York: Oxford University Press, 1994.
Henney, Nella Braddy. *Anne Sullivan Macy: The Story Behind Helen Keller*. Garden City, NY: Doubleday, Doran, 1933.
Herrmann, Dorothy. *Helen Keller: A Life*. New York: Knopf, 1998.
Hill, Calvin C. "Reminiscences," typescript, n.d., Mary Baker Eddy Library, Boston, MA, 183–85, 190, © The Mary Baker Eddy Library Collection. Used by permission.
Hill, Mary A., ed., *Endure: The Diaries of Charles Walter Stetson*. Philadelphia: Temple University Press, 1985.
Hoff, Ann K. "'How Love May Be Acquired': Prescriptive Autobiography in Millay's 'Fatal Interview.'" *CEA Critic* 68, no. 3 (Spring and Summer 2006): 1–15.
Hyman, Laurence Jackson, ed. *The Letters of Shirley Jackson*. New York: Random House, 2021.
Jackson, John Andrew. *The Experience of a Slave in South Carolina*. London: Passmore & Alabaster, 1862.
Jackson, Shirley. *The Bird's Nest*. New York: Farrar, Straus, 1954.
———. *Four Novels of the 1940s and 1950s*. New York: Library of America, 2020.
———. *Hangsaman*. New York: Farrar, Straus, 1951.
———. *The Haunting of Hill House*. New York: Viking, 1959.
———. *Life Among the Savages*. New York: Farrar, Straus, 1953.
———. *The Lottery; or, The Adventures of James Harris*. New York: Farrar, Straus, 1949.
———. *Novels and Stories*. New York: Library of America, 2010.
———. *Raising Demons*. New York: Farrar, Straus, 1957.
———. *The Road Through the Wall*. New York: Farrar, Straus, 1958.
———. *The Sundial*. New York: Farrar, Straus and Cudahy, 1958.
———. *We Have Always Lived in the Castle*. New York: Viking, 1962.
———. *The Witchcraft of Salem Village*. New York: Random House, 1956.
Jewett, Jon. "Elizabeth Hardwick." *The Castine Visitor* 18, no. 1 (Spring 2008): 8.
Jewett, Sarah Orne. *Betty Leicester, A Story for Girls*. Boston: Houghton, Mifflin, 1889.
———. *Country By-Ways*. Boston: Houghton, Mifflin, 1881.
———. *A Country Doctor*. Boston: Houghton, Mifflin, 1884.
———. *The Country of the Pointed Firs*. Boston: Houghton Mifflin, 1896.
———. *Deephaven*. Boston: James R. Osgood, 1877.
———. "Looking Back on Girlhood." 1892. In *Novels and Stories*. New York: Library of America, 1994, 754–60.
———. *A Marsh Island*. Boston: Houghton, Mifflin, 1885.
———. *The Mate of the Daylight, and Friends Ashore*. Boston: Houghton, Mifflin, 1884.
———. *A Native of Winby and Other Tales*. Boston: Houghton, Mifflin, 1893.

———. *Novels and Stories*. New York: Library of America, 1994.
———. *Old Friends and New*. Boston: James R. Osgood, 1879.
———. *Play Days: A Book of Stories for Children*. Boston: James R. Osgood, 1878.
———. *The Story of the Normans*. New York: Putnam's, 1887.
———. *Strangers and Wayfarers*. Boston: Houghton, Mifflin, 1890.
———. *Tales of New England*. Boston: Houghton, Mifflin, 1894.
———. *The Tory Lover*. Boston: Houghton, Mifflin, 1901.
———. *A White Heron and Other Stories*. Boston: Houghton, Mifflin, 1886.
Johanningsmeier, Charles. "Sarah Orne Jewett and Mary E. Wilkins (Freeman): Two Shrewd Businesswomen in Search of New Markets." *New England Quarterly* 70, no. 1 (1997): 57–82.
Johnson, Thomas H., and Theodora Ward, eds. *The Letters of Emily Dickinson*. Cambridge, MA: Belknap Press of Harvard University Press, 1958.
Jones, Jacqueline. *A Dreadful Deceit: The Myth of Race from the Colonial Era to Obama's America*. New York: Basic Books, 2013.
Keller, Helen. *Midstream*. New York: Doubleday, 1929.
———. *Out of the Dark*. New York: Doubleday, 1913.
———. *Selected Writings*, ed. Kim E. Nielsen. New York: New York University Press, 2005.
———. *The Story of My Life: The Restored Edition*, ed. James Berger. 1903. New York: Modern Library, 2003.
———. *Teacher: Anne Sullivan Macy; a tribute by the foster-child of her mind*. Garden City NY: Doubleday, 1955.
———. *The World I Live In and Optimism*. 1908, 1903. Mineola, NY: Dover, 2009.
Keyser, Catherine. "Edna St. Vincent Millay and the Very Clever Woman in 'Vanity Fair.'" *American Periodicals* 17, no. 1 (2007): 65–96.
Kirkpatrick, Melanie. *Lady Editor: Sarah Josepha Hale and the Making of the Modern American Woman*. New York: Encounter Books, 2021.
Lancaster, Jane. "A Web of Iniquity? Race, Gender, Foreclosure, and Respectability in Antebellum Rhode Island." *Rhode Island History Journal* 69 (Summer–Fall 2011): 72–92.
Lane, Ann J. *To Herland and Beyond: The Life and Works of Charlotte Perkins Gilman*. New York: Pantheon, 1990.
LaPlante, Eve. *Marmee and Louisa: The Untold Story of Louisa May Alcott and Her Mother*. New York: Free Press, 2012.
Lee, Hermione. *Edith Wharton*. New York: Knopf, 2007.
Lewis, R.W.B. *Edith Wharton: A Biography*. New York: Harper & Row, 1975.
Leyda, Jay. *The Years and Hours of Emily Dickinson*. New Haven, CT: Yale University Press, 1960.
Lippman, Laura. "The Women of Peyton Place." *Baltimore Sun*, June 14, 1999.
Longfellow, Samuel L. *Life of Henry Wadsworth Longfellow*. 3 vols. Boston: Ticknor, 1886.
Longsworth, Polly. *Austin and Mabel: The Amherst Affair and Love Letters of Austin Dickinson and Mabel Loomis Todd*. New York: Farrar, Straus and Giroux, 1984.
Lowell, Robert. *The Dolphin*. New York: Farrar, Straus and Giroux, 1973.
Macdougall, Allan Ross, ed. *Letters of Edna St. Vincent Millay*. New York: Harper & Brothers, 1952.
Mars, Laura. "Edna St. Vincent Millay's Steepletop." *Berkshire Magazine* 11, no. 4 (August 2022): 70–75.
Maryniak, Ben. "Errant Chaplain of the Iron Brigade: Biography of the Reverend James C. Richmond, 2nd Wisconsin." *Military Images* 16, no. 4 (January–February 1995): 28–30.
Matteson, John. *Eden's Outcasts: The Story of Louisa May Alcott and Her Father*. New York: Norton, 2007.
Matthiessen, F.O. *Sarah Orne Jewett*. Gloucester, MA: Peter Smith, 1965.
McCarthy, Mary. *Birds of America*. New York: Harcourt, Brace, 1975.
———. *Cannibals and Missionaries*. San Diego: Harcourt, Brace, 1979.
———. *The Company She Keeps*. New York: Harcourt Brace, 1942.
———. *The Group*. New York: Harcourt, Brace, 1963.
———. *The Groves of Academe*. New York: Harcourt, Brace, 1951.

———. *Hanoi*. New York: Harcourt, Brace, 1964.
———. *How I Grew*. New York: Harcourt Brace Jovanovich, 1987.
———. *Intellectual Memoirs: New York, 1936–1938*. New York: Harcourt, Brace, 1992.
———. *The Mask of State*. New York: Harcourt, Brace, 1974.
———. *Memories of a Catholic Girlhood*. New York: Harcourt, Brace, 1957.
———. *The Oasis*. New York: Random House, 1959.
———. *Vietnam*. New York: Harcourt, Brace, and World, 1967.
McFarland, Philip. *Loves of Harriet Beecher Stowe*. New York: Grove Press, 2007.
McKenzie, Daisette Stocking. "Reminiscences." Typescript, n.d., Mary Baker Eddy Library, Boston, MA, 27–28. Letters and Reminiscences, ©The Mary Baker Eddy Collection. Used by permission.
Metalious, Grace. *No Adam in Eden*. New York: Simon & Schuster, 1963.
———. *Peyton Place*. New York: Julian Messner, 1956.
———. *Return to Peyton Place*. New York: Julian Messner, 1959.
———. *The Tight White Collar*. New York: Julian Messner, 1960.
Milford, Nancy. *Savage Beauty: The Life of Edna St. Vincent Millay*. New York: Random House, 2002.
Millay, Edna St. Vincent. *Aria da Capo*. New York: Appleton, 1924.
———. *The Buck in the Snow*. New York: Harper, 1928.
———. *Collected Poems*, ed. Norma Millay. New York: Harper & Row, 1982.
———. *Edna St. Vincent Millay: Selected Poems*, ed. J.D. McClatchy. New York: Library of America, 2003.
———. *Fatal Interview*. New York: Harper, 1931.
———. *A Few Figs from Thistles*. New York: Frank Shay, 1920.
———. *The Harp Weaver and Other Poems*. New York: Harper, 1923.
———. *Huntsman, What Quarry?* New York: Harper, 1939.
———. *The King's Henchman: A Play*. New York: Harper, 1927.
———. *Mine the Harvest*. New York: Harper, 1954.
———. *Renascence and Other Poems*. New York: Harper, 1917.
———. *Second April*. New York: Mitchell Kennerly, 1921.
———. *Wine from These Grapes*. New York: Harper, 1934.
Myerson, Joel, and Daniel Shealy, eds. *The Selected Letters of Louisa May Alcott*. Boston: Little, Brown, 1987.
Oppenheimer, Judy. *Private Demons: The Life of Shirley Jackson*. New York: Putnam, 1988.
Paley, Grace. *The Collected Stories*. New York: Farrar, Straus and Giroux, 1994.
———. *Enormous Changes at the Last Minute*. New York: Farrar, Straus and Giroux, 1974.
———. *Just As I Thought*. New York: Farrar, Straus and Giroux, 1998.
———. *Later the Same Day*. New York: Farrar, Straus and Giroux, 1985.
———. *Leaning Forward: Poems*. Penobscot, ME: Granite Press, 1985.
———. *The Little Disturbances of Man*. New York: Doubleday, 1960.
Perkins, Frederick B. *Devil-Puzzlers and Other Stories*. New York: G.P. Putnam, 1877.
Pickard, Samuel T. *Life and Letters of John Greenleaf Whittier*, 2 vols. Boston: Houghton, Mifflin, 1895. Republished as *Letters of John Greenleaf Whittier*, 2 vols. Cambridge, MA: Harvard University Press, 1975.
Quimby, P.P. "To the Sick in Body and Mind," ppquimby.com.
Reisin, Harriet. *Louisa May Alcott: The Woman Behind Little Women*. New York: Macmillan, 2010.
Reynolds, David S. *Mightier Than the Sword: Uncle Tom's Cabin and the Battle for America*. New York: W.W. Norton, 2012.
Rhode Island and Providence Plantations. "Preliminary Survey Report, Town of Middletown, June 1979."
Rich, Adrienne. "Caryatid: A Column." *American Poetry Review* 2 (September–October 1973): 3442–44.
Richmond, James C. *The Rhode Island Cottage*. 1st English edition. Newport, Isle of Wight: R.J. Denyer, 1849.

Roman, Margaret. *Sarah Orne Jewett: Reconstructing Gender*. Tuscaloosa: University of Alabama Press, 2017.
Rugoff, Milton. *The Beechers: An American Family in the Nineteenth Century*. New York: Harper & Row, 1981.
Samra, Matthew K. "Shadow and Substance: The Two Narratives of Sojourner Truth." *Midwest Quarterly* 38, no. 2 (January 1, 1997): 158–71.
Sanborn, F. B., and William T. Harris. *A. Bronson Alcott: His Life and Philosophy*. 2 vols. Boston: Roberts Brothers, 1893.
Scharnhorst, Gary. *Charlotte Perkins Gilman: A Bibliography*. Metuchen, NJ: Scarecrow Press, 1985.
Schenkman, A.J. "Preservation Failures: The Hardenbergh House." *New York Almanack*, July 18, 2013.
Serlin, David. "'Yours Is a Different Understanding of Architecture': Helen Keller's House in Easton, Connecticut," afb.org.
Sewall, Richard B. *The Life of Emily Dickinson*. Cambridge, MA: Harvard University Press, 1980.
Shealy, Daniel Lester. "The Author-Publisher Relationships of Louisa May Alcott." Ph.D. dissertation, University of South Carolina, 1965.
Stowe, Calvin. *Origin and History of the Books of the Bible*. Hartford, CT: Hartford Publishing Company, 1867.
Stowe, Charles Edward. *Life of Harriet Beecher Stowe Compiled from Her Letters and Journals*. Boston: Houghton Mifflin, 1889.
Stowe, Harriet Beecher. *Dred*. Boston: Houghton Mifflin, 1856.
_____. *The Key to Uncle Tom's Cabin*. Boston: Jewett, 1853.
_____. *Lady Byron Vindicated*. London: Sampson, Low, 1870.
_____. *Mayflower*. New York: Harper & Brothers, 1843.
_____. *The Minister's Wooing*. New York: Derby and Jackson, 1859.
_____. *My Wife and I*. New York: Ford, 1872.
_____. *Oldtown Folks*. Boston: Houghton, Mifflin, 1869.
_____. *Palmetto Leaves*. Boston: Osgood, 1873.
_____. *The Pearl of Orr's Island*. Boston: Ticknor and Fields, 1862.
_____. *Pink and White Tyranny*. Boston: Roberts Brothers, 1871.
_____. *Poganuc People*. New York: Fords, Howard, & Hulbert, 1878.
_____. *Uncle Tom's Cabin*. Boston: John P. Jewett, 1852.
_____. *We and Our Neighbors*. Boston: Houghton, Mifflin, 1873.
Strickland, Charles. "A Transcendentalist Father: The Child-Rearing Practices of Bronson Alcott." *History of Childhood Quarterly* 1, no. 1 (Summer 1973): 4–51.
Taggart, Cynthia. *Poems*, 3d ed. New York: Barlow, 1848.
Tarbell, Ida. *All in the Day's Work*. New York: Macmillan, 1939.
_____. *The Business of Being a Woman*. New York: Macmillan, 1914.
_____. *The History of the Standard Oil Company*. 2 vols. New York: McClure, 1904.
_____. *In the Footsteps of the Lincolns*. New York: Harper, 1924.
_____. *The Life of Abraham Lincoln*. New York: Doubleday, McClure, 1900.
_____. *The Life of Judge Gary*. New York: McClure, 1925–26.
_____. *A Life of Napoleon Bonaparte*. New York: McClure, Phillips, 1901.
_____. *A Life of Napoleon Bonaparte: With a Sketch of Josephine, Empress of the French*. New York: McClure, Phillips, 1901.
_____. *Madame Roland*. New York: Scribner's, 1895.
_____. *Owen D. Young, a New Type of Industrial Leader*. New York: Macmillan, 1932.
_____. *Peacemakers—Blessed and Otherwise*. New York: Macmillan, 1922.
_____, and Cather, Willa, writing as Georgine Milmine. *The Life of Mary Baker Eddy and the History of Christian Science*. 1909. Lincoln: University of Nebraska Press, 1993.
Thaxter, Celia. *Among the Isles of Shoals*. Boston: James R. Osgood and Company, 1873.
_____. *The Cruise of the Mystery and Other Poems*. Boston: Houghton, Mifflin, 1886.
_____. *Drift-weed*. Boston: Houghton, Osgood and Company, 1878.
_____. *Idyls and Pastorals*. Boston: D. Lothrop, 1886.

———. *An Island Garden*. 1894. Boston: Houghton Mifflin, 1904.
———. *Poems*. Cambridge, MA: Hurd and Houghton, 1872.
———. *Poems for Children*. Boston: Houghton Mifflin, 1884.
Thaxter, Rosamond. *Sandpiper: The Life of Celia Thaxter*. Sanbornville, NH: Wake-Brook House, 1962.
Titus, Frances W. "Sojourner Truth." *Daily Inter Ocean* (Chicago), September 24, 1893.
Tomlinson, Rev. Irving C. *Twelve Years with Mary Baker Eddy*. Boston: Christian Science Publishing Association, 1945.
Toth, Emily. *Inside Peyton Place: The Life of Grace Metalious*. Garden City, NY: Doubleday, 1981.
Totten, Gary. "Selling Wharton." In *Edith Wharton in Context*, ed. Laura Rattray, 127–36. New York: Cambridge University Press, 2012.
Treckel, Paula. "Ida Tarbell and the Business of Being a Woman," https://sites.allegheny.edu/tarbell/ida-tarbell-and-the-business-of-being-a-woman/.
Truth, Sojourner, with Gilbert Vale. *Fanaticism; its source and influence, illustrated by the Simple Narrative of Isabella*. 2 vols. New York: G. Vale, 1835.
———, with Olive Gilbert. *The Narrative of Sojourner Truth*. Boston: The Author, 1850.
Vollaro, Daniel R. "Lincoln, Stowe, and the 'Little Woman/Great War' Story: The Making, and Breaking, of a Great American Anecdote." *Journal of the Abraham Lincoln Association* 30, no. 1 (Winter 2009): 18–34.
Warner, Charles Dudley. "The Story of *Uncle Tom's Cabin*." *Atlantic Monthly* 78 (September 1896): 312–13.
Washington, Margaret. *Sojourner Truth's America*. Urbana: University of Illinois Press, 2009.
Wharton, Edith. *The Age of Innocence*. New York: D. Appleton, 1920.
———. *A Backward Glance*, in *Novellas and Other Writings*. New York: Library of America, 1990.
———. *The Buccaneers*. Incomplete. New York: Penguin, 1938.
———. *The Children*. New York: D. Appleton, 1928.
———. *The Custom of the Country*. New York: Scribner's, 1913.
———. *Ethan Frome*. New York: Scribner's, 1911.
———. *The House of Mirth*. New York: Scribner's, 1905.
———. *Italian Villas and Their Gardens*. 1904. New York: DaCapo, 1988.
———. *The Mother's Recompense*. New York: D. Appleton, 1925.
———. *Novels*. New York: Library of America, 1985.
———. *A Son at the Front*. New York: Scribner's, 1923.
———. *Summer*. New York: Scribner's, 1917.
———, and Ogden Codman, Jr. *The Decoration of Houses*. 1897. Rev. and expanded ed., New York: Norton, 1978.
Whipple, Frances Harriet. *See* Green, Frances Harriet Whipple.
White, Barbara A. *The Beecher Sisters*. New Haven, CT: Yale University Press, 2003.
Wilson, Richard Guy. *Edith Wharton at Home*. New York: Monacelli Press, 2012.

Index

Numbers in ***bold italics*** indicate pages with illustrations.

activism, political 16, 17, 54–55, 61–62, 74, 128, 198, 202, 204
Addams, Jane 173
agents, literary 40, 152–153, 154, 155, 193
Alcott, Louisa May: family of 90–92, 94, 95, 97–98; finances of 96–97, 98; health of 94, 95, 98; homes of 90–92, ***93***–94, 95, ***96***, 97, 98; pseudonyms 96; works of 95–97
Allegheny College 32
American Ladies Magazine 182
American Magazine 40
Amherst Academy 99
Amherst College 99, 102, 107
Anagnos, Dr. Michael 10–12
Andover Theological Seminary 24
Anthony, Susan B. 3, 27, 147
Appledore House Hotel 78, ***79***, 82, 85, 87
Arcan Ridge 18–***19***
Atlantic Monthly 4, 26, 29, 46; and Alcott 95; and Gilman 171; and Jewett 47–49, 50, 52; and Paley 202; and Thaxter 80, 81, 83, 84
Auden, W.H. 198–199
autobiography 13–14, 17, 40, 48, 62, 116, 167, 176, 204; *see also* memoirs

Baker, George Waldron 139
Barnard College 70
Baumgarten, Bernice 193
Beauvoir, Simone de 58, 64
Beecher, Catharine 22, 23
Beecher, Henry Ward 25, 27–29
Beecher, Isabella 22, 24, 25, 28, 167
Beecher, Lyman 21
Beecher, Thomas 28
Bell, Alexander Graham 10, 11
best sellers 14, 61, 74, 154, 190, 191, 192, 194
Bianchi, Martha Dickinson 107
Bingham, Millicent Todd 107
Bishop, Elizabeth 54
Bishop, John Peale 71
Blackwell, Elizabeth 146, 148
Blackwood, Lady Caroline 62–63
Bloomingdale Asylum 112, 182
Boissevain, Eugen 72–76, ***73***
Bowdoin College 21, 23, 30

Bowles, Samuel 103, 104
Brandt, Carol 193, 195
Bridgman, Laura 10–11
Broadwater, Bowden 57, 61
Burlingame, Edward 34

Canby, Margaret 12
Canfield, Cass 75–76
Cather, Willa 52
Century Magazine 15, 40, 49, 122, 127
Chambrun, Jacques 152–153, 154, 155
Channing, Grace 170, 171, 172, 176
Chautauqua Institution 33–34
Chautauquan 33–34
Child, Lydia Marie 95
Christian Science Association 135–136
Christian Science Journal 136
Christian Science Monitor 140
Civil War 24, 95, 104, 133, 144, 147–148
Codman, Ogden 122, 124, 128
collaboration, in writing 113–114, 116–117
Collier's 40
Columbia University 202
Copeland, Charles Townsend 13
copyright 47, 82, 98, 118, 144
Cosmopolitan 138
Crowell Publishing Co. 39
Crowninshield, Frank 127
Cutts Farm 84–85

Dana, Richard Henry 78
defamation 28, 64, 113, 138
Dell, Floyd 71
Detroit Free Press 49–50
Dickens, Charles 10, 26, 51, 81, 85
Dickinson, Emily: family of 99–100, 102, 104, 105; friends of 100, 103, 104; health of 105, 106; homes of 99, 100–***101***, ***102***, 107; posthumous publication of poems 106–107
Dillon, George 74–75
divorce 54, 56–57, 58, 61, 63, 67, 127, 134, 150, 155, 168, 172, 202
The Dolphin (Robert Lowell) 63
Doubleday 200
Doubleday, McClure 35

227

Index

Dove Cottage 91–92
Dumont, John 109–110

Eddy, Asa Gilbert 135–136
Eddy, Mary Baker: family of 131–133, 138–139; founds *Christian Science Monitor* 140; health of 133–134; homes of 131, **132**, 133, 134, 135, 136–138, **137**, 139–140; hostility toward 135–136, 138–139; marriages of 131, 132, 134, 135; writings of 135, 136
Eldridge, Elleanor **165**; business career of 161; courtship of 161; domestic work of 160–161, 162; family of 160, 161, 162–163; finances of 162–163, 166; homes of 162, 166; legal problems of 162–163; memoir 164–166
Elliott, James 96
Ellison, Ralph 187, 190
Emerson, Ralph Waldo 3, 50, 51, 81, 85, 91, 93, 145
Encounter 58
Epstein, Barbara 60, 66
Epstein, Jason 60
Esquire 194, 202
The Evergreens 100, 102, **103**, 107
Everybody's Magazine 49

Farrar, Straus 188, 189, 193
Ficke, Arthur 70, 71
Fields, Annie 29, 146; and Jewett 50–52; and Thaxter 80–85
Fields, James 4; and Alcott 95; and Jewett 50–51; and Thaxter 80–85
Folger, Ann 112–113
Folger, Benjamin 112–113
Forerunner 174–175
Frank Leslie's Illustrated Newspaper 96
Freedmen's Aid Society 119–120
Fruitlands 91–92
Fugitive Slave Law 22, 117
Fullerton, William Morton 127

Garrison, William Lloyd 117, 166
Gilbert, Olive 115–117
Gilder, Richard Watson 122, 127
Gilman, Charlotte Perkins **176**; as artist 169; autobiography 176; family of 167–168; fiction by 171, 174; founds *Forerunner* 174–175; friends of 169, 172; health of 169, 170, 176; homes of 167–**168**, 170, 171, 174, 175–**176**; on housekeeping 169, 175; as lecturer 173–174; marriages of 169–170, 172, 174; nonfiction by 174–175; poetry of 172; productivity of 171–172, 174–175; on Tarbell 39
Gilman, George Houghton 173–**176**
Glover, George Washington 131–132
Glover, George Washington II 132–133, 138–139
Godey, Louis 145–146, 149
Godey's Lady's Book 145–147, 149
Good Housekeeping 189
Greeley, Horace 4, 117, 145
Green, Francis Whipple 164–166

Hale, Sarah Josepha: and Bunker Hill Monument 144; as editor 143–144, 145–148; family of 141–142, 143, 148; homes of **142**, 148; marriage of 142; politics of 147–148; and seamen's welfare 144; and Thanksgiving 148; works of 142–143, 144–145, 147
Haley House 78
Harcourt, Brace 55
Hardenbergh family 108
Hardenbergh house **109**
Harmonia Commune 118
Hardwick, Elizabeth: edits William James's letters 58; education of 55; founds *New York Review of Books* 60; homes of 53, 58, 59–60, **65**; marriage of 56, 58; politics of 61–62; works of 55, 58–59, 60, 66
Harper (book publisher) 75–76
Harper's 34, 49, 59, 81, 189
Harvard University 19, 58, 91, 107
Hassam, Childe 85, 86
Hawthorne, Nathaniel 50, 85, 93, 94
Hawthorne, Sophia 51
Hellman, Lillian 64
Higginson, Thomas Wentworth 78, 79, 103, 104, 106
Hillside **93**–94
Holmes, Oliver Wendell 29, 51, 81, 85, 95
Hooker, Isabella Beecher 22, 24, 25, 28, 167
Hoppin & Koen (architects) 124, **125**
Hotel des Artistes 60
Houghton Mifflin 48
housekeeping, attitudes toward 4, 80, 129, 151–153, 169, 175
Howells, William Dean 49, 50, 51, 84, 85
Hull House 173
Hurd and Houghton 83
Hyman, Stanley Edgar 185, 187–188, 190

Ipswich Academy 100
Isles of Shoals 77, 87; *see also* Thaxter, Celia
"It'll Do" (house) 151–152, 153, 155
Ivy Green 8–**9**

Jackson, John Andrew 22
Jackson, Shirley: ancestors of 184; children of 186, 188, **189**; fiction by 185, 189, 190–192; finances of 186, 188, 190, 192, 193–194; health of 190, 191, 194, 195; homes of 184, 185, 186, **187**, **189**, 190, 191–**192**; image of 190, 196; "The Lottery" 188; marriage of 185, 186; nonfiction by 187, 188, 190, 191–192; parents of 184–185, 195
James, Henry 127
James R. Osgood and Company 47–48, 83
Jewett, John P. 23
Jewett, Sarah Orne: and Annie Fields 50–52; approach to writing 47–49; children's books by 47–48; family of 44–46, 58; friends of 50, 85; health of 46, 52; homes of 44, **45**, 45–46, 48; income of 50–51;

Index   229

pseudonyms of 46–47; and Stowe 29; works of 47–49, 52
Johnsrud, Harold 54

Keller, Helen: activism of 16, 17; autobiography 13–14; education of 11–14; engagement of 16; family of 8–11; films about 17, 19; homes of *9*, 14, *15*, 17, 18, *19*; honors 19–20; as speaker 13; on Tarbell 39; in vaudeville 17; works by 14, 16, 19
Keller, Kate Adams 8–10, 16, 18
Knapp, Adeline 172

Ladies Home Journal 13, 37
Ladies' Magazine 143–144
Land's End 122
lecture tours 16, 29, 39–40, 172–174, 176, 195
libel 28, 64, 113, 138
The Liberator 117
Lincoln, Abraham 24, 25, 35, 41, 118, 119–120, 148
Longfellow, Alice 48
Longfellow, Henry Wadsworth 3, 11, 22, 23–24, 50, 51, 81, 85, 95, 96, 145
Longfellow, Samuel 79
Lord, Judge Otis 103
Lowell, Harriet 59, 66
Lowell, James Russell 51, 80, 85
Lowell, Robert 56, 58, 59, 60, 62–63
The Lyric Year 70

Macy, Annie Sullivan 10–14, 16–19
Macy, John Albert 14–15
Mademoiselle 189
magazines 3, 4, 37, 48; payment by 21, 25, 40, 49, 57, 95–96, 126, 144, 174–175, 186, 189
Mailer, Norman 61
Martin, Thomas James (TJ the DJ) 155–156
Mathews, Robert 112–113
"Matthias" (Robert Mathews) 112–113
May, Samuel 91, 92, 94, 115
McCall's 40
McCarthy, Mary: family of 53–54; fiction by 54, 57, 61; homes of 53, 55, 62, *63*; honors 64–65; and Lillian Hellman 64; marriages of 54, 56–57, 61; memoirs by 57, 66; nonfiction by 61; politics of 54–55, 61; at Vassar 54
McClure, Samuel 39, 138
McClure Newspaper Syndicate 4, 34–35, 49–50
McClure's Magazine 35, 36, 37, 138
McCormick, Ken 200
Melville, Herman 3, 66
memoirs 4, 45, 64, 66, 164, 204; *see also* autobiography
Merry's Museum (magazine) 96
Messner, Julius 152
Messner, Kitty 153
Metalious, George 150–151, 153, 155, 156
Metalious, Grace *154*; family of 150;

finances of 153, 154–155, 156; health of 151, 155–156; homes of 150, 151–152, 155; housekeeping of 151, 152, 153; image of 152, 153; later novels of 155, 156; marriages of 151, 155–156; *Peyton Place* 152–155, 156–157
Millay, Edna St. Vincent *73*; activism of 74; as actress 69, 71; diaries of 69; family of 67–68; finances of 74; health of 72, 75; homes of 67–69, 72–*73*; honors 72; marriage of 72, 74–75; poetry collections of 70–72, 74, 76; relationships of 71; short stories of 71, 72; translation by 74
The Miracle Worker 19
Mitchell, Dr. Silas Weir 170–171
The Mount 123–126, ***125***, ***127***
Mount Holyoke Female Seminary 100
Mount Washington Female Seminary 78
Mudgett homestead 155
Muni, Paul 74

The Nation 54, 55
National Era 23
Neely, John 108–109
Nevler, Leona 152, 153
New England Magazine 171
New Republic 40, 54, 185, 186
New School for Social Research 198
New York Post 57
New York Review of Books 60, 61, 66
New Yorker 57, 58, 59, 186, 188
newspaper syndicates 4, 34–35, 49–50
newspapers 34, 49–50, 60, 103
Nichols, Bob 202–203
Niles, Thomas 96–97
Nook Farm 25–27
North American Review 138
Northampton Association of Education and Industry ("the Community") 114–115

Oakholm 26
Oceanic Hotel 82, 87
Orchard House 95–97, ***96***

Paine, John Knowles 85
Paley, Grace ***203***; activism of 198, 202, 204; children of 200, 201, 202; homes of 197–198, 199–200, ***203***; honors 202; marriages of 199, 202; memoir 204; parents of 197–198, 199; poetry of 198, 202, 204; short story collections of 200, 202; siblings of 198, 200, 202
Paley, Jess 199, 200
"Pandora in Blue Jeans" 153, ***154***
Partisan Review 54–56, 58, 59
Patterson, Daniel 132, 133, 134
Pavillon Colombe 128
Perkins, Frederick 167–168
Perkins, Mary Beecher 24, 25, 167
Perkins Institution for the Blind 10–12
Perry, Dr. William 45
Pictorial Review 49

Index

Pierson, Elijah 112–113
Pleasant View *137*
Portland Evening Courier 133–134
Pratt, William Fenno 102
Provincetown Players 71
pseudonyms 46, 96
Pulitzer, Joseph 138–139
Pulitzer Prize 56, 63, 72, 128

Quimby, Phineas Parkhurst 133–134

Radcliffe College 10–14, 20
Rahv, Philip 54–55
Reader's Digest 190
Red Cross Magazine 40
Rees, John 156
"rest cure" 170–171
Revolutionary War 177–178
Reynolds, Paul 40
Rhinecliff 121
Rich, Adrienne 63
Richmond, James C. 178–180, 182
Riverside Magazine for Young People 50
Rogers, Henry Huttleston 14, 36–37
Romance Magazine 49
royalties 14, 35, 148, 192; and house purchases 1, 26, 37, 190; negotiating 50, 97, 126
Rukeyser, Muriel 54

St. Nicholas Magazine 50, 69, 81
Sarah Lawrence College 202
Saturday Evening Gazette 95
Saxton, Eugene 75
Scribner's (book publisher) 35, 126
Scribner's Magazine 34, 35, 49, 81, 124
Scudder, Horace 47, 50
"separate spheres" 143, 147, 149
Sewanee Review 55
slander 28, 64, 113, 138
Spaulding, John S. 14
Standard Oil Co. 31, 36–37
Steepletop 72–74, *73*
Stetson, Grace Channing 170, 171, 172, 176
Stetson, Katharine 170–172, 174, 176
Stetson, Walter 169–170, 171, 172, 174
Stowe, Calvin 21, 22–24, 26, 29
Stowe, Harriet Beecher **28**; family of 21–25, 27–29, 168; homes of 21, 22, *23*, 24, *25*, 26–27; and Jewett 50; later works by 22–24, 27, 29, 46; *Uncle Tom's Cabin* 21–24
suffrage, women's 9, 25, 39, 120, 147, 170, 171, 173
Sullivan, Annie 10–14, 16–19
Syracuse University 185

Taggart, Cynthia: family of 177–180, 182; health of 179; home of 178–*179*; poetry of 179–181; poverty of 179, 182; work published 182
Taggart, William 177–178, 182
Tarbell, Ida: autobiography 40; as editor 36–37, 39–40; family of 31–32; *History of the Standard Oil Company* 37–38; homes of 31, 32, *33*, 36, 37–*38*, 39; as lecturer 39–40; in Paris 34–35; as teacher 32; on women's rights 39; works of 34, 35, 37–38, 39, 40
Thaxter, Celia Laighton: family of 77–78, 79–80, 82, 85; finances of 81, 84; friends of 81, 85; garden of 85–*86*; homes of 77, 78, *79*–80, *81*, 82, 84–85; marriage of 79; painting by 84; poetry collections of 83, 84, 85; prose writings of 83–84, 85–86
Thaxter, Levi Lincoln 78, 79–80, 85
Thaxter, Lucy 78
Ticknor and Fields 4, 50, 51, 81
Time 195
Todd, Mabel Loomis 104–107
Trilling, Diana 64
Truth, Sojourner: carte de visite *119*; conversion of 111; as evangelist 111–112; family of 108, 110–111, 115, 119, 120; *Fanaticism (Simple Narrative)* 113–114; finances of 117, 118; homes of *109*, 115–*116*, 118, 120; itinerant preaching 114–115; in Matthias scandal 112–114; names of 110, 114; *Narrative* 116–117; as orator 117–120; "owners" of 108–110
Twain, Mark 26, 36, 85, 138
Twin Oaks (Washington, D.C.) 35
Twin Oaks (Easton, CT) 37–*38*, 39

University of Rochester 185

Vale, Gilbert 113–114
Vanity Fair 71, 72, 127
Vassar College 54, 57, 61, 70, 146
Victoria (magazine) 81
Viking Press 193, 194
Von Wagenen, Isaac D. 110
Von Wagenen, Isabella *see* Truth, Sojourner

Ward, Samuel 182
West, James 61, 62
Wharton, Edith: family of 121; fiction of 123, 127, 128, 129; finances of 126; friends of 127; honors 128; houses of 121, 122, 123–126, *125*, *127*, 128; marriage of 122, 127; nonfiction of 122, 129; in World War I 128
Whittier, Elizabeth 82
Whittier, John Greenleaf 29, 50, 51, 82, 83, 85, 145
Wilkens, Laurie 152, 153
Wilson, Edmund 55–57, 61, 71
Wilson, Reuel Kimball 55, 61
Woman's Home Companion 49
Woman's Journal 173
Woodbury, Josephine 138
Woolf, Virginia 3

Yale Review 55
Youth's Companion 13, 81